Springer Series on Social Work

Albert R. Roberts, D.S.W., Series Editor

Advisory Board: Joseph D. Anderson, D.S.W., Barbara Berkman, D.S.W.,
Paul H. Ephross, Ph.D., Sheldon R. Gelman, Ph.D., Nancy A. Humphreys, D.S.W.,
Louise P. Shoemaker, D.S.W., and Julia Watkins, Ph.D.

Thomas Owen Carlton, D.S.W., M.S.W., is Associate Professor of Social Work, and Chairman of the Health Social Work Curriculum Specialization of the Master of Social Work degree program at Virginia Commonwealth University in Richmond, Virginia. He earned his master's degree at the University of Southern California and his doctoral degree at the University of Pennsylvania. In addition, he holds degrees in international relations and comparative government. A former Peace Corps Volunteer in the Philippines, Dr. Carlton was a teaching fellow at the University of Pennsylvania School of Social Work prior to joining the faculty of Virginia Commonwealth University. His practice experience includes social casework with families and social group work with physically incapacitated fathers.

Clinical Social Work in Health Settings

A Guide to Professional Practice with Exemplars

Thomas Owen Carlton, D.S.W.

With Contributors

Foreword by Hans S. Falck, Ph.D., A.C.S.W.

Springer Publishing Company
New York

Springer Publishing Company, Inc.
200 Park Avenue South
New York, New York 10003

84 85 86 87 88 / 10 9 8 7 6 5 4 3 2 1

Library of Congress Cataloging in Publication Data

Carlton, Thomas Owen.
    Clinical social work in health settings.
    (Springer series on social work ; v. 4)
    Includes bibliographical references and index.
    1. Medical social work—United States—Addresses, essays, lectures. I. Title. II. Series.
[DNLM: 1. Social work. 2. Delivery of health care. 3. Sociology, Medical. W 322
C285c]
HV687.5.U5C37   1984   362.1′0425′0973   84-3914
ISBN 0-8261-4400-4

Printed in the United States of America

For Susan, Ricky,
Christopher, and Elisabeth,
who make everything possible.

Contents

Part II: Exemplars

Foreword

It is fortunate that social work in the health field has a clear and distinct history. It has produced some of the top leaders in the profession. And it takes scholars of Carlton's caliber to make sense of their contributions. Carlton's major merit is synthesizing ideas over time, within a profession, across specializations, and weaving them together to provide perspective as well as guidelines for current practice.

The existence and applicability of ideas depend on the specific context of those ideas; thus, the future of ideas is directly related to what one makes of them. In this book, the ideas expressed through the membership model of social work practice are examined for their usefulness in the health field. The practice model gains its validity from its application to real work with clients. In the health field, the clients are the patients in hospitals, clinics, and institutions, and their significant others. The clients are also the countless social workers and students who will be enriched because the author of this volume brings to them understanding and insights never before available.

Carlton's application of the membership model to social work in the health field fleshes it out, and makes manifest characteristics that can only be discovered by trying it out on a more limited basis rather than by attempting to cover the entire profession at once.

This volume, however, has significance for the whole of social work. Not only does the author draw on the writings of others in the health field, but he constantly reflects developments in social work as a profession. One attribute of social work has been, and still is, its concern with its uniqueness. This is reflected in the competition that exists among a number of professions for clients and patients, money, influence, and social prestige. Thus, so the reasoning goes, the more territory a profession can claim for itself, the less incursion by unwelcome outsiders there will be. Social work is not alone in this, otherwise there would be no reason for competition.

There exists a danger, however, that in the drive for uniqueness one overlooks a far more profound consideration: that is, that a profession is better defined by its central characteristics than by its relations with other professions at its boundaries. What social work in 1984 clearly needs is a central definition that reflects a centripetal rather than a centrifugal logic. Social work is best defined by its central elements, those aspects which are so irreducible that without them social work would not be social work. That was, is, and has remained the intent of the membership model which guides so much of Carlton's book.

In evaluating Carlton's book, one sees that his kind of analysis of the contributions of others lends the field a definition it has long sought. Carlton calls attention to Bartlett's contributions which gave the medical social work of the 1950s a strong push toward systematic analysis. In doing so, Bartlett laid the groundwork for an analysis of social work practice itself that is still heavily indebted to her original ideas. Her ideas were and are broad enough to accommodate variations, including some early ones hardly intended by Bartlett which could have set the profession back by nurturing some of its earlier atomistic biases. Carlton has set straight the record that Bartlett left for us.

What all of us are learning through Carlton's approach is that theory cannot develop much ahead of practice. But, we are also learning that the university-based scholar is indispensable to the development of practice. The implication is that generalization is one of the fundamentals for specific practice. This book shows us that this is indeed the case. It also shows us how to link theory-based generalizations and specific practice to each other. Carlton has presented the readers of this book with some of what others have written, but the book is his synthesis. He has, thereby, rendered a contribution that will long be remembered and appreciated.

Hans S. Falck, Ph.D., A.C.S.W.
Professor of Social Work
School of Social Work;
Professor of Psychiatry
Medical College of Virginia;
Virginia Commonwealth University
Richmond, Virginia

Preface

This book is about one dimension of health social work—clinical practice. It is the result of study and experiences over the last fifteen years that have led to a number of conclusions about social work in general and about health social work in particular. Together, they lead to the position from which the book proceeds. Primary in this position are the following beliefs:

1. Social work is a profession whose purpose, logic, and underlying rationale differ from those of other professions.
2. Health social work is a highly specialized form of social work that differs from social work in other fields because: it responds to a specific set of problems which involve particular kinds of human needs; it takes place in a highly complex, multidisciplinary system that is grounded in scientific habits of thought and action and has its own characteristics, purpose, and configuration of participants; and it requires, therefore, a different synthesis of social work and nonsocial work knowledge and specialized practice skills.
3. Because of its specialized nature, mastery of the essential elements of social work's common base—its values, purpose, knowledge, and methods—is a necessary precondition but not a sufficient base in and of itself for effective health social work practice.

In considering these belief statements, particularly numbers 2 and 3, one could argue that they apply to all specialized fields of social work practice. Such arguments would be for the most part correct. The differences and similarities in social work as it is practiced in the different fields become visible only when the specifics of these two items are spelled out for each field. To conceptualize and describe some of these specifics as they occur in clinical social work in health settings is an overall objective of this book.

In another sense, the book reflects a commitment to social work in the health field, admiration for its contributions to social work and social work education over the years, appreciation of its great potential, and recognition of some of the problems it has faced in the past, faces in the present, and sometimes shares with other fields of social work.

Beginning in 1905, and continuing for more than half a century, social work in the health field provided the locus for some of social work's most intensive and consistent developments in theory, practice, and professional education. Health social workers were the first to organize professionally and from their ranks emerged leaders who not only pushed outward the boundaries of social work knowledge, expertise, and activity in the health field, but also provided leadership to the profession as a whole. Such health social workers as Ida M. Cannon, Gordon Hamilton, Janet Thornton, and particularly Harriett M. Bartlett, have achieved almost legendary status in the profession.

Following social work's achievement of professional consolidation and integration in the 1950s, however, the focused development that had characterized health social work for more than 55 years became fragmented and its developmental momentum declined. Although the mainstream of health social work was diverted during the period from the early 1960s to the middle 1970s, these years were not unproductive ones for health social workers. During these years, they contributed substantively to the identification and understanding of the essential elements of social work that constitute the common base of social work in all fields.

By the end of the 1970s, however, the circle began to close. Today, there is increasing acceptance of the position taken by White more than 30 years ago that despite commonalities in purpose, responsibility, knowledge, skills, and philosophy, "All social work practice is specific; there is no generic practice of social work (White, 1951, p. 33). As a consequence, health social work has reemerged as a specific, identifiable field of specialized social work and the demand for specialized educational preparation for practice in the field has expanded accordingly. Health social work is once again one of the profession's most rapidly growing and dynamic fields of practice.

The need for a book like this is apparent. Because of the fragmentation of health social work's development during the 1960s and 1970s, there has been a lag in the production and publication of literature for health social work practice. Indeed, Bartlett's book on medical casework—originally published in 1940 by the American Association of Medical Social Workers, revised in 1952 by the inclusion of a new preface and a retrospective chapter, and reissued in 1958 by the National Association of Social Workers—remained for many years the principal framework for direct social work practice in the health field.

While the flow of new health social work literature has accelerated in recent years, the gap in the development of conceptual frameworks for clinical social work in the field persists. The persistence of this gap represents a serious deficit inasmuch as the majority of professional social workers in the health field hold direct practice positions.

This book is an attempt to help bridge that gap. Its preparation was guided by two major objectives which derive from its basic position. The first was to identify and emphasize those things that are central to social work and its clinical practice. The second was to consider the application of these central elements in terms of the special requirements which are posed by the problems of central concern to the health field—physical illness, disability, and injury.

The first objective reflects concern about the perceived consequences of the ever-increasing demands posed by the burgeoning social needs, rapid production of new knowledge, and proliferation of interventive techniques that have impacted social work for the last 20 or more years. Because of the pressing nature of these demands, there has been a tendency to assume responsibility for the amelioration of problems beyond the ken of social work and to incorporate that responsibility into its professional mission. Similarly, new knowledge and interventive techniques have been incorporated into professional practice without sufficient analysis of their appropriateness, function, or pertinence for the realization of social work purpose. The results, as perceived here, have included a diffusion of effort, a confusion of purpose, and sometimes a loss of identity. These results, in turn, have led to what appears to be a growing inability to distinguish social work, especially its clinical practice, from other helping professions, and an inability to communicate clearly to social work novices and to colleagues in other professions what it is that social workers think about and do and why they think and act as they do.

The second objective reflects concern about what is perceived here to be an unanticipated consequence of the concerted effort, institutionalized in the middle 1950s, to identify the common core of social work practice. While there can be no question that this effort was a necessary step—indeed, a crucial step—in the profession's development, attention to the commonalities eclipsed the differences between social work in the various fields. Despite Bartlett's observations in 1957 that far "more is involved than just the application of social work knowledge and skill to one setting or another"; that social work is incomplete "until the welding of generic with specific is completed"; and that analysis of how the special features and requirements of each field determine the selective use of the common social work core and additions to it remained unfinished (pp. 24ff), generic formulations in practice theory and in social work curricula took on lives of their own. These developments virtually ignored the implications of the characteristics of and knowledge specific to the various fields in which social work is practiced, discounted their particular missions, and downplayed their problems of central concern. Thus, in an effort to overcome the deficits inherent in the overspecialization that had characterized the field in the past, social workers located and defined a common core; the unintended outcome was the substitution of one extreme for the other.

In response to these two objectives and the concerns they reflect, the focus of this book is on those elements of social work's common core that are deemed essential to the profession's purpose and its clinical practice as that practice occurs in the health field. This focus is one of complementarity, and has as a goal avoidance of the dichotomies posed by overemphasis on either generic or the specific.

Because many of the essentials of clinical social work considered in the pages that follow express aspects of social work's common base, this book can be of help to social work novices seeking to understand and master that base. Because these elements are discussed in relation to the particular requirements and characteristics of the health field, the book can serve as a guide to social workers who wish to specialize their knowledge and skill for practice in health settings. Because it regards the generic and specific elements of social work as complementary aspects of one whole, it may be used by experienced health social workers in support of their ongoing efforts to clarify the particular synthesis of social work and nonsocial work knowledge that informs their practice, the factors that distinguish social work from other health professions, and the similarities and differences between their clinical practice and that of clinical social workers in other fields. With respect to this last consideration, social workers in nonhealth settings may also find the chapters that follow of interest.

Part I of the book is divided into seven chapters. The first chapter introduces the developmental context of social work in the health field, major social work concepts, and their functions in clinical social work in health settings. In general terms, Chapter 1 begins the process of weaving past and present, generic and specific, into a conceptual framework. In doing so, it sets the stage for the following six chapters.

The second chapter continues the process of building the conceptual framework by considering ways in which elements of social work's common core and knowledge from the health field and other pertinent sources can be organized to form a knowledge base that informs the social worker's clinical practice. The remaining chapters deal with specific aspects or dimensions of clinical social work and their application to the health field: clinical process and relationship; clinical diagnosis and intervention planning; clinical social work methods of intervention; collaborative practice; and functions inherent in the clinical social work role, including research. Figures and tables illustrate or summarize important ideas and concepts at various points in the book.

Part II of the book consists of articles selected as exemplars of the general content of the chapters. Some of these articles are classic statements by health social workers that are no longer readily available outside of special library holdings or private collections. Others are more current and some are published here for the first time. The intent of this particular organization is to combine the book's chapters and relevant readings into a single volume, an approach that differs from the more common practice of publishing texts and readings in separate volumes.

Winding its way through the book is the perspective of membership. Indeed, the book might well have been subtitled, "A Membership Perspective." This perspective, as introduced here, was formulated by Hans S. Falck and is based on his study, practice, and teaching over a period of years. Its origins can be found in his writings, many of which are cited in the chapters that follow.

From the perspective of membership, people are viewed as simultaneously social and psychological in nature and neither can be reduced from the other. Further, membership in a variety of social groups is perceived as fundamental to human life. People and their groups, including those usually described in social work literature as environments, society, and institutions, are regarded as one whole. From these basic points of departure, the membership perspective becomes a means for maintaining focus on factors that are central to social work, thereby making possible a reconciliation of dichotomies and dilemmas that have plagued the profession in the past. Thus, social work and its practice can be more readily distinguished from other professions and their practice.

This book is the first to apply the membership perspective to a field of social work practice. By applying and extending it into previously unconsidered dimensions of clinical practice in the health field, many ideas and concepts—hitherto associated with particular and sometimes conflicting schools of social work theory—have been reformulated into a new conceptualization of practice. As such, this book illustrates the potential of the membership perspective, not only for understanding clinical social work, or social work in the health field, but also for clarifying the dimensions of other forms of social work, and social work in other fields.

It will be noted that the material in the chapters of this book is conceptualized primarily in terms of clinical social work in secondary and tertiary health settings. This is because most health social workers today continue to practice in secondary and tertiary settings where the care and treatment of people who are physically ill, disabled, or injured is the central purpose. For those who practice in primary settings, where the maintenance of physical health is the major purpose, some minor modifications of the formulations in the chapters of this book may be needed.

Where and how such modifications should be made will be apparent to those health social workers whose major efforts are directed to the prevention of adverse health conditions and problems.

As a final introductory comment, it should be pointed out, perhaps, that except for an occasional reference in some of the exemplars, clinical social work in relation to mental health is not included as an aspect of health social work in this book. This is because the position this book takes is that health and mental health are separate fields. It is recognized that in some schools of thought they are considered parts of a single field, and it is also recognized that each has implications for the other. As ongoing research yields new knowledge and understanding, it may be that health and mental health will form a single field. The advances that have been made in the use and effectiveness of psychotropic drugs and recent findings which suggest that many of the mental conditions previously thought to be of nonorganic origin do, in fact, appear to be of organic etiology suggest that this may indeed come to pass. Nevertheless, with the possible exception of those settings where health and mental health social workers practice under a unified administrative structure and employ a unified approach, the characteristics and problems of central concern, the policy, the organization and structure, and the funding patterns which shape the health and mental health systems in this country appear to be sufficiently different at the present time to warrant regarding each as a field of practice in its own right.

It will be apparent to readers of this book that many of the formulations in its chapters draw on the ideas, concepts, and understanding of many notable social workers of the past and present. In some instances, their work is the basis for specific conclusions about certain aspects of professional social work. In other instances, they point the way to new formulations or reformulations of important ideas. In part, their work chronicles the origins and constants in social work thought and practice. As such, they suggest the richness of social work and its professional growth. Together, they represent the heritage that is each social worker's professional legacy.

References

Bartlett, Harriett M. *Some Aspects of Casework in a Medical Setting.* Chicago: American Association of Medical Social Workers, 1940. Reprinted by the National Association of Social Workers, 1958.

Bartlett, Harriett M. *50 Years of Social Work in the Medical Setting: Past Significance, Future Outlook.* New York: National Association of Social Workers, 1957.

White, Grace. The distinguishing characteristics of medical social work. *Medical Social Work*, September 1951, 1:1, 31–39.

Acknowledgments

Writing the chapters of this book has made me acutely aware of how many people have contributed to it, and how very large my debt to them is. Not only is the debt large, it is also ongoing. One's views, thoughts, and ideas do not spring into existence full-blown. Rather, they evolve and—like social work itself—are always "in process." The best one can do, it seems to me, is to freeze that process for a moment in time and try to acknowledge the debts one owes at that moment, with full realization that some who have contributed significantly in the past will remain unidentified in the present.

With this thought in mind, I would like to thank those social workers whom I have never met, but whose writings are such rich gifts. Among them are Harriett M. Bartlett, Felix Biestek, Gordon Hamilton, Helen Harris Perlman, and Jessie Taft. There are others as well, but the contributions of these social workers are representative of the legacy from which all members of the profession are free to benefit, as I have.

Early teachers also had a hand in shaping the chapters of this book. Norris E. Class, Helen Northen, and Barbara Solomon are among those who first helped me to find my way in social work. They set standards which serve as constant goals, but are sometimes difficult to attain. I have had other teachers too, not in the formal sense, but in the sense of always gleaning something important from even the most casual interactions. These "teachers" include H. Otto Dahlke, Emanuel E. Tropp, and Ruth E. Smalley.

I depend on my colleagues for helping me to stay on the track, for pulling me out of the ditch when I stumble, and for prodding me along when I go into a stall. I am indebted to Hans S. Falck, who gives so much so freely. Our discussions have expanded my thinking in new directions and have helped me to rediscover and clarify the central dynamics of social work and the language which explains its fundamental unity. Indeed, he will find much in these pages that reflect his thinking and his influence and, hopefully, some new ideas as well.

I owe a very special debt to Dojelo C. Russell, who struggled with me through the entire process of writing this book. She read every page of manuscript and asked all the necessary "so what?" questions. As in the past when she has been of so much help in so many different situations, her questions, comments, and suggestions made a difference.

Jaclyn Miller was of great help in spotting problematic passages in many sections of this book, particularly in the chapters on methods and collaboration. Thanks are also due to Frances Raphael, whose model of the casework process served as the basis for the process outline in Chapter 5; to Marcel Charpentier, director of social work at the Memorial Hospital in Pawtucket, Rhode Island; to Amanda Cummings of the North Charles General Hospital in Baltimore, Maryland, who contributed the case material in Chapters 3 and 4, respectively; and to Charlotte Schrieberg and Ruby Walker who commented on portions of the draft. Lila Patterson helped by typing many parts of the manuscript and by overseeing the seemingly endless flow of pages through the copying machine.

Elaine Rothenberg, former dean of the Virginia Commonwealth University School of Social Work, has my gratitude for making it possible to transform an idea into reality. She found the time in my schedule and the tangible means necessary to support the writing of this book.

Finally, I would like to thank the authors and publishers of the articles and papers that appear as exemplars in this book. Their cooperation is deeply appreciated.

The help received from these people, and from others who supported me in this undertaking, cannot be adequately acknowledged. Suffice it to say, they prove the reality and the benefits of collegial membership.

Contributors

Marcel O. Charpentier, M.S.W., A.C.S.W., is the director of social work at the Memorial Hospital in Pawtucket, Rhode Island. He earned his social work degree at Virginia Commonwealth University.

Sarah N. Cohen, M.S.W., A.C.S.W., is a partner in Options for Aging, a consultation service for older adults and their families in New York City. At the time her article was written, she was a home care social worker at the Lenox Hill Hospital in New York City.

Randy Lee Comfort, M.S.W., is a social worker in private practice in Denver, Colorado. At the time her article was written, she was a social worker providing family services in the office of a pediatrician in private practice in Commerce City, Colorado.

Amanda Cummings, M.S.W., is a social worker at the North Charles General Hospital in Baltimore, Maryland. She earned her social work degree at Virginia Commonwealth University.

Bernadette Egan, M.S.W., A.C.S.W., is a social worker supervisor with the International Ladies Garment Workers Union Health Center in New York City. At the time her article was written she was a home care social worker at the Lenox Hill Hospital in New York City.

Hans S. Falck, Ph.D., A.C.S.W., is professor of social work at the School of Social Work and professor of psychiatry at the Medical College of Virginia, Virginia Commonwealth University. Formerly the Regenstein Distinguished Professor of the Social Sciences at the Menninger Foundation in Topeka, Kansas, he is the author of numerous articles and monographs. Dr. Falck is a Fellow of the Royal Society for Health, serves on the editorial boards of the *Journal of Clinical Supervision, Social Work in Health Care,* and *Social Work with Groups.* He is the editor of the *Journal of Education for Social Work.*

Louise F. Galvin, M.D., was the director of the Bureau of Crippled Children of the Virginia State Health Department in Richmond, Virginia, from 1947 to 1967. Prior to service as its director, Dr. Galvin served as a pediatrician in the Bureau's specialty clinics. She is presently retired and residing in Richmond, Virginia.

Archie J. Hanlan, D.S.W., was an associate professor of Social Work at the University of Pennsylvania School of Social Work. Prior to joining the faculty of the University of Pennsylvania, he was a member of the faculty of the George Warren Brown School of Social Work of Washington University in St. Louis.

Jeanette Hertzman was formerly a case work supervisor in the Social Service Department of the Montefiore Hospital in Pittsburgh, Pennsylvania.

Rosalie A. Kane, D.S.W., is a social scientist at the Rand Corporation in Santa Monica, California, and teaches at the School of Social Welfare at the University of California at Los Angeles. She is also the editor of *Health and Social Work.*

Michael S. Kappy, M.D., is a pediatrician at the Department of Pediatrics, Miller Health Center of the University of Florida School of Medicine. At the time his article was written, he was in private practice in Commerce City, Colorado.

Margaret A. Kauffman, Ed.D., M.S.N., earned her doctoral degree from the University of California and her master's degree from Western Reserve University. At the time her article was written, she was assistant professor of medical-surgical nursing at the School of Nursing, University of California.

Barbara Leff, M.S.W., A.C.S.W., was a clinical social worker with the Veterans Administration Hospital in New York City at the time her article was written.

Judith Poole, M.S.W., is director of social work at the Retreat Hospital in Richmond, Virginia. She earned her master's degree at Virginia Commonwealth University.

Edith Shapiro, M.S.W., was an instructor in social work at the University of California and a clinical social worker at the Veterans Administration Hospital in Los Angeles, California, at the time her article was written.

Grace White, M.A.S.S.A., was president of the American Association of Medical Social Workers from 1944 to 1946. She chaired the Association's Education Committee and its subcommittee on teaching medical students, and served on many of its other committees. Formerly on the staff of the Council on Social Work Education, she earned her Master of Social Service Administration degree from the University of Chicago and currently resides in Lexington, Kentucky.

Rachel Wyman was formerly a social worker at the Hospital for Joint Diseases in New York City. At the time her article was written, she was senior medical social worker at the Montefiore Hospital in Pittsburgh, Pennsylvania.

A Guide to
Professional Practice

1

The Context and Concepts of Clinical Social Work in the Health Field

Introduction

Health social work was born of concern for social factors as aspects of health and illness care. Its beginnings in Great Britain, Europe, and the United States date back to the end of the nineteenth century. It is one of the oldest established fields of professional social work practice (Butrym, 1967; Cannon, 1913).

The full history of health social work will not be recounted here. Others have recounted it in rich detail elsewhere (Bartlett, 1957, 1975; Cabot, 1919; Cannon, 1952; Kerson, 1981; Stites, 1955; Nacman, 1977). It is necessary, however, to note that history as the sphere of activity in which concepts that flow from the common base and purpose of social work intersect with the special demands of physical health, illness, disability, and injury to form a separate field of social work practice.

In the United States, early medical-social concerns crystallized in 1902 in an emphasis on social factors in the education of medical students at Johns Hopkins Hospital. Similar concern developed among visiting nurses who were often part of a hospital or dispensary service. In 1904, this concern led to the offering of elective courses which emphasized social aspects of medical care in the nursing program at the New York Presbyterian Hospital (Cannon, 1913). These beginnings laid the groundwork for the emergence of health social work as a distinct field of social work practice in America.

First known as hospital social work, and later as medical social work, health social work began in the United States in 1905 at the Massachusetts General Hospital where Richard C. Cabot, M.D., organized and directed the first health social work service with Garnet I. Pelton as the first American health social worker. One year later, Ida M. Cannon, a registered nurse who had completed a formal program of social work education at

Simmons College, joined the staff. Together, Cabot and Cannon influenced the development of health social work for nearly five decades.

After 1905, the new social work specialization spread rapidly to other hospitals and sectors of medical and public health care. By 1919, social workers were found in some 200 hospitals in the United States, and by 1930, the number of hospital social service departments stood at more than 1,000. As many as 40 to 50 social workers were employed in a single social service department in some of these hospitals, while others employed only one (Cabot, 1919; Beckly and McMahon, 1933).

Today, some 45,000 social workers are employed in hospitals, in the public health service, in community health clinics and centers, in health maintenance organizations, and in other sectors of the health system (Miller and Rehr, 1983). Of these, 25,000 social workers are found in nearly 7,000 hospitals. Approximately 4,000 social workers are employed by the Veterans Administration alone (Berkman, 1977; Bracht, 1978).

In 1918, at the National Conference of Social Work—after several years of informal meetings—health social workers formally associated by establishing the American Association of Hospital Social Workers, the first professional social work organization in the United States. In 1934, the name of the organization was changed to the American Association of Medical Social Workers to reflect the movement of social work into nonhospital sectors of health care. The Association took a leading role in the advancement of theory and standards for social work practice in the health field and in the evolution of professional education (Stites, 1955).

The American Association of Medical Social Workers was one of the seven professional organizations that merged in 1955 to form the National Association of Social Workers.* Through units of the National Association, health social workers have continued to provide leadership for the development of both general and specialized practice. Their work has been particularly noteworthy in, for example, the Medical Social Work Section (1955-63), the Commission of Social Work Practice (1955-63), the Joint Committee on Participation in Medical Education (1961), the Council on Social Work in Medical and Health Services (1963-76), and the Health Standards Quality Committee (1976-Present).

In 1966, the Society for Hospital Social Work Directors of the American Hospital Association was organized with focus on social work administration and standards in health care facilities. A joint committee of the American Hospital Association and the National Association of Social

---

*The six other associations that joined the American Association of Medical Social Workers to form the National Association of Social Workers were: The American Association of Social Workers, American Association of Psychiatric Social Workers, American Association of Group Workers, Association for the Study of Community Organization, National Association of School Social Workers, and the Social Work Research Group.

Workers makes possible joint activity by the two organizations (Beck, 1977; Phillips, 1977).

This brief historical sketch serves as background for the identification of concepts deemed essential to social work and its clinical practice in the health field. These concepts are discussed briefly in the sections that follow. First, however, for purposes of clarity and consistency, the terms *health social work* and *clinical social work in health settings* need definition. As used here, these two terms parallel the older terms, *social work in medical settings* and *medical social work*.

Health Social Work

The term *health social work* refers to all of social work in the health field. It refers to the totality of the profession's contribution to both health and illness care. Thus, it includes much more than clinical practice. It is a term inclusive of the range of social work roles and functions in the health field that, at a minimum, includes: practice in relation to institutional, community, state, and federal health policy formation; program planning and administration; the educational preparation of social workers and other professionals for practice in the health field; and social research.

Bartlett's (1961b) analysis represents the first comprehensive examination of health social work as a whole. The more recent examination of health social work by Bracht (1978) expands the focus on the whole of health social work to include specific guides to a variety of social work roles and functions in the health field. Germain (1977, 1981) has developed a comprehensive theory of practice applicable to a variety of social work roles and functions in the health field; and Coulton (1979) and Hubschman (1983), among others, have examined specific, nonclinical dimensions of health social work in some detail.

Clinical Social Work in Health Settings

Akin to the older concept of *medical social work*, the term *clinical social work* first came into use in federal hospitals and out-patient clinics where it was coined to describe the practice of social workers with and on behalf of patients. It gained particular currency in hospitals of the Veterans Administration where its definition includes the collaborative activities of social workers with members of the medical and paramedical professions (Lustman, 1959; Bartlett, 1961b).

In recent years, controversy has developed over the definition of clinical social work. For some, clinical social work is synonymous with individual psychotherapy. Frank's (1979) definition of clinical social work as "a process of treatment which addresses itself to the support, promotion, and increase of internal resources (psychic equipment) in people" (p. 14) is supportive of this view. For others, such definitions are too narrow to allow for the full realization of social work purpose and have the disadvantage of limiting the worker's clinical practice to a method that is generic to a variety of professions.

The definition of clinical social work developed in this book is broader than those that focus only on the internal resources of people. It is also more consistent with the generally accepted position that clinical social work does not rest on any single theory or interventive approach, but selects both "in accordance with the needs of each client and situation" (Ewalt, 1979, p. 90).

As understood here, clinical social work includes the full range of social work diagnosis, goal establishment, interventive foci, and methods. No single custom, protocol, theory, or etiquette governs the clinical social workers' decision to work with the client/patient, family, or significant others, including other health professionals, singly or in groups. This understanding informs the following definition of clinical social work in the health field:

> Clinical social work in the health field is a mutual process of face-to-face interventions in which the professional social worker provides social work services to clients, including services on behalf of those clients, who use them to resolve mutually identified and defined problems in client social functioning precipitated or exacerbated by actual or potential physical illness, disability, or injury.

With these definitions in mind, we now turn our attention to a consideration of concepts deemed essential to social work and its clinical practice.

Concepts Central to the Clinical Practice of Social Work in the Health Field

The concepts of social functioning and social stress have combined throughout social work history to form the profession's raison d'étre. They are fundamental to the practice of clinical social work—the direct provision of social work services to clients in health settings. Since they are central to professional practice, these two concepts unify the activities of health social workers in diverse settings into a single field of practice and, in turn, they bind that field to the profession. Clarity about the meaning of these ideas is, therefore, important.

Social Functioning

Emphasis on social functioning is present, in some form, even in the earliest writings of the profession (Cheyney, 1926; Richmond, 1899, 1907, 1930). It runs through the development of social work and its specialized practice in various fields and settings. At times, when attention is directed to other factors important to the expansion of social work theory or practice, it seems to fade in importance. At other times, it seems to receive only lip service. But, it is present, in one form or another, throughout the profession's history (Bartlett, 1970). It is central to the logic of social work practice, and it remains its most enduring constant.

> Whatever the problem, such as illness or delinquency, social work is always concerned with the same aspect, namely, the lessening of social stress and the improvement of social functioning. Hence, its role is consistent throughout. (Bartlett, 1961a, p. 11)

The term *social* refers to life in companionship with others, to life in community. It involves the mutual relations of people living in an organized society. Bartlett (1957) identified two meanings that have been included in social work's definition of the term: "the system of social relationships between people and the system of cultural values in society" (p. 31).

Function refers to something that is related to or dependent on other factors that together operate in a particular way. Thus, the gears and cogs of a clock operate in relation to one another in such a way that the clock, more or less accurately, keeps track of the passage of time. In social terms, function refers to the behavior of people. More specifically, it refers to the way they perform the tasks and meet the demands of life in some relation to the social requirements and cultural norms of the community or communities of which they are part.

From a social work perspective, then, *social functioning* is the ability of people to perform the tasks of daily life and to engage in mutual relationships with other people in ways that are gratifying to themselves and to others and meet the needs of an organized community.

Social Stress

The term *stress*, on the other hand, refers to action on a body of balanced forces whereby strain or deformation occurs which interferes with the body's normal equilibrium. In social terms, stress is strain or tension that interferes with the ability of people to satisfactorily perform daily tasks or live satisfactorily in community with others.

Social stress may be physical or social, mental or emotional in character. Its roots may be in physiological, socioeconomic, or psychological factors, or in any combination of these. It may be manifested physically as illness or disability, or socially in the interpersonal relationships of people, or in the interaction of people with their social institutions.

Bartlett (1961b) underscores the need for social workers to "be clear that the concept covers not only pressures, burdens, and conflicts but also deprivations, i.e., anything that is stressful" (p. 138). She identifies "loneliness" as a deprivation since it is the emotional manifestation of the "lack of essential relationship." It is, therefore, a form of psychosocial stress. Because of the impact of social stress, Bartlett also notes the related need of social workers to understand the ways people cope biologically, psychologically, and socially since these strategies influence ability to function.

Thus, the concept of social functioning and the related concept of social stress give form and direction to the purpose and practice of social work as a profession.

> Social work is a profession whose body of knowledge skills and techniques are and may be learned for the sole purpose of helping human beings in social difficulties whether the malfunction occurs because of interpersonal dysfunction or environmental stress. (Brock, 1969, p. 23)

Focus on social functioning and social stress is particularly vivid in the literature and practice of health social work (Berkman, 1978). Like social work in general, it is based on belief in the value of people as human beings. Also like social work in general, its primary focus is on the social functioning of people, but since health social work is practiced in organizations and institutions where illness and disability—their diagnosis, treatment, cure, and/or prevention—constitute the problem of central concern, the lens through which social functioning is assessed is the impact of illness and disability. Health social work seeks to help ill or disabled people to maintain, attain, or regain a mode of living that is satisfactory to them and helps them make a socially positive contribution to the human groups and communities of which they are part.

Related Concepts

A number of related concepts flow from the theme of social functioning and social stress that reflect social work purpose and activity and distinguish them from the purpose and activity of other professions in the multidisciplinary settings that constitute the American health system. It is to these elements that attention will now be directed since they are basic to the foundation upon which clinical social work in the health field rests.

The Client Is a Social Being

In the early writings of Cannon and Cabot are found rudimentary definitions of concepts in health social work that are consistent with social work's core purpose. The first of these is that human beings are social beings who engage in multiple relationships with other people and have membership in a variety of human groups.

In the first book written on health social work, Cannon (1913) noted that the patient's physical condition is only one aspect of the client that the hospital social worker needs to take into account.

> As the doctor sees the diseased organ not as isolated but as possibly affecting and being affected by the whole body, so the hospital social worker sees the patient not merely as one unfortunate person occupying a hospital bed but as belonging to a family or community group that is altered because of the ill health of one *member*.* (p. 16)

One need not be an experienced health social worker to see this notion acted out on a daily basis in hospitals and other health settings across the country. Even the client in the hospital for a minor medical condition, requiring only one or two days hospitalization, may be visited as soon after admission as possible by his or her spouse, children, parents, other relatives, and/or friends from the neighborhood, from work, church, social club, or other group in which the client holds membership. As one hospital social work director put it, "The patient doesn't have to be here long before somebody from his family and every group he is a member of starts to march in and out of his room."

Others visit the client too. Physician, nurse, and social worker soon join the parade, for while a hospital patient the client also shares membership with these and other health professionals and hospital staff in a series of relationships that are precipitated by the client's health status.

Two years after the publication of Cannon's book, Cabot (1915) expanded on the notion of the person as a social being. He identified family relationships, friendships, neighborhood ties, and those relationships based on common interest as among the most satisfying human ties (pp. 49–50). Cabot's ideas anticipate the biopsychosocial view of the person and the

---

*Emphasis added. The concepts of member and membership further define the person and social functioning and hence are germane to social work's core purpose. They will be dealt with in more detail in Chapter 2.

concept of social functioning. He conceptualized the person in relationship terms which suggest a variety of human groupings: age, sex, race, residence, occupation, economic status, social status, social environment, and educational level (pp. 72–74). These are attributes long familiar to social workers for they date back to the profession's earliest formulations of its practice (Richmond, 1917, 1922), and they define, in part, those aspects of the person that make him or her a social being.

Cabot recognized the roles of subconscious and conscious factors, including the instinctual needs of humans for food, shelter, and "procreation," and their interaction with social factors as forces that influence human behavior (pp. 72–73). Cabot wrote, however, while sociology was still in its infancy and before the contributions of dynamic psychology had major impact on social work thought, and the notion of the person as a multidimensional being, with biological, psychological, and social attributes was more fully developed by others who followed him.

Even in these early writings, however, the notion of the person as a social being stands out clearly, if not completely developed. As Smalley (1967) has pointed out, early social work thought included awareness of the importance of the family to the person, the place of the person in his or her family, and "the importance of family relationships for individual development and well-being" (p. 19).

Cannon clearly perceived the person in multidimensional terms. She cites James's tripartite notion of "the material me, the social me, and the spiritual me" to explicate her view (p. 30).

> As man's me is the sum total of all he can call his, not only his body and his psychic powers, but his clothes and his house, his wife and children, his ancestors and friends, his reputation and works, his lands and horses, and yacht and bank account. (James, 1905, p. 291)

This multidimensional perspective remains a feature of social work thought. It is, for example, the basis for the distinctions between individuation and individualism made by Falck (1976).

> Individuation has to do with that process in early growth which provides us with a sense of *who we are within the context of relationship to others* . . . *Individuation is a social process*, a process that describes relationships in such a way that one understands that they occur as part of group life. (p. 33)

Glick (1977) and Reiner (1979) also maintain the multidimensional perspective that animates Falck's work. They believe that individualistic behavior denies the essentially social nature of human beings. Like Falck, they regard it as a precipitating factor in the evolution of impersonal, bureaucratic society which, in turn, leads to a sense of personal irrelevance. Falck stresses the fact that people are born into groups and derive a sense of belonging, identity, and autonomy within them. Glick asserts that individualistic behavior transforms the concept of personal freedom into one of license, and that it tends to deify the "isolated self," as seen in demands for instant gratification of desires and wishes as a right unrestricted by social obligations or norms. Individualism, the underlying rationale for such behavior, overlooks the fact that self-actualization and a sense of worth are by-products of socially productive living.

Glick describes the results of individualistic behavior as a sense of loss, a longing for love and security, an increasing sense of impotence, and transitory quests for intimacy. Reiner describes a "diagnostic picture" of such behavior in which failure or inability to be an essential part of a group, to be cared for, to have opportunity to lead a disciplined life, to find safe ways to express anger, and to be responsible for one's actions are reflected as major components.

To Falck, individualism and its associated behavior are presocial in nature and are, therefore, inadequate and inappropriate as a basis for social work practice. Glick credits loss of the social perspective as a source of serious difficulty for social work since the results are a tendency to regard "the family and society," human groups and institutions, "as social barriers to clients," and a failure to recognize "the pursuit of self" as a cause of conditions that necessitate social work intervention. He stresses, therefore, "the healthy or functional social context of behavior" (p. 584). Similarly, Reiner concludes that "the cure for individual feelings of irrelevance can be found only in collectives in which the person is relevant" (p. 10).

From a social work perspective, then, the person is an essentially social being with physical, psychological, and social attributes, who derives a sense of identity, personal autonomy, and meaning from relationships with other people. Group membership is the essence of human life. Within groups, the person acts and is acted upon, creates and is created, cares and is cared for, uses and is used to learn and master the autonomous tasks of daily living. Through membership in groups, the person engages in activities that lead to a sense of worth, accomplishment, well-being, and fulfillment.

The person is neither a passive being created by external forces alone, nor a self-contained being created solely by internal forces, but a dynamic participant in the process of his or her development as a human being. This view recognizes what Smalley (1967) describes as the limits on human development imposed by genetic endowment and "the irrational, the unconscious, the powerful potentially crippling effects of life's experiences, particularly early experiences and relationships within the immediate family," and it also recognizes "the push toward life, health, and fulfillment as primary in human beings" (p. 66).

Thus, the concept of the person as a social being is a key one for social work in general, and for health social work in particular. As Bartlett (1961a) aptly notes: "Physical illness can be regarded as a social deviation because it incapacitates the individual for carrying on his social responsibilities and thus causes social loss" (p. 42).

Illness and Disability as Social Phenomena

Bartlett's notion that the consequences of ill health represent a social loss suggests another important concept in health social work. That is, illness and disability, as well as health at the other end of the continuum, are social phenomena which relate directly to the ability of people to function in community with others. Cabot (1915) asserted that the "essence" of social work, or "that which corresponds to diagnosis and treatment as the center of the . . . medical sciences," is the "study of character under adversity and the influences that mold it for good or ill" (pp. 55–56). While reflecting the early period of health social work in which he wrote, Cabot's formulation does suggest aspects of current social work formulations of social functioning, social stress, and the social nature of people. As already noted, these are concepts which give form and direction to clinical social work, whatever the field of practice.

Adversity is a misfortune that acts against or is contrary to something, in this case, the social functioning of people. Cabot recognized that how a person deals with adversity is determined to a considerable extent by social-psychological factors, such as family, culture, religion, and the attitudes and behavior these and other group memberships foster. These are variables that influence the person "for good or ill." In this instance, the adversity or difficulty is illness or disability which disrupts normal body systems and requires medical intervention on the one hand, and which may disrupt social relationship and functioning on the other.

The ability of the ill or disabled person to participate in social, religious, or cultural activities may be curtailed or eliminated. Ability to earn a living or support a family may be diminished or ended, thus requiring others, family members or society, to contribute to or provide financial income and support. The cost of medical and follow-up care may drain available resources causing more social and psychological stress.

Thus, it is clear that the impact of ill health or disability is not limited to the ill or disabled person alone. Moos and Tsu (1977) underscore the fact that "family members and friends, as well as patients, are affected by the crisis, encounter many of the same or closely related adaptive tasks, and use the same types of coping skills" (p. 8). Family roles and friendships may be affected. Certain medical regimens, involving specific tasks, new ways of thinking and acting, or special equipment, may be imposed that require changes in living arrangements, standards, or style. How the ill or disabled person and others involved in the situation cope with these and other demands are determined by such social membership variables as age, sex, religion, race, ethnicity, culture, level of education, and socio-economic status.

> Illness is a social event that affects not only the ill person, but also his family and may cause disruption in all aspects of their living. Illness is inexorable in its choice and plays no favourites; poor and rich alike are its victims. Indisputably, the dislocation caused by sickness and hospitalization varies in degree according to the person, without reference to the diagnosis or severity of the disease or the economic status of the patient. (Brock, 1969, pp. 29–30)

Adversity, or misfortune, has another dimension relative to the definition of health, illness, and disability as social phenomena. This dimension concerns the roles social and psychological factors play in the etiology of poor health. As early as 1913, Cannon noted that "the common occurrence of sickness and poverty together has long been recognized as more than a coincidence" (p. 23). During the 17 years that followed Cannon's observation, health social workers expanded their understanding of the relationship between social factors, health status, and medical care (Wulkop, 1926). It was increasingly recognized that social factors influence health status in many ways and in many combinations, and thinking developed to the point where Thornton (1930) was able to classify social factors in health care according to three basic categories:

1. Social conditions which bear directly on the health of the patient, either inducing susceptibility to ill-health, or helping or hindering the securing and competing of medical care.
2. Social distress caused to others by the illness of patients; such as, loss of income, neglect of children, etc.
3. Social problems not having direct cause-and-effect relation to the health condition, but collateral to it. Such problems would exist independently of sickness. (p. 59)

These variables, and their interacting functions, generally became known as the social component of medical care (Thornton, 1937). Bartlett (1961b) has commented on the soundness of this approach that "required medical social workers to identify those social factors that were actually influencing the medical situation and describe the nature of the inter-action" (p. 134). She finds in Thornton's first category health social work's most important theme because it demonstrates the interaction of medical and social factors and provides the rationale for social work's role in health maintenance and illness care. The second category demonstrates the reciprocal nature of social factors and health status in which the "social distress caused to others by illness, tends to react on the patient in turn." To illustrate this point, Bartlett provides the example of a man who is "unable to support his family because of ill health," becomes anxious, "and not infrequently wishes to leave the hospital and return to work before his physical condition permits." Bartlett's analysis suggests that the third of Thornton's categories was less important in the long run because "situations in which social difficulties can be regarded as collateral to the medical situation . . . are not frequently found."

Beginning in the late 1930s and continuing through the 1940s and into the 1950s, the definition of the social component tended to narrow as psychiatric theory and thought permeated social work. An emphasis on the psychological aspects of the social component had the effect of singling out the meaning of illness to the patient as the major aspect of the situation calling for social work intervention (Bartlett, 1940; Goldstine, 1954). Awareness that the illness had meaning for the patient's family, however, was never lost and today a more balanced view prevails in health social work which defines the influence of both psychological and social factors in health and illness in terms of their manifestations in the social behavior of the people involved in the situation. The term *psychosocial* is often used to describe this balance, and the concept of *life style* has recently been coined to describe the function of these variables in relation to health and illness status (Bracht, 1978).

Nevertheless, whether referred to as the social aspects of medicine, the social component of medical care, the meaning of illness to the patient and family, the psychosocial component of health and illness care, or the relationship between life style and illness patterns, there is consistent recognition in health social work that health status is a social phenomenon and that illness and disability are social events in the lives of those affected by disease and handicapping conditions.

It has long been known that social stress can make an individual sick, and longer recognized that sickness can and does cause fear, depression, a break-down in family and other relationships, economic hardship because of loss or lowering of income or changes in personal and family standards of living. For all or any of these conditions the results may be broken homes and broken lives. There are other social dysfunctions too, some of which are becoming more urgent with every year of scientific change and technological progress, such as the need for post-discharge care adjustment of the pattern of living of the nuclear family and provision and use of medical services after hospitalization. (Brock, 1969, p. 30)

The Social Nature of the Health System and Health Practice

Wherever one looks at the American health system, it is apparent that it is made up of a range of social organizations and institutions in which representatives of an array of professions, disciplines, and occupations engage in separate and joint activities related to some aspect of health as the problem of central concern. In many ways, the hospital, because of its purpose and complex organization, demonstrates this most clearly. There are, however, several ways in which the various components of the health system can be viewed which suggest its social nature.

First, as Smalley (1967) has pointed out, hospitals, community health clinics, public health services, and the like, are among those social institutions which society supports through public, private, or sectarian means. Society supports these institutions in its own interest, as well as in the interest of its members who are served by them. This support takes various forms of social expression, the most obvious of which is financial. However, support is also indicated by the policies, procedures, and actions of regulatory bodies, by accountability procedures, and by service on the boards of directors of various health agencies. In this sense, the components of the health system are institutional representations of society's interest and stake in health and illness care.

In another sense, health institutions are social by virtue of the multidisciplinary nature of the services they provide and those who provide them. This perspective is not new. In writing about medical social service in 1943, for example, Rubinow described the hospital as "probably as complex and intricate a piece of social machinery as has been devised," the purpose of which is "to provide necessary and appropriate care for the sick" (p. 14). This complexity results, in part, from two characteristics of health care: the intricate, highly specialized knowledge and skill of each professional and staff member in the organization; and the synthesis of this knowledge and skill in the provision of services which are often given in collaboration or by health teams. Again, the hospital provides an apt example:

> The modern hospital, staffed by qualified personnel from many professional disciplines using a variety of work skills and administered professionally, is indeed a community resource. Society uses it as one of its instruments to promote physical, social, emotional, and mental health, and it is in this context that hospitals have to be considered. Modern hospitals normally subscribe to

two fundamental principles determining and governing their role and function in society. First, they conceive of themselves as an instrument shaped and used by society to give *total care* to the sick. Secondly, taking this as their mandate, they must provide and make available the many different and special resources, both in personnel and equipment, necessary to give total care. (Brock, 1969, p. 34)

In this connection, Butrym (1967) points out that a health agency cannot adequately fulfill its purpose if it does not consider the social needs of its clients, the range of which can be very wide. She notes, "It is by no means easy to distinguish between the relatively simple welfare needs which can be met without the intervention of a trained social worker and social problems which require professional assessment and skilled help" (pp. 28–29).

Cannon (1913) was aware of the social implications of institutionalized hospital care and the behavior of its personnel from the client's perspective. She describes the visiting staff, resident physicians, and nurses as "parts of a smooth-running machine ready daily to care for the sick and suffering." "But," she asks, "what of the patient?"

> The patient's point of view is in sharp contrast to that of nearly everyone he meets. All about him he sees people apparently indifferent where he is excited, comfortably unconscious of his pain, swiftly and easily passing him through their hands as a sailor coils a rope. To this big, strange place he comes, absorbed in consciousness of his own danger and discomfort, only to find he is one of many, a small part of a confusing mass. He is fortunate if he can enter into his hospital experience with a knowledge of the language and with some spirit of adventure to meet the incidents of life there. Too often, however, the hospital expects him to conform to rules and standards which he does not comprehend and to which he sometimes cannot quickly adjust himself. (pp. 26–27)

Wulkop (1926) also drew attention to the distress the patient experiences upon admission to the hospital and its source in what is seen or heard in the health setting. Client, family, and friends encounter in the health setting rules and procedures related to the demands of health and medical care that govern their behavior in ways that often produce anxiety, possibly fear or depression, and sometimes awe or exhilaration.

For most of this century, the orientation of clinical social work to practice in health settings has included recognition of this form of stress as an important dynamic in the provision and use of health care. It has also recognized it as an important factor in the client's perception of his or her role in the process. Although the situation has doubtlessly improved since Cannon and Wulkop made the observations cited above, the fact remains that this stress is expressed by the patient in his or her response to, and role in, the giving and taking of help.

All health professionals, therefore, need to draw on a common base of knowledge of human behavior from the social and behavioral sciences to better understand the patient, family, and colleagues in order to provide services effectively through a social process in which all play a part. It has sometimes been claimed that understanding of and skill in the use of relationship distinguishes social work from other helping professions. This, however, is not the case, nor is it the basis for social work's role in health care. All health professionals make use of relationship skills in their practice. Although it may be argued that social work education historically has placed greater emphasis on the development of relationship skills than has been the case in education for other helping professions, the use of relationship skills is not unique to social work. Rather, it is the core purpose, or that which is central to each profession, that distinguishes it from others, and the use of relationship skills by all health professionals, as a means to attain resolution of the problem for which the patient has sought help, is the common process which underscores the social nature of health and medical care practice.

The Authority and Sanction of Clinical Social Work in the Health Field

As noted, hospitals and other health agencies are social institutions which society supports in its own interest and in the interest of members served by them. They have, on occasion, been described by social workers, however, as "host agencies" in which social work plays a secondary kind of role. Use of this unfortunate term may be the result of somewhat confused efforts to distinguish between social agencies that are purely social work agencies in purpose and practice, and social agencies which respond to problems that are interdisciplinary in character and require, therefore, multidisciplinary practice. In addition to placing social work in the impossible role of perpetual guest, causing confusion among other health professionals, and producing dismay among social workers, this view overlooks the fact that medical and social work "are branches split off a common trunk:—*the care of people in trouble*" (Cabot, 1915, p. 91).

In this connection, Cannon (1913) referred to an "enlarged understanding" of health care, an understanding which takes into account human relationships, community life, temperament, and financial circumstances and combines these and other social considerations with the physician's knowledge of physical conditions to form a basis for sound medical-social judgment and action. Within such a framework, the value of the clinical social worker's contribution to the care of the patient "depends on [the] very fact of its being drawn fre n another field" (p. 107). In the revised version of her book, Cannon str esses the need for

> . . . the co-operation of one skilled in understanding social problems and equipped by training and experience to guide a patient in solving those personal problems that may arise from his illness or to which his illness may have been due in part. Thus, the medical social worker becomes a component part of organized medicine. (Cannon, 1923, p. 30)

Thus, it is clear that clinical social work, since its beginnings in the health field, has not been conceptualized as a secondary function, but as an integral part of direct patient care.

Smalley (1967) asserts that the community supports hospitals, and other multidisciplinary health agencies for that matter, as social institutions and that it engages social work to help hospitals realize their purpose as hospitals. The services of physicians, nurses, social workers, and others are, therefore, interdependent in the same way that physical and social conditions are interdependent. In addition, since physical and social factors must be considered in admission, diagnosis, and treatment, patients should, as Cannon points out, be discharged socially as well as medically when they leave the hospital.

Social work, then, is one of the many professions required for adequate and effective provision of health and medical care. No single profession is sufficient; all are needed. Social work's authority, like that of all the health professions, derives, therefore, from two major sources: society's sanction of its role and function; and its own knowledge and expertise in relation to health and illness care.

> . . . the degree and effectiveness of social work's professional self-direction will inevitably correspond to the profession's awareness, understanding, and control of its own purposes, resources, and actions, and of the complex social environment in which it operates. (Bartlett, 1961a, p. 12)

Conclusion

Health social work, as we have seen, is one of social work's oldest fields of specialized practice. It makes its contributions to health and illness care in a variety of social institutions which have as their central concern some aspect of health, illness and/or disability. These organizations are supported by society as expressions of its interest and stake in health and illness care.

Clinical social work in the health field draws on concepts from the common base of professional social work practice and applies them to work with clients who seek help with one or more of the problems for which the health system has been created. In doing so, the concepts of social functioning and social stress give form and direction to the practice of clinical social work in health agencies. These concepts are closely related to a perception of the person as a social being with biological, psychological, and social attributes. Illness and disability, a form of social as well as medical stress, represent social phenomena and social events in the lives of those they impact. Thus, clinical social work in health agencies seeks to help people maintain, attain, or regain ability to function socially when this ability requires changes in behavior necessary to maintain health or when that ability has been impacted by social stress in the form of illness or disability.

Social work pursues this purpose as one of the health care professions in recognition of the interrelatedness of social factors with health and medical factors. It is an integral part of the health system by virtue of its knowledge and expertise and by virtue of society's recognition and sanction of its contributions to health maintenance and illness care.

References

Bartlett, Harriett M. *Some aspects of social casework in a medical setting.* Chicago: American Association of Medical Social Workers, 1940. Reprinted by the National Association of Social Workers, 1958.

Bartlett, Harriett M. *50 years of social work in the medical setting: Past significance, future outlook.* New York: National Association of Social Workers, 1957.

Bartlett, Harriett M. *Analyzing social work practice by fields.* New York: National Association of Social Workers, 1961. (a)

Bartlett, Harriett M. *Social work practice in the health field.* New York: National Association of Social Workers, 1961. (b)

Bartlett, Harriett M. *The common base of social work practice.* Washington, DC: National Association of Social Workers, 1970.

Bartlett, Harriett M. Ida M. Cannon: Pioneer in medical social work. *Social Service Review,* June 1975, 49:2, 208-229.

Beck, Bertram M. Professional associations: National Association of Social Workers. In John B. Turner (Ed.), *Encyclopedia of Social Work,* II, 17th issue. Washington, DC: National Association of Social Workers, 1977, pp. 1084-1093.

Beckly, Helen & McMahon, Kate. Hospital Social Work. In Fred S. Hall (Ed.), *Social work yearbook.* 2nd issue. New York: Russell Sage Foundation, 1933, pp. 223-226.

Berkman, Barbara. Social services in health care. In Francine Sobey (Ed.), *Changing roles in social work practice.* Philadelphia: Temple University Press, 1977.

Berkman, Barbara. Knowledge base and program needs for effective social work practice in health: A review of the literature. Commissioned by the Society for Hospital Social Work Directors of the American Hospital Association, 1978.

Bracht, Neil F. *Social work in health care: A guide to professional practice.* New York: The Haworth Press, 1978.

Brock, Mary Gaughan. *Social work in the hospital organization.* Toronto: University of Toronto Press, 1969.

Butrym, Zofia. *Social work in medical care.* London: Routledge & Kegan Paul, 1967.

Cabot, Richard C. *Social service and the art of healing.* New York: Moffat, Yard & Company, 1915. Reprinted by the National Association of Social Workers, 1973.

Cabot, Richard C. *Essays on the meeting ground of doctor and social worker.* New York: Moffat, Yard & Company, 1919. Reprinted by the Arno Press and The New York Times, 1972.

Cannon, Ida M. *Social work in hospitals: A contribution to progressive medicine.* New York: Russell Sage Foundation, 1913 (rev. ed., 1923).

Cannon, Ida M. *On the social frontier of medicine: Pioneering in medical social service.* Cambridge: Harvard University Press, 1952.

Cheyney, Alice S. *The nature and scope of social work.* New York: American Association of Social Workers, 1926.

Coulton, Claudia J. *Social work quality assurance programs: A comparative analysis.* Washington, DC: National Association of Social Workers, 1979.

Ewalt, Patricia L. Social work process as an organizing concept. In Patricia L. Ewalt (Ed.), *Toward a definition of clinical social work.* Washington, DC: National Association of Social Workers, 1979, pp. 87-91.

Falck, Hans S. Individualism and communalism: Two or one? *Social Thought,* Summer 1976, II:3, 27-44.

Frank, Margaret Galdston. Clinical social work: Past, present, and future challenges and dilemmas. In Patricia L. Ewalt (Ed.), *Toward a definition of clinical social work.* Washington, DC: National Association of Social Workers, 1979, pp. 13-22.

Germain, Carel B. The ecological perspective on social work practice in health care. *Social Work in Health Care,* Fall 1977, 3:1, 67-76.

Germain, Carel B. Social work identity, competence, and autonomy: The ecological perspective. *Social Work in Health Care,* Fall 1981, 6:1, 1-10.

Glick, Peter M. Individualism, society, and social work. *Social Casework,* December 1977, 57:10, 579-584.

Goldstine, Dora. *Readings in the theory and practice of medical social work.* Chicago: University of Chicago Press, 1954; Midway Reprint, 1973.

Hubschman, Lynn, ed. *Hospital social work practice.* New York: Praeger Publishers, 1983.

James, William. *The principles of psychology,* vol. 1. New York: Henry Holt and Co., 1905.

Kerson, Toba Schwaber. *Medical social work: The pre-professional paradox.* New York: Irvington, 1981.

Lustman, Claire R. Development of research in a clinical social work service. *Social Work*, July 1959, 4:3, 77–83.

Miller, Rosalind S., & Rehr, Helen, eds. *Social work issues in health care.* Englewood Cliffs, N.J.: Prentice Hall, 1983.

Moos, Rudolf H., & Tsu, Vivien Davis. The crisis of physical illness: An overview. In Rudolf H. Moos (Ed.), *Coping with physical illness.* New York: Plenum Medical Book Company, 1977.

Nacman, Martin. Social work in health settings: A historical review. *Social Work in Health Care*, Summer 1977, 2:4, 407–418.

Phillips, Beatrice. Social workers in health services. In John B. Turner (Ed.), *Encyclopedia of social work*, I, 17th issue. Washington, DC: National Association of Social Workers, 1977, pp. 615-625.

Reiner, Beatrice Simcox. A feeling of irrelevance: The effects of a nonsupportive society. *Social Casework*, January 1979, 59:1, 3–10.

Richmond, Mary E. *Friendly visiting among the poor: A handbook for charity workers*, 1899. Reprinted by Patterson Smith Publishing Corporation, with an introductory essay by Max Siporin, 1969. Montclair, New Jersey: Publication No. 92, Patterson Smith Reprint Series in Criminology, Law Enforcement, and Social Problems.

Richmond, Mary E. *The good neighbor in the modern city.* Philadelphia: J. B. Lippincott Company, 1907.

Richmond, Mary E. *Social diagnosis.* New York: Russell Sage Foundation, 1917.

Richmond, Mary E. *What is social case work? An introductory description.* New York: Russell Sage Foundation, 1922.

Richmond, Mary E. The social case worker's task. In Joanna C. Colcord (Ed.), *The long view: Papers and addresses by Mary E. Richmond.* New York: Russell Sage Foundation, 1930, pp. 397-401. (Reprinted from Proceedings of the 44th Annual Session of the National Conference of Social Work, Pittsburgh, Pennsylvania, June 6-13, 1917, pp. 112-115.)

Rubinow, Leonora B. Medical social service. In Dora Goldstine (Ed.), *Expanding horizons in medical social work.* Chicago: University of Chicago Press, 1955, pp. 14-25. (Originally published in *Hospitals*, Vol. 17, No. 3 [March 1943], pp. 95-100.)

Smalley, Ruth E. *Theory for social work practice.* New York: Columbia University Press, 1967.

Stites, Mary A. *History of the American Association of Medical Social Workers.* Washington, DC: American Association of Medical Social Workers, 1955.

Thornton, Janet. *The functions of hospital social service.* Chicago: American Association of Hospital Social Workers, 1930.

Thornton, Janet. *The social component in medical care.* In collaboration with Marjorie Strauss Knauth. New York: Columbia University Press, 1937.

Wulkop, Elsie. *The social worker in a hospital ward.* With Comment by Richard C. Cabot, M.D. New York: Houghton Mifflin Company, 1926.

Organizing the Essential Knowledge Base
2 for Clinical Social Work Practice in Health Settings

Introduction

Effective clinical social work in any field requires a synthesis of knowledge from two essential sources. The first source is the common base of social work practice. The second source is the particular field itself. The synthesis of knowledge selected from these two essential sources yields the characteristics of social work practice in the particular field.

Bartlett (1961a) conceptualized this configuration of knowledge and its resulting practice in terms of three frames of reference: (1) the essential elements of social work practice; (2) characteristics of the particular field; and (3) social work practice in the particular field. Subsequently, Bartlett (1961b) applied these three frames to an analysis of social work in the health field to illustrate their utility for grasping the dimensions of the specialized nature of social work practice in that field. More recently, Meares (1981) made use of Bartlett's framework for a consideration of graduate level education designed to prepare social workers for specialized practice, thereby demonstrating its continuing utility and also its capacity for flexible application and modification.

Figure 2.1 presents Bartlett's framework for analysis with modifications suggested by Meares: the addition of "Forces of Change" to Frame #2, and qualification of Frame #3 to reflect recent decisions of the National Association of Social Workers (1978) and the Council on Social Work Education (1982) that specialized practice is the purview of graduate level social workers. A review of Figure 2.1 suggests that in addition to its use as a framework for analyzing the whole of social work in a given field, it can also be used to consider a specific dimension of social work practice in a particular field—in this case, clinical practice in the health field.

The framework also suggests that mastery of the first frame, the essential elements of social work practice, is a prerequisite for specializa-

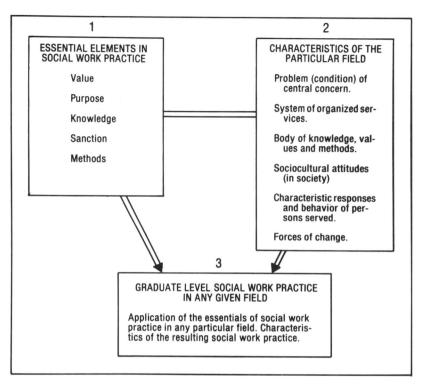

FIGURE 2.1 Social Work Practice in any Given Field

Adapted in part from "Frames of Reference for Analysis of Social Work Practice in Any Particular Field," in Harriet M. Bartlett, *Analyzing Social Work Practice by Fields* (New York: National Association of Social Workers, Inc.), 1961, p. 19, as further adapted in "Educating Social Workers for Specialization," by Paula Allen Meares, SOCIAL WORK IN EDUCATION, Vol. 3, No. 2 (January 1981), p. 45.

tion. Some of the elements in the first frame were considered in Chapter 1: the concept of the person as a social being, which reflects primary social work values; the concepts of social functioning and social stress, which give form and direction to social work's purpose as a profession; and the authority and sanction of social work. Some of the elements in the second frame were also considered briefly in Chapter 1: health status as the problem of central concern to the health system; the variety of professions, with their particular knowledge and skills, necessary for effective health care; and the social nature of the American health system—one of the forces that stimulates evolution and change in the system itself. In addition, illness and disability, as specific phenomena, reflect the perceptions of both social work and other professions in the health field since they are forms of stress that are both biological and social.

In this chapter, more focused attention is given to those knowledge elements in the second frame which are essential for the effective practice of clinical social work in health settings—the problem of central concern, characteristic responses and behavior of the persons served, and socio-cultural attitudes and variables. These knowledge elements will be considered with reference to those elements central to social work. Finally, the concept of membership is introduced as a way of thinking about and unifying these two sets of elements into a single knowledge base for clinical intervention.

The Unifying Concept of Membership

To establish a base for practice, the social work clinician must organize knowledge from social work and the health field into four basic categories and consider these with regard for a fifth. These categories are: (1) the purpose of the particular ordering of knowledge; (2) the physical nature of health problems or of the particular somatic condition involved; (3) the general response patterns and coping mechanisms of people confronted by health problems or by the particular health problem involved; (4) social variables that influence response patterns and the selection of coping mechanisms; and (5) the implications of this understanding for clinical social work intervention. In ordering this knowledge, social work values play a prominent role since they provide basic motivation and guide the ways in which the social worker applies knowledge in practice to realize the profession's purpose.

Frameworks for integrating diverse knowledge elements into a unified base for social work practice, and language to express that unity, have proven difficult to formulate. The tasks involved have proven even more difficult when generic social work knowledge must be integrated with that of other professions and disciplines in a specialized field of practice, such as health care.

Attempts to develop appropriate conceptual frameworks are evident in such common social work concepts as: human behavior and the social environment; the person-in-situation; the client as a social system; the individual-in-the-group; the person and the family; and so on. The problem inherent in these and similar formulations is that they conceptualize the person and his or her social context separately while at the same time trying to maintain some sense of connection between the two. Another problem is evident in the interpretations and applications of the term *biopsychosocial* which such formulations yield. In many interpretations, the biological elements are ignored for the most part and the psychological elements are found at one end of the continuum, while the social elements are found at the other. Such conceptualizations fragment the fundamental unity of the person as a human being. Terms like the person-in-situation and the frameworks they represent, however, do indicate awareness that bio-polarities and dichotomies need to be reconciled to serve effectively as a base for social work knowledge development and practice.

Regensburg (1978), for example, employs the term *biopsychosocial integrity* to denote "the wholeness, oneness, and indivisibility of every human being" (p. 9). The notion of wholeness which the term is meant to convey breaks down, however, because it is premised, as are similar constructs, on the "primacy of the individual" as a "fundamental inherent human value unrelated to such specific characteristics as sex, age, color, creed, ethnic grouping, and intellectual acuity, or to social status determined by such factors as level of education, income, and type of occupation" (p. 4). Yet, it is precisely from these and similar attributes, both positive and negative, that each person derives his or her sense of being. To strip the person of all the attributes that constitute his or her particular self does not reveal a person, but a biological organism instead. To attempt to do so in the interest of social work values overlooks the fact that human values are derived by people from their social contexts and experiences.

The issue here seems to be a confusion of the social work principle of nondiscrimination in practice on the basis of a person's specific characteristics and social status, and opposition to such discrimination elsewhere, with a person's inherent value as a social being. To oppose discrimination against people because of their specific characteristics and social status does not mean, however, that people should be denuded of them. Rather, such differences are to be respected and valued as aspects of each person's present and/or potential ability to grow as a contributing member of his or her social groups and society in general. The person's value as a person stems from his or her ability as a human being to grow, develop, change, overcome adversity, and contribute socially, whatever the person's circumstances and genetic endowment may be.

Regensburg's description of the person as "a social human being" supports the notion of wholeness and the social basis of each person's inherent value. She cites the value given by social work to the "family as a social institution" and, more importantly, stresses the value of "maximum self-determination" and "social justice" which qualify the absolute "primacy of the individual."

Maximum self-determination, for example, denotes the reciprocal relationships between each person and "his or her family, other reference groups, and the society in which he or she lives."

The social worker believes that rights are balanced by obligations and that therefore the right to self-determination has limits and boundaries which are implied in the word *feasible*. The exercise of an individual's rights to decide and to make judgments and choose according to his or her preferences, wants, and desires is limited by the obligation to respect the rights of others, to avoid endangering himself or herself and others, and to add to, rather than detract from the general social welfare. (p. 5)

Social justice, as a concept, has a similar limiting quality. As a social work value, it embodies the notions of "equity, fairness, impartiality, and equality of opportunity" and, as Regensburg points out, "social workers hold these qualities to be morally good and right" (p. 5).

The importance of clarity about social work values at the outset for a balanced ordering of knowledge for intervention with clients who are affected by illness or disability cannot be overlooked, for balance is crucial to the realization of social work's purpose as a profession. This fact is underscored by Mailick's assertion (1980) that social workers new to practice in health settings have a tendency to overemphasize the psychological component in their practice and do "not sufficiently value or productively use available biosocial data in their assessments and interventions" (p. 38). Such practice represents a distortion of social work values and of professional purpose.

A balanced concern for the biopsychosocial integrity of people is, therefore, the starting point for ordering knowledge for health social work practice. Based on a synthesis of psychoanalytic object-relations theory, symbolic interactionism, and social process, Hans S. Falck has formulated an approach designed to maintain this balance. It builds on the notions of social functioning and social stress, focuses on the fundamental unity of human beings, and is identified by its basic concept, *membership*.

. . . membership occurs when persons experience themselves as part of others and become significant to each other. That significance may be negative or positive, may rest on loving or destructive behavior, but being significant still, makes people part of each other and thus members. (Falck, 1979, p. 162)

The concepts of *member* and *membership* rest on social behavior and proceed from the view that people are "both social and psychological by definition, i.e. that neither precludes or may be reduced from the other." Put another way, personality is simultaneously social and psychological; it occurs in a single process, both in origin and in development (Falck, 1980). This conceptualization underscores the social nature of human beings since it views intrapsychic structure and social process as part of the same phenomenon, one in which the person contributes to and is the product of those to whom he or she is significant and who, in turn, are significant to him or her (Falck, 1978).

In an objective sense, membership can be identified by such observable criteria as blood relationships, marriage, occupations, common interest, and by such life states as age, shared conditions, and so on. In a subjective sense, membership consists of mutual experience and is dependent on the quality and meaning of that experience as perceived by those who share it. In this sense, membership is also irreversible.

> The meanings may change . . . yet one cannot resign emotionally from one's family. This is furthermore said of other relations. One can resign from one's place of work, but the memory-stored affects about one's co-workers indicate the permanence of meaning per se in time—even when long "forgotten." One may divorce but one keeps the membership of meaning. One may lose someone through death and yet the meaning of the "broken" relationship is sharply modified into a past tense; it is not abolished or unexperienced. (Falck, 1980, p. 23)

The consequences of membership as a social work concept are multiple. It unifies the array of values, knowledge, and understanding required for effective clinical intervention. The person and the social environment are viewed as parts of one whole. The person's biopsychosocial integrity is defined in irreducible terms that reflect a social work perspective. The sick person who is a social work client, therefore, is not simply a being with a diseased body or defective body parts. The affected client is far more than this. He or she is the sum total of all of his or her social memberships and experiences, past and present, simultaneously internal in terms of psychological make-up and external in terms of social relationships.

Illness and disability cannot be viewed from a social work perspective as organic disturbances only, for they have heavy implications for memberships. Nor can the ill or disabled person be considered apart from his or her social environment. How the affected person and his or her significant others respond to the health disturbance will be determined by the quality of their memberships. Quality, in this sense, involves their particular personalities, patterns of behavior, and their social interaction as members. The person, therefore, is not just an individual with a tacked-on family, age, race, socioeconomic status, or religion. The person *is* all of these things because they define each person as a biopsychosocial being, a member, as Figure 2.2 illustrates.

As a unifying concept, membership provides a conceptual lens for considering the diverse knowledge elements necessary for clinical social work practice in health settings while systematically maintaining focus on those things that are central to social work.

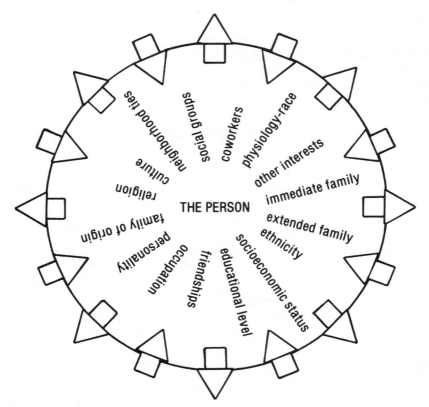

FIGURE 2.2 The Person as Member

The General Purpose of the Knowledge Base

The clinical social worker's purpose in establishing a particular knowledge base is to enhance his or her practice in ways that are consistent with the profession's purpose. In health social work, this requires understanding of the ways disease and disability impact human relationships and ability to function socially. To achieve this understanding, the clinician needs to have greater familiarity with the various states of physical health—knowledge that flows from the health system and its central concerns—than is true of social workers in other fields of practice. In addition, the health social worker needs more specific understanding of how the meaning of disease and disability to people, and their health-related behavior, are influenced by socioeconomic, cultural, racial, ethnic, religious, and other membership variables. The clinical social worker in a health agency seeks, therefore, to augment his or her generic social work understanding of human behavior by adding to it understanding of physical illness and handicapping conditions.

Since the health professions draw on common knowledge sources in varying degrees, it is important for the social work clinician to keep social work's purpose and values clearly in mind when nonsocial work knowledge is explored with the view of integrating it into his or her knowledge base. Just as physicians and nurses turn to knowledge from the social and behavioral sciences to better understand their patients as persons so that they can provide better medical and nursing care, the social worker seeks knowledge from medicine and other medical sciences to better understand the physical problem for which the client originally sought help, in order to provide better social intervention.

The integrity of social work and its contributions to health care require clarity of social work's own psychosocial goals and values in relation to the clients it serves within the framework of the health agency's objectives. To function effectively in the health field, the clinical social worker must retain and maintain social work's professional integrity (Kumabe, et al., 1977).

By considering social work's professional purpose of lessening social stress and improving social functioning through the lens of membership and by applying that purpose to practice in the health field, we reach the following specialized definition: The central concern of clinical social work in the health field is the ability of clients to manage their social memberships when those memberships are or may be disturbed and made problematic by episodic, long-term, or chronic physical disease, disability, or injury. Its purpose is to provide professional service to people so affected to help them regain, retain, maintain, or enhance their ability to manage effectively their memberships in various social groups.

Thus, whether the clinician's goal is to better understand the factors involved in health and medical care in general, or to deepen understanding in relation to a particular health condition or group of conditions, clarity of professional purpose and values provides the focus for knowledge acquisition and integration.

The Physical Nature of Illness, Disability, and Injury: The Health Field's Problem of Central Concern

To inform and enhance their practice, social work clinicians who work with people whose lives are disturbed by a physical illness, disability, or injury need to understand the physical manifestations and treatment of the particular health condition. This need is present whether the health condition is episodic, chronic, terminal, or simply a potential health problem.

Knowledge in this category is biological in character. It focuses on the person as a discrete physical being composed of specific interrelated body parts which, "when infused with the mystery of life, [interact] in such a way that the person appears as a closed entity, a self-propelled, adequate machine." In biological terms, "there is a distinct discontinuity between each person and other persons" (Falck, 1981b).

The biological perspective is basic to medicine and to the other medical sciences since it is the physical attack by disease, disabling conditions, injuries, and similar phenomena on the body's ability to function as an organic unit that constitutes the central concern of these professions. Adverse health states may temporarily or permanently impair the body's ability to function or they may eliminate that ability altogether, with death the result. The implications of such physical phenomena for effective social functioning are obvious and they underscore the need of clinical social workers in health settings to understand them. Such biomedical knowledge includes a basic understanding of the etiology, signs and symptoms, medical diagnosis, treatment procedures and protocols, and the prognosis for any given health condition. Epidemiological factors, such as indices of high risk and other variables, are important as well. Mailick (1980) points out that deficits in biomedical knowledge constitute a serious burden for social workers in a health setting because they seriously impede effective interprofessional collaboration.

It should be noted, however, that understanding of biomedical factors is also important for effective intervention with clinical social work clients, who are also medical patients, or potential patients, and their significant others, because deficits in biomedical knowledge also impede the clinician's ability to understand what clients are experiencing physically, emotionally, and socially, and how they are experiencing it. To have such understanding, the clinical social worker must turn to knowledge outside of social work's own domain, that is, to medicine and other biomedical sciences.

Characteristic Response Patterns and Behavior in Relation to Adverse Health Conditions

Knowledge in the previous category focused on the somatic condition causing biological stress to the person's body and on the various medical procedures and protocols designed to lessen and, hopefully, eliminate that stress. In this category, focus is directed to the psychosocial stress caused by the somatic condition and how people respond to and deal with it. Knowledge in the previous category, therefore, is directed to understanding how the body behaves under adverse biomedical circumstances, while knowledge acquisition in this section is directed to understanding the internal and external responses of people to that stress. In other words, the objective is to understand the ways people behave when their social memberships are impacted by adverse somatic conditions and their consequences.

There are a variety of models that draw on knowledge from a variety of disciplines to explain human behavior in relation to physical illness, disability, and injury. Because ongoing research constantly yields new knowledge, any given explanatory model is subject to modification, total revision, even abandonment as new knowledge produces new understanding. Despite the initial promise of some models, it is unlikely that any single framework for understanding human behavior in relation to adverse physical health will remain unchallenged and unchanged by future research.

To test the appropriateness of any given explanatory model for social work, the clinician needs to determine whether it: (1) is consistent with social work values; (2) permits a balanced perception of social and psychological factors in relation to biological elements; and (3) allows for the realization of social work purpose. For purposes of illustration, three models are examined in this section, two briefly and one in more detail.

In the 1930s and 1940s, psychosomatic medicine incorporated medical and psychodynamic concepts into theoretical constructs which attempted to associate particular personality characteristics with specific somatic disorders in cause-effect relationships. This approach gained widespread currency and was adopted by health social workers as a means for synthesizing knowledge for practice in the health field. Since psychiatric approaches were gaining wide acceptance throughout social work during this period, the use of this approach by health social workers seemed both logical and promising. It found expression in clinical social work by almost exclusive emphasis on the psychological/emotional meaning of the biomedical event to the patient. Because it focused primarily on intrapsychic phenomena, however, it eventually proved too narrow to serve as a framework for building a knowledge base for health social work practice.

Since the 1950s, research in medicine, psychiatry, and the social sciences has greatly expanded understanding of human behavior in relation to health and illness. This new and ever-expanding knowledge and social work's deepening appreciation for the importance of social and cultural influences on human behavior have stimulated health social workers to seek out more comprehensive and flexible frameworks that synthesize knowledge and provide an appropriate base for practice.

The Parsonian model of the "sick role" has proven helpful to many social workers. According to Bracht's (1978) summary of the model, the person in the sick role is: (1) not responsible for the illness since it is beyond his or her control; (2) free from normal social role obligations; (3) obligated to seek help which is technically competent; and (4) "expected to cooperate in the process of getting well" (p. 112). The Parsonian model makes clear that somatic disorders have social meaning as well as medical (biological) and psychological meaning. Examination of the model for possible limitations in its utility from a social work perspective, however, is suggestive of some of the problems health social workers often encounter when ordering a multidisciplinary knowledge base for practice.

Contrary to the model, for example, the person in the sick role can be viewed as fully or partially responsible for his or her health problem if it is a result of his or her own behavior, for example, smoking and eating habits as etiological factors in heart disease; sexual preference and behavior in the incidence and transmission of venereal disease; irresponsible automobile driving and physical injury. How do such possibilities square with social work views on the reciprocity of rights and obligations and responsibility for one's own behavior in relation to others?

Other problems related to social work values and purpose may be involved. For example, are the obligations to seek technically competent help and the expectation of cooperation in the Parsonian model too strongly premised on the precepts of Western medicine to incorporate social work concerns? Is there sufficient leeway in this framework for it to accommodate social and cultural difference? Can it, for example, accommodate the behavior of a Filipino with a health problem who relies on an *albolaryo* or a *maghihilot* for the treatment of illness or orthopedic problems when he or she regards these folk practitioners as technically competent and follows their treatment prescriptions carefully?

If the answers to such questions are negative or doubtful, the health social worker is likely to be confronted by serious value dilemmas stemming from the nonresponsiveness of the model in question to the value accorded by social work to the person as a social being, to the person's right to social self-determination, to cultural and other variations in human behavior. If a model is unresponsive to social work values, can it serve as a basis for the realization of social work purpose?

Moos and Tsu (1977) have developed a model which can be used to illustrate in more detail how a given way of explaining health-related behavior can be explored in terms of the three social work requisites specified above. Since the concept of membership incorporates these requisites, it will be used in the course of the examination.

The Moos and Tsu model hinges on the person's need for biopsychosocial equilibrium. Accordingly, physical illness, disability, and injury are seen as disruptive of biological equilibrium which, in turn, disrupts the affected person's psychosocial ability to function. This aspect of the model is compatible with the concepts of the biopsychosocial integrity of the person, social stress, and social functioning and it relates to the ability of people to manage their social memberships.

According to the model's next premise, when the disruption is serious enough to render habitual behavior patterns inadequate, a biopsychosocial crisis results which "leads to a state of disorganization often accompanied by anxiety, fear, guilt, and other unpleasant feelings which contribute to further disorganization" (p. 7). Since the model holds that disequilibrium cannot continue indefinitely and homeostasis must be restored in some way, the crisis is regarded as a transitional period in which efforts to restore balance may indicate a healthy or a maladaptive response. The concept of crisis as a transition period suggests that the approach allows for the realization of social work purpose since the services offered by the social work clinician are designed to help affected clients cope with the crisis in ways that promote psychosocial growth and social functioning.

The Moos and Tsu model specifies seven sets of adaptive tasks which must be accomplished if a health adaptation to the crisis is to occur. Three of these are related to the particular health condition involved. The remaining four are more general in nature, but must also be accomplished. The model's seven task sets are summarized in Table 2.1.

Falck (1981a) hypothesizes three levels of membership. Table 2.2 lists and describes the three levels.

A review of the seven adaptive task sets summarized in Table 2.1 in terms of the level of membership described in Table 2.2 suggests further

TABLE 2.1 Adaptive Tasks in Health Crises

Illness-Related Tasks	*General Tasks*
1. Dealing with pain and incapacitation.	1. Preserving a reasonable emotional balance.
2. Dealing with the hospital environment and special treatment procedures.	2. Preserving a satisfactory self-image.
3. Developing adequate relationships with professional staff.	3. Preserving relationships with family and friends.
	4. Preparing for an uncertain future.

Adapted from Rudolf H. Moos and Vivien Davis Tsu, "The Crisis of Physical Illness: An Overview," in *Coping with Physical Illness,* edited by Rudolph Moos. New York: Plenum Medical Book Company, 1977, p. 9.

TABLE 2.2 Levels of Membership

Levels	Characteristics
Primary membership	Face-to-face interaction.
	Affective intimacy, i.e., blood relationships, marriage, close friendships.
	Intense meaning and impact, i.e., love, hate, fear, rage.
Secondary membership	Face-to-face interaction.
	Nonintimate in the main, i.e., work groups, church, neighborhood associations, acquaintances.
	Professional interactions, i.e., social casework interviews.
Tertiary membership	Non-face-to-face interaction.
	Nonintimate in nature.
	Complex configurations, i.e., populations, large corporations, government.
	Dealt with by and through secondary membership groups, i.e., representational groups.

Adapted from Hans S. Falck, "Social Work as the Management of Membership: An Interactionist Perspective." School of Social Work, Virginia Commonwealth University, 1981, p. 13. (Mimeographed.)

that the Moos and Tsu model is responsive to social work need for a broadly based explanation of health behavior.

All of the illness-related (I-R) tasks, for example, plus general (G) tasks 1 and 2 appear to have meaning for the secondary membership of the health client and those professionals involved in his or her overall treatment and care configuration. G tasks 3 and 4 seem related, for the most part, to the client's primary membership, while G tasks 1, 2, and 4 may impact tertiary as well as primary and secondary client membership. Thus, it appears that accomplishment of the seven adaptive task sets to the maximum extent possible requires simultaneous interaction at all three membership levels. If this is so, the model is responsive to social work's purpose and permits opportunities for its realization.

From another perspective, I-R tasks 1 and 2 appear to relate primarily to the patient's biological attributes, as does G task 2 to some extent. I-R tasks 2 and 3 and G tasks 1, 2, 3, and 4 appear to be concerned with the ill person's psychosocial attributes. If this is so, all seven tasks, regardless of category, reflect a balanced perception of the person's biopsychosocial integrity.

To render effective service, the clinical social worker often needs to expand the definition of the term *client* beyond that of the person who is the medical patient. From a social work point of view, the other people in the client's primary membership groups, particularly the family, may also be clients. Kumabe et al. (1977) underscore the importance of this expansion of the term client in any given case. They define the family as the source of the person's primary relationships and note that it is the "most important social context within which health is maintained" or within which "illness occurs and is resolved."

As the basic unit of health management, the family exhibits characteristic patterns of health practices, definitions of medical services. Its commitment to protect its members through stressful situations makes the management of illness more than an individual function and focuses on the family as a significant source of strength—or weakness—in the individual's coping process. The patient who appears at a health facility is seldom a single individual seeking help; rather, he is a member of a family which has exhausted its known internal and external resources to deal with the problem. The health, growth, and development of each member reflects, and in the case of young children is determined by, the health of the group as a whole. (p. 25)

From a social work point of view, therefore, we can conclude that an adverse health condition is not a solitary event experienced only by the client/patient, nor are the adaptive tasks confronted by the client/patient alone. This conclusion is supported by Kaplan, Grobstein, and Smith (1976) who studied 40 families with children diagnosed and treated for leukemia. They found that 88 percent of the families studied experienced psychosocial problems precipitated by the child's illness. Of these, 80 percent experienced problems only after the diagnosis was made. The problems experienced by these families were wide-ranging and included marital and sibling problems, difficulty in fulfilling major social role responsibilities, health problems such as ulcers, colitis, hypertension, alcoholism, and morbid grief.

The question arises then as to whether the Moos and Tsu model permits an expanded definition of the concept of the client. It would appear that the model can accommodate such an expansion. Moos and Tsu assert that the patient and his or her family encounter "the same or closely related adaptive tasks." It can be assumed, therefore, that accomplishment of these tasks is as important for family, and intimate friends by extension, as it is for the client/patient.

The next major component of the model consists of seven types of coping skills which the model contends are used to accomplish the seven adaptive task sets. The model permits consideration of anything a person

TABLE 2.3 Major Coping Skills in Response to Adverse Health Conditions

Skills	Examples	Functions
Denying or minimizing the seriousness of the crisis.	Claiming myocardial disease is indigestion.	Self-protection.
	Shopping for cures after the diagnosis is accepted.	Rescues the person from being overwhelmed.
	Suppression, projection, or displacement of anger.	
	"Clinical detachment."	Provides time to garner other coping resources.
Seeking and using relevant information.	Using information and intellectual resources effectively.	Relieves anxiety caused by uncertainty, misinformation, and guilt.
	Questioning physicians and nurses about hospital procedures.	Restores a sense of control.
	Reading newspapers, magazines, and professional journals for the latest information.	Helps to come to terms with expected loss.
Requesting reassurance and emotional support from significant others.	Expressing feelings.	Relieves tension.
	Opening up to comfort.	Provides reassurance.
	Joining special groups, i.e., for relatives, spouses, siblings; may be national or local, formal or ad hoc.	Provides psychosocial support.
Learning specific health condition related procedures.	Feeding, caring for the affected person.	Confirms personal ability and effectiveness.
	Using special machines, i.e., dialysis.	Source of pride; patient can care for self.
	Giving injections.	
		Source of relief; relatives are able to offer "concrete" help.
Setting concrete goals.	Breaking problems into small, manageable parts.	Provides something meaningful to look forward to.

36

(continued)

TABLE 2.3 (continued)

Skills	Examples	Functions
	Re-learning to walk.	Provides a sense of achievement.
	Attending a special event.	Progressive desensitization of self and others.
Rehearsing alternative outcomes.	Mental preparation (anticipation and rehearsal).	Prepares for expected difficulties.
	Discussion of possible outcomes with family and friends.	Allays anxiety.
		Eases fears; restores a sense of confidence.
	Anticipatory mourning.	Acknowledges an impending loss.
Finding a general purpose or pattern of meaning.	Belief in a divine purpose.	Provides consolation.
	Belief in the general beneficence of a divine being.	Provides encouragement to do one's best to deal with difficulties.
	Transcendental redirection.	
		Restores a sense of value.
		Provides a long-term perspective which makes events seem more manageable.

Adapted from Rudolf H. Moos and Vivien Davis Tsu, "The Crisis of Physical Illness: An Overview," in *Coping with Physical Illness,* edited by Rudolf H. Moos. (New York: Plenum Medical Book Company, 1977), pp. 12-15.

does as a coping skill if it facilitates accomplishment of the adaptive tasks. Further, it holds that coping skills are seldom exclusive and that several may be invoked simultaneously. Table 2.3 summarizes, gives examples of, and describes the functions of the major skills identified in the model.

Considering the clinical social worker's objective of decreasing stress caused by illness, disability, or injury as a means of helping health clients to maintain, regain, attain, or enhance their level of social functioning to a mutually satisfactory degree, the coping skills identified in the model are consistent with social work purpose. The functions and outcomes of the skills are designed to decrease stress, the disruption caused by illness, in order for clients to regain biopsychosocial equilibrium. They are skills necessary for the effective management of social memberships.

Finally, the model directs attention to background and personal characteristics, illness-related factors, and features in the physical and social environments as influences on health-related behavior and determinants of its outcomes. In terms of environmental variables, the model includes human relationships, sociocultural norms and expectations, and social supports in the health care system and in the wider community. As care givers, health professionals are expected to know and understand their own responses to various health crises. By extending this injunction to the level of secondary memberships, it would seem that as health care professionals participate with the client/patient and his or her significant others in accomplishing the adaptive task sets they would use the same coping skills, albeit, perhaps, to different degrees and in varying ways.

On the basis of this review, the Moos and Tsu model appears to explain the characteristic response patterns and behavior of people affected by adverse health conditions in a way that meets the three social work requisites explicated earlier. The model appears to pose no serious value dilemmas for clinical social workers. It does regard biopsychosocial factors in relation to one another and in a balanced way. And, it appears to be sufficiently generic to the health professions to allow for the realization of social work purpose.

While, as already noted, no model is free from the possibility of revision as research generates new knowledge and understanding, it is also true that no single model can, by definition, provide the clinical social worker with all of the data and other information needed for practice in health settings. The Moos and Tsu model, for example, provides no specific information about sociocultural norms, even though it does note their importance as factors in health- and illness-related behavior. For this kind of specific knowledge and for knowledge about the influence of other membership variables, the clinician must turn to other data sources.

Sociocultural Attitudes and Other Membership Variables that Influence Health Behavior and Illness Responses

A range of variables indicative of other social memberships may also influence the health status and health related perceptions, responses, and behavior of patient/clients, family, friends, and professional care providers. These variables often indicate factors beyond the control of the patient/client and beyond the control of those with whom he or she shares primary and secondary membership.

Among the factors that influence behavior in relation to health maintenance, illness prevention, and psychosocial responses when illness, disability, or injury occur, and also recovery from them, are: socioeconomic status; educational level; culture; race; ethnicity; sex; and religious affiliation and practice. Bracht (1978) notes that research supports a positive relationship between social and health variables and points out that this relationship constitutes one of the basic premises upon which social work in the health field rests (pp. 24-25).

Factors such as these are often thought of in terms of tertiary memberships and this perception is often accurate. People belonging to specific socioeconomic classes, ethnic groups, or religions, for example, share those affiliations with millions of other people whom they will never meet or know. Yet, they often feel a profound sense of membership with these unseen and unknown people with whom they share identifiable membership criteria. Moreover, beliefs and practices and the physical conditions of life associated with tertiary memberships can be strong determinants of health behavior and response patterns when illness, disability, or injury occur.

These factors have been categorized in a variety of ways. Berkanovic and Reeder (1973), for example, identify three models of alternative determinants of behavior relative to the use of health services. Each model is based on one of three concepts central to it: (1) unequal access; (2) poverty; and (3) cultural and social psychological differences related to ethnicity and socioeconomic status. It is difficult to consider these or any of the other factors separately, however, because they do not exist separately in reality. Instead, they and the physical conditions they represent overlap to a considerable extent.

Kosa (1975) asserts that a characteristic of the disadvantaged is the lack of some of life's privileges, which are defined by prevailing standards and include access to services that promote health and a healthy life. Kosa's assertion suggests the interrelatedness of socioeconomic status (privileged, disadvantaged), culture (prevailing standards and deviations from them), and health status. One national study (DHEW, 1979) notes that, historically, differences in mortality and morbidity have characterized the socioeconomically privileged and underprivileged. Economic poverty and poor health tend to function in a circular fashion. Poor health is an obstacle to economic opportunity and betterment, and poor economic circumstances, in turn, contribute to poor health.

Perkins et al. (1975) offer two paradigms to explain the propensity for illness consistently demonstrated by lower socioeconomic groups in research studies. Each paradigm relates to the interaction of conditions in the physical environment and the social behavior of economically disadvantaged people in relation to their health status. The first holds that adverse "socioeconomic conditions lead to certain behaviors which in turn result in the exposure of the individual to noxious conditions or to the denial of essential substances of behaviors." The second is that "prolonged stress causes the production of noxious metabolic products and these products direct tissue liability or weakened resistance" (p. 537).

There is support, then, for the view that socioeconomic status, educational level, culture, race, and other membership variables are not isolated phenomena. Further, a number of models exist which explain the simultaneous interaction of these variables and their influences on health status and behavior.

The clinical social worker, however, needs to take additional steps to inform his or her general knowledge base. First, knowledge of variables that operate in given health configurations, and in what combinations, needs to be reconceptualized in ways that enhance the clinician's social work practice base. Table 2.4 suggests one way knowledge can be extrapolated for this purpose. It combines generalized data from a national study with membership variables.

The health conditions and incidence data reported in Table 2.4 appear in combination with membership variables which indicate certain tertiary memberships of the people affected. From this general understanding, the clinician's next step is to discover the kinds of meaning and influence these memberships have for the health perceptions and behavior of the people involved. That meaning may come from within the group itself or from nonmembers outside the group. Falck (1981a) explains this in terms of membership by object-introjects, interaction, and symbolization.

> According to this approach, psychological in nature, persons internalize each other through transference, countertransference and other phenomena. When this occurs, the receiver, while treating the impact of the other as external at the beginning, eventually converts the messages, called introjects, and makes them his/her own, only to project them as part of what pre-existed them but [is] now integrated into the recipient's personality, to others.
>
> Another quality of membership lies in interactionism. . . What it refers to is in essence no more than social exchange, a series of behavioral phenomena. . . It is altogether empirical and overt and is the easiest of all membership forms from the standpoint of observability and quantifiability.
>
> Symbolization . . . has to do with the subjective perceptions and interpretations of what is exchanged and derives its importance from the pragmatic use of what is exchanged from the standpoint of social action. In other words, symbolization touches heavily and significantly on the habit of persons to act on the basis of what they think is real from a phenomenological, subjective standpoint [rather] than from the vantage point of objective reality. It is the difference between what is said and what is heard, what is and what one may think or feel something to be. (pp. 14-15)

TABLE 2.4 Relationships Between the Incidence of Selected Health Conditions and Membership Variables

Health Condition	Membership Variable	General Findings
General life expectancy	Race	Expectation for minority group members is five years less than for whites.
Infant mortality	Race: general	Mortality rate almost twice as great for racial minority group members as whites.
	Race: Black American	Greatest negative differential.
	Race: Native American	Greatest positive gains.
Maternal mortality	Race: general	Mortality rate for racial minority group members three times greater than whites.
		No significant change in past twenty-five years (1950–75).
Genetic disorders	Race and ethnicity	Sickle cell anemia primarily among blacks.
		Cystic fibrosis primarily among whites.
		Tay-Sachs among Jews of Northeastern European origin.
		Thalessemia primarily among people from Mediterranean countries.
		Phenylketonuria (PKU) greater incidence among people of European descent than among blacks or Eastern European Jews.
Acute diseases	Socioeconomic status and race	Highest incidences among highest income whites.
		Lowest incidence among lowest income minority groups.
	Race and sex	Highest incidence among male members of racial minority groups.

(continued)

41

TABLE 2.4 (continued)

Health Condition	Membership Variable	General Findings
		Lowest incidence among female members of racial minority groups.
Chronic diseases	High socioeconomic groups	Highest incidence of breast cancer.
	Low socioeconomic groups	Highest incidence of heart disease, cancer, stroke, diabetes.
Injuries and accidents	Race and socioeconomic status	*Rate* of injury lower among racial minority and low-income groups; higher among white and high income groups.
		Impact (i.e., degree of activity restriction, mortality) greater for minority and low income groups; less for white and high income groups.

Adapted from Department of Health, Education, and Welfare. *Health Status of Minorities and Low-Income Groups.* Washington, D.C.: U.S. Government Printing Office, 1979, pp. 5–8.

The kinds of meaning derived from object-introjects, interaction, and symbolization can be glimpsed in a situation discussed by Kumabe et al. (1977). This situation suggests how the meaning of economic conditions can influence decisions to use or not to use health and medical services.

> The cost of services, as an economic issue, has three components: (1) money spent in obtaining services, including the cost of health insurance or other third-party payments; (2) money lost at time away from employment, including the existence (or lack) of sick leave; and (3) the incurring of "obligations for services" to one's neighbors and/or friends, or to the family network providing interim services or interim financing in the event of illness. (p. 27)

Kumabe et al. also point out that other factors, such as education, ethnicity, residence, cost, and quality of services need to be considered if the decision is to be fully understood.

Coulton's (1978) consideration of the interactive influence of socio-cultural norms and sanctions on health behavior suggests other examples of the meanings group membership have for their members. She identifies readiness to engage in preventive health behavior, beliefs regarding the etiology of illness, its severity, and the best means to prevent it as particularly important. By pointing out that ethnic group beliefs may support or oppose the premises of Western scientific medicine, Coulton further suggests how differences in the group memberships of health professionals and clients can lead to different perceptions of and behavior in relation to the same events. Citing Saunders (1954), she notes that:

> Mexican-American culture prescribes certain health practices that are qualitatively different from those prescribed by Western medical practitioners. Individuals whose social relationships are mainly ethnically endogamous are more likely to engage in those activities prescribed by their ethnic groups than those prescribed by scientific medicine. (p. 301)

Coulton cites Zabrowski who studied the responses to pain of 103 male patients, while controlling for ethnic group membership. Zabrowski found that Italian and Jewish patients expressed their responses outwardly. Irish and Anglo-Saxon patients, in contrast, were likely to withdraw. Understanding gained by considering knowledge germane to the health system in social work terms helps the clinician to begin to identify where problems are likely to exist and to suggest points of clinical help.

One final membership variable will be considered here. Religious affiliation is a membership variable that has received little attention in social work literature, but religious beliefs, practices, and behavior can have major importance in health care. This importance derives from the introjection and symbolization of religious tenets and these may determine both health maintenance behavior and responses to illness, disability, or injury. A physically or mentally impaired child born to an orthodox Roman Catholic family, for example, may be regarded as a special gift from God, who will judge the quality of love and care the child receives from his or her parents and family members. Beliefs of other religious groups may prohibit practices designed to preserve health or life, such as immunizations, blood transfusions, surgery, or other medical care. On the other hand, religious prohibitions against smoking and the ingestion of alcohol or other drugs may contribute to the good health of those who follow these religiously based dictates.

The impact of religious affiliation is most clear when serious illness occurs, death is imminent, or death has occurred. The situation of the nonpracticing Roman Catholic who faces death provides insight. Often, this person and his or her significant others display acute anxiety until the person whose death is imminent has confessed and received the last rites from a priest. These preparations for death take different forms in different religions, but those who avail themselves of religious ministrations often display a marked decrease in anxiety and fear, while their families and friends display acceptance of the inevitable.

Gowen (1980) cites Leming who studied the validity of Homans' thesis that the anxiety experienced by people when they encounter death is basically socially ascribed. This thesis holds that the religious emphasis on immortality and impending judgment increases death anxiety, but once religious ceremonies have been completed and requirements met, anxiety decreases markedly. Leming found that religious commitment was the most significant factor in the relationship between a person's religious beliefs and death fears. That is, he found that a high degree of religious commitment relieves the fear of death it originally provoked and dispels anxiety caused by the social effects of death.

Leming's finding has meaning for both the affected person and those of whom he or she is a part. The intensification of religious beliefs, practices, and ceremonials when death is imminent may well be the catalyst for mending damaged memberships in family and other social groups, as well as religious ones. In addition, religious practices provide means for survivors in the deceased person's membership groups to separate and continue living in a positive manner. *Shivah*, the seven-day mourning period following the funeral in Judaism, provides structure for such outcomes, as do requiem masses, the saying of rosaries for the deceased, and other death-related rituals.

As Doeltz and Adamson (1968) point out, religion can be a major factor that helps the patient and those of whom he is a part "meet with dignity and forbearance the trial of illness and possible death, the interruption of family life, and the anxieties associated with physical illness." As a result, they conclude that illness "can be a meaningful life experience that leads to spiritual and social growth" (p. 413).

Implications for Clinical Practice

As is true of the general purpose of the knowledge base, the physical nature of adverse health states, patterns of responses to and coping with adverse health conditions, and other variables related to health, the implications of this understanding can be viewed in three ways by the health social worker. In the first instance, specific knowledge can be integrated into a general framework of understanding to inform clinical practice. This approach requires a broadly based study of pertinent research and literature in each of the areas explicated and the sifting of findings from this study through a social work perspective to determine general implications and applications for practice. The first approach is akin to the one followed in this chapter.

The second approach makes use of a narrower focus as study is directed to a specific health condition and its implications for clinical social work practice. Attention might be directed exclusively, for example, to Tay-Sachs disease, an inherited condition clinically apparent within the first six months of life and invariably fatal by the fourth year. In this instance, focus is on the etiology, signs and symptoms, diagnosis, and prognosis of this specific genetic disease. Understanding of preventive measures and the population at risk—Jews of northeastern European origin—also needs to be included. General psychosocial response patterns of parents at risk and potential risk need to be explored with attention given to the impact of membership variables on these patterns. Finally, this information is screened through a perspective involving social work purpose, values, knowledge, and role(s) in health care to provide general principles for clinical intervention.

Midway between these two approaches is one that combines elements of both. It is less general than the first and less specific than the second. It focuses on a specific group of health conditions, such as cancer or the pediatric leukemias. Again, however, the process is the same: the acquisition of knowledge in all four areas and the sifting of that knowledge through a social work screen to provide guidelines and principles for clinical practice.

Regardless of focus, the clinician draws practice implications in a systematic manner from analysis of the material studied. Distinction between what is known and what is thought to be on the basis of practice experience or wisdom must be carefully maintained. Implications based on what is known and reported yield guidelines and principles for practice. Implications based on practice wisdom require conversion into hypotheses and documentation. Knowledge for use is the baseline in such considerations as these. The clinician who can answer the question of how reported knowledge in these areas can be used in social work practice is in a position to improve his or her practice and make it a more effective, helpful service to clients.

Table 2.5 summarizes the parts of the approach presented in this chapter, regardless of focus.

Conclusion

A broadly based understanding of the essential elements in social work practice and the characteristics of the health field, including its problems of central concern, are indispensable ingredients in the knowledge base for clinical social work in health settings. The relationship between ill health and psychosocial events in the lives of people is apparent. Adverse

TABLE 2.5 A Study Outline for Social Workers in the Health Field

Knowledge Area	Content and Process
Purpose	What is the subject/focus of the study?
	Why is this subject/focus of importance to clinical social work practice in health settings?
	How does this study relate to social work's professional purpose?
The physical nature of the health condition	Etiology, signs and symptoms, pathology, diagnosis.
	Treatment procedures and protocols.
	Prognosis for recovery.
	Incidence rates, high-risk populations.
Psychosocial responses to the health condition	What perceptions and tasks are involved?
	How do people cope, psychologically and socially, with the health condition?
	What special equipment, conditions, procedures, or care is required?
	What are the signs and symptoms of maladaptive responses?
Other social factors involved	What kinds of conditions or states are factors in this health condition, i.e. socioeconomic status, sex, age, race, culture/ethnicity, sexual predispositions and behavior, etc.?
	How do memberships in social groups suggested by these conditions and states influence the meaning of the health condition to people and their behavioral responses to it?
Implications for clinical social work intervention	On the basis of analysis of findings in the other areas, how can this knowledge be used in clinical practice?
	What memberships are involved?
	What social work skills and processes are required?
	How do/can social work knowledge, skill, and process compliment/augment/contribute to overall intervention plans?

health conditions are life events that may require changes in family structure and in primary and secondary memberships. Education, occupation, residence, religion, and economics may be involved (Kumabe et al., 1977).

With a firm knowledge base, clinical social workers can help people to emerge from conditions of adverse health with a renewed sense of being and purpose in life, productive of health and growth. Such an outcome is no mean accomplishment for clinician and client alike.

References

Bartlett, Harriett M. *Analyzing social work practice by fields.* New York: National Association of Social Workers, 1961. (a)

Bartlett, Harriett M. *Social work practice in the health field.* New York: National Association of Social Workers, 1961. (b)

Berkanovic, Emil & Reeder, Leo G. Ethnic, economic, and social psychological factors in the sources of medical care. *Social Problems*, Fall 1973, 21:2, 246-259.

Bracht, Neil F. *Social work in health care: A guide to professional practice.* New York: The Haworth Press, 1978.

Coulton, Claudia. Factors related to preventive health behavior: Implications for social work intervention. *Social Work in Health Care*, Spring 1978, 3:3, 297-310.

Council on Social Work Education. Curriculum policy statement. Adopted 1982; effective, 1983.

Department of Health, Education, and Welfare. *Health status of minorities and low-income groups.* Washington, DC: U.S. Government Printing Office, 1979.

Doeltz, Doloris & Adamson, Duane. The collaboration of chaplin and social worker in hospital care. *Social Casework*, July 1968, 49:7, 410-413.

Falck, Hans S. The individuality-groupness effect: Phenomenology, social values and clinical applications. *Social Thought*, Summer 1978, IV:3, 29-49.

Falck, Hans S. The management of membership: The individual and the group. In Sonia Leib Abels and Paul Abels (Eds.), *Social work with groups: Proceedings of the 1979 symposium on social work with groups.* Louisville, Kentucky: Committee for the Advancement of Social Work with Groups, 1979, pp. 161-172.

Falck, Hans S. Aspects of membership: On the integration of psychoanalytic object-relations theory and small group science. *Social Thought*, Winter 1980, VI:1, 17-26.

Falck, Hans S. Social work as the management of membership: An interactionist perspective. School of Social Work, Virginia Commonwealth University, 1981. (a) Mimeographed.

Falck, Hans S. *The "seen" and the "unseen" group in clinical social work.* Richmond: The Virginia Organization of Health Care Social Workers, Monograph #3, Health Social Work Practice Series, 1981. (b)

Gowen, Patricia A. Selected medical, psycho-social, and religious aspects in Duchenne's muscular dystrophy: Implications for micro social work practice.

School of Social Work, Virginia Commonwealth University, 1980. Mimeographed.

Kaplan, David M., Grobstein, Rose & Smith, Aaron. Predicting the impact of severe illness in families. *Health and Social Work*, August 1976, 1:3, 71–82.

Kosa, John. The nature of poverty. In John Kosa and Irving Kenneth Zola (Eds.), *Poverty and health: A sociological analysis*. Cambridge: Harvard University Press, 1975.

Kumabe, Kazuye; Nishida, Chikae; O'Hara, David; & Woodruff, Charlotte. *A handbook for social work education and practice in community health settings*. Honolulu: University of Hawaii School of Social Work, 1977.

Mailick, Mildred. Designing a new course offering for health practice: A cooperative venture of school and agency. In Phyllis Caroff and Mildred Mailick (Eds.), *Social work in health services: An academic practice partnership*, with the assistance of Grace Fields. New York: Prodist, 1980.

Meares, Paula Allen. Educating social workers for specialization. *Social Work in Education*, January 1981, 3:2, 36–52.

Moos, Rudolf H. & Tsu, Vivien Davis. The crisis of physical illness: An overview. In Rudolf H. Moos (Ed.), *Coping with physical illness*. New York: Plenum Medical Book Company, 1977, pp. 3–21.

National Association of Social Workers. Specialization in the social work profession. Washington, DC: Task Force on Specialization, 1978.

Perkins, Robert A.; Parker, Jack B.; & Daste, Barry M. Multiple-influence paradigms in illness. *Social Casework*, November 1975, 55:9, 531–537.

Regensburg, Jeanette. *Toward education for health professions*. New York: Harper & Row, 1978.

Saunders, L. *Cultural differences in medical care*. New York: Russell Sage Foundation, 1954.

Process and Relationship as Aspects of Clinical Social Work Practice in Health Settings

3

Introduction

In the previous chapter, we focused on the ways in which elements in the first and second frames of Bartlett's schema can be combined to form a basis for clinical social work in the health field. In this chapter, we direct our attention to aspects of the third frame which, as Figure 2.1 (see Chapter 2) indicates, draws on the first two. Focus here, therefore, is on some of the specialized dimensions of clinical social work practice in health settings.

Accordingly, two aspects of clinical social work practice are considered in this chapter: (1) the nature of clinical social work process, including attributes of clinical membership and activity; and (2) the concept of relationship, which is the connection and quality of clinical membership. Clinical social work diagnosis and methods of intervention will be considered in subsequent chapters.

Process as an Aspect of Clinical Membership

Clinical social work in health and illness care is predicated on the intersection of health problems and social problems. Because of this intersection, clients, including but not limited to the patient, may experience problems in managing their social memberships, that is, social functioning. To address the social impact of the health condition or problem, a new membership group is formed consisting of the social worker and the clients. Depending on the circumstances, the size of this group may vary from the clinician and one client to the clinician and two or more clients.

When the clinical process begins, the client members are already related to one another and their significance to one another, as parts of one another, continues after the process has come to a close. In contrast, the social worker becomes related to the clients in order to help them resolve the social problem(s) they experience attendant to the health problem or condition. The social worker, therefore, becomes part of or significant to the clients in the sense of face-to-face relationship only for a limited time, whereas the face-to-face relationship of the clients to one another is usually ongoing. Thus, the clinical social worker's membership with clients stems from and is inherent in the social work role in the clinical process.

The Nature of Clinical Process

To consider the nature of clinical social work process, it is first necessary to distinguish *process* from *method*. These terms are sometimes used interchangeably in social work but, as Bartlett has pointed out (1961), such usage leads to problems in social work thinking. One might add that it leads to problems in social work practice as well. Even the briefest consideration of Bartlett's point suggests the kinds of problems such usage can create. Failure to define key terms leads to inconsistency in their use. Inconsistency, in turn, leads to inability to distinguish between process and method and the failure to recognize them as separate elements in practice. In health agencies, the results include ineffective social work practice and confused communication between social workers and other professionals in a field where precision and expertise in thought and practice are highly valued.

Process is a dynamic concept. It refers to progress in the sense of forward movement. In natural phenomena, it is characterized by gradual changes leading toward particular results. These results can be positive, negative, or neutral. When applied to human beings, it refers to physical growth, development, and change throughout the life cycle as well as to the social interactions that lead to psychosocial growth, development, and change.

As a social work concept, Bartlett defines process as "the social worker's intervention and participation in social interaction in the effort to bring about change" (pp. 36-37). In this sense, clinical social work process rests on a shared purpose and consists of the movement of clinician and client toward attainment of mutually agreed-upon change objectives.

In contrast, *method* is limited by definition to an orderly, systematic procedure. In social work, the term has referred historically to the traditional methods of social casework, social group work, and community organization. In recent years, however, other formulations of social work method have developed and gained acceptance.

Methods of clinical social work will be discussed in more detail in

Chapter 5. At this point, however, it is important to note that while social work methods are employed by clinician and clients in their movement toward the attainment of agreed-upon objectives, the clinical process is not dependent on or limited by method. Process is a broader, more dynamic, and comprehensive concept than method. It makes use of the social work method or methods appropriate for the resolution of particular problems in social functioning.

Like all processes, clinical social work process takes place within identifiable time sequences. In social work, these are known as beginnings, middles, and ends. Smalley's (1967) consideration of these time phases illustrates important dimensions of clinical process, aspects of which are summarized in Tables 3.1 and 3.2 and discussed briefly in the sections below. Smalley identifies skill in the conscious use of time as generic to professional social work. The overall objective of this skill is to enable clients to make full use of each time phase so that they may attain maximum benefit from each. In this regard, each time phase has its own objective.

Table 3.1 builds on Smalley's notion that each time phase can be exploited for use by clients. It summarizes the general objectives of each time phase and in so doing suggests the kinds of activities that characterize each sequence in the helping process.

In health social work, the particular health condition or problem and its impact on the abilities of clients to manage their social memberships is the

TABLE 3.1 Objectives of the Time Sequences in Clinical Social Work Process

Time Sequence	Objective of the Time Sequence
Beginning phase	To establish a common base for joint activity by clinician and clients designed to resolve an agreed-upon problem in social functioning; to begin.
Middle phase	To deepen the mutual engagement of clinician and clients in task performance geared toward problem resolution.
Ending phase	To assess the clinical process and its outcomes including affirmation of the clients' sense of accomplishment and ability to manage their social memberships.
	To affirm mutually the end of the process, the separation of clinician and clients from clinical membership, and the continuing of the clients on their own as a new beginning for them.

TABLE 3.2 Some Examples of Typical Member Behaviors and Their Purpose in the Time Phases of Clinical Social Work Process

| Time Phase | Typical Client Behaviors | | Typical Clinician Behaviors (Techniques) | |
	Manifestation	Purpose	Manifestation	Purpose
Beginning phase	Expressions of hope and excitement.	Mobilizes energy.	Encouragement of expression of feelings.	Affirms client integrity.
	Opposition or resistance.	Denotes fear and/or uncertainty.	Makes unknowns known.	Lessens client fears and uncertainties.
	Expressions of doubt in ability to solve problem(s).	Denotes a sense of being overwhelmed.	Partialization of the problem/situation.	Helps clients to take hold and begin.
Middle phase	Searches for ways to withdraw from the process.	Denotes possible discouragement or depression.	Use of new content or tasks to revitalize mutual activities.	Helps clients gain a renewed sense of their abilities.
	Seeks reassurance and encouragement.	Denotes a need for sustenance and support.	Expression of professional concern.	Helps clients to continue and accept responsibility for their part in the process.
	Deepens engagement in process and task performance.	Denotes acceptance of own part in the process.	Expression of respect for client integrity.	Helps clients maintain a sense of worth.
Ending phase	Attempts to postpone ending the process.	Denotes possibility of doubt in own ability.	Recognition of client accomplishments.	Affirms client abilities.
	Attempts to end the process prematurely.	Denotes possible fear of separation or loss.	Encouragement of expression of feelings.	Affirms client's sense of worth.
	Expression of readiness to end.	Denotes sense of accomplishment and ability.	Recapitulation of the process and its meaning.	Mutual evaluation of outcomes and affirmation of client's ability to begin again.

content of the clinical process. The resolution of problems in social functioning stemming from this impact is the purpose of the clinical process. The exchange of knowledge, cognitive information, and the expression of feelings and actions that lead to or indicate understanding of the meaning of both pertinent data and affect are dynamics of the clinical process.

Attributes of Clinical Membership and Activity

As members, the behavior of the social worker and clients is guided by the clinical social work process which provides the vehicle for joint problem-solving activity. Social worker and clients differ, however, in attributes of clinical membership and activity. The clinician, for example, brings professional social work expertise to the membership group. In turn, clients make use of the clinician's knowledge and skill in the mutual process of problem assessment (diagnosis), task definition (planning), task implementation (intervention), and evaluation of outcomes.

While engaged in this joint activity, both social worker and clients are simultaneously members of other ongoing social groups and, while they share this human characteristic, they differ in terms of the use made of the content that flows from their other group memberships. The clinical process requires that the social worker control the influence of his or her other social memberships in order that they not distort the process or be imposed on clients. In contrast, attributes of the clients' other social memberships—family, friendship network, profession, religion, culture, and so on—are at the heart of the clinical process; these attributes contribute to its content, and are the primary concern of its focus and purpose.

The factor of time suggests other ways in which social worker and clients differ as members. Table 3.2 suggests some of the different ways clients behave and the purpose of that behavior in the time phases of the process. It also suggests some of the ways the social work clinician responds to client behavior (techniques) and the reasons for the responses.

The patterns of behavior that clients bring to each phase of the process are diverse and, as Smalley observes, derive from the particular past experiences of clients and the particular approaches they have developed over time for dealing with new beginnings, ongoing interactions, and endings. It is important, therefore, to bear in mind that the client and clinician behaviors included in Table 3.2 are only illustrations of the possibilities within each time phase. Clients may behave in any or all of the ways suggested in Table 3.2 or in ways not included. Similarly, the underlying purpose of their behavior may vary from client to client. Finally, the social worker may employ any or all of the behaviors (techniques) noted in Table 3.2 in any combination or may use other techniques deemed appropriate to the situation.

The important point is to recognize that each time phase constitutes an opportunity that can be exploited by the clinician and clients for the growth and development of the client members. The social worker brings to the process an understanding of time that facilitates the use of what Smalley calls "each present and passing moment" in each time phase. In this sense, time is the medium of the helping process (Taft, 1962).

Finally, for the process as a whole and within each time sequence, the social worker carries responsibility for managing the use of time so that the potential inherent in each time phase of the process, and in the process as a whole, may be fully realized for the clients. The clinician does this through a series of actions, some of which are included in Table 3.2. These actions are not disparate techniques, but rather indications of skill in what Smalley identifies as "ways of relating to and making appropriate professional social work use of time" that reflect an understanding of its significance as a generic principle of social work practice (pp. 150-151).

An Illustration from Practice

The following case material provides a synopsis of clinical social work process as it occurred over a nine month period. As is often true, the medical patient in this case is not the social work client. This material is notable in several respects. It summarizes clinician-client interactions and interactions by the clinician on behalf of the clients as aspects of a single process. It demonstrates how clinician and clients can collaborate with representatives of other professions—in this case, law—in mutual efforts designed to help clients continue to function when they are confronted by catastrophic events. These two factors suggest the artificiality of attempts to separate so-called concrete services from other clinical interventions when, in fact, they are aspects of one process of giving and taking help. Throughout the material, the clinician freely relates, often in dramatic terms, the simultaneous impact of stressful events on the clients and on himself, thereby demonstrating the power of the meaning of mutuality in the process of clinical membership.

The Case of Gary

Medical Situation   The patient, Gary L., a nine-year-old boy, was admitted to the hospital's intensive care unit (ICU) immediately following his arrival from a county about 90 miles away. While crossing a road near his home, Gary was struck by a medium-sized truck carrying logs. Upon admission, he was described in the medical chart as having sustained an open depressed skull fracture with extensive brain damage, a fractured pelvis with bladder contusion, fractures of the right elbow (compound) and right ankle, multiple contusions and abrasions, and was showing hematuria with internal bleeding of unknown origin. Gary was unconscious and neurologically unresponsive.

Nine days after his admission, Gary was referred to the social work department for an assessment of an apparent need for financial assistance. After reading Gary's chart in the morning, and viewing his mangled body, I felt this young boy would die in a matter of days. I had little grasp of the tragically extended journey upon which I was about to embark with Gary, his mother, and his family.

Referral to Social Work

I returned to the ICU in the early afternoon and found a woman, about 35 years old, standing alongside Gary's bed, holding his left hand tightly, and saying, "Gary, this is Mama. Mama is here with you, honey. Talk to Mama." Gary remained unresponsive. As I approached Gary's bed, I inquired, "Mrs. L?" In response, she turned abruptly toward me and stated, "Oh! You surprised me! I'm Mrs. L." I smiled as I introduced myself and clarified who I was and why I had come to see her—to offer social work assistance to her and Gary throughout Gary's hospital stay. As I explained my role and clarified my purpose, Mrs. L expressed satisfaction at "having someone to talk to." Mrs. L, talking very quickly and darting her eyes back and forth between Gary and me, told me about her son's accident, injuries, and emergency surgery. Throughout our initial contact, Mrs. L kept stimulating Gary verbally in futile attempts to elicit some type of response from him, whether it be a grunt, moan, squeezed hand, or any other sign of awareness. Standing at Gary's bedside, Mrs. L and I conversed intermittently. My role was essentially that of concerned listener.

Beginning Phase

Beginning establishment of common base for joint activity

Expression of hope

Affirmation of client's integrity

The ICU atmosphere was eerie. Gary was in a bed near the left wall of a room containing four beds in a row, all surrounded by beeping, buzzing, pulsating mechanical devices connected through wires and tubes to the inanimate bodies of mostly comatose patients. In addition to the relatives of other patients, a group of medical staff stood to the left of us, in the rear, adding to the already socially cumbersome environment in which we tried to achieve some semblance of privacy to talk.

Impact of setting

The latter part of our first interaction took place in the hallway, where I learned that Mrs. L was the thirty-five-year-old mother

Family membership group

of five children, ages four through 16. Her husband, who worked the day shift in a factory near their home, was able to visit Gary only infrequently. Mrs. L spent five days each week at the hospital and returned home only on weekends.

Partialization

Expression of
doubt/fear

During this first interview, I chose to explain only peripherally the reason for the social work referral, which was procurement of financial resources to cover the costs of Gary's extended hospitalization. This choice was made in response to Mrs. L's overwhelming and realistic concern for the present moment, the life or death situation of her son. My role as concerned listener continued as Mrs. L freely shared with me the fears and anxieties she felt as a result of this unforeseen catastrophe. The anguish of her loneliness in suffering was compounded by her fears about the possibility of Gary's long impairment, disability, and ultimate death which increased the anxiety aroused in her by being in a large hospital, in a strange city, a long distance from family and friends.

*Intervention on
behalf of clients*

Preparation for
making unknowns
known

Following our interview, I telephoned the Health Department to determine possible financial assistance for severely injured children. I had been referred to the Department by the Social Service Bureau where I had been informed that Mrs. L could apply for Medicaid in Gary's name, but that the application would have to be completed in person at the Bureau. I also contacted the local Crippled Children's Bureau, and was told to contact the Health Department to arrange for a public medical evaluation and to have the information forwarded to them as part of their intake process. In the meantime, Gary's physical status was to be evaluated by a nurse from the Crippled Children's Bureau.

**Transition to
Middle Phase**

Expression of
doubt/fear

Expression of
professional concern

Help for the client
to continue

During the following week, my interaction with Mrs. L continued to focus primarily on Mrs. L's spontaneous emotional reactions to Gary's tenuous hold on life. We also dealt with the beginning integration of the full impact of Gary's accident on Mrs. L and his family. Specifically, Mrs. L was discouraged by Gary's unresponsiveness and his apparent lack of progress in comparison to other ICU patients. I tried to reassure Mrs. L by first explaining that Gary had been injured severely and for this reason, his body would likely be slower in healing compared to some of the other patients in the unit. I then commented that although waiting would not be easy, we would have to be patient with Gary, and would wait together. I frequently encouraged Mrs. L to share her concerns with me in this way since it helped her to release tension and to obtain the emotional support necessary in a time of crisis.

Although describing her son's appearance immediately following admission to the hospital as resembling a "monster," Mrs. L never lost sight of Gary's innate humanness, despite physical deformities. For myself, especially after Gary's head bandage was removed, it took several visits before I was able to view his smashed head without being visually repulsed.

Impact of patient's medical condition

During the remainder of Gary's stay in the ICU, prior to his transfer to pediatrics, I helped Mrs. L to cope with her depression over her inability to get a response from Gary despite her repeated and frustrated daily efforts. I acknowledged Mrs. L's frustration while reassuring her that her attempts to communicate with Gary were very important since not even the physicians could be sure that Gary could not hear her voice.

Help for client to maintain a sense of ability and worth

During the first fifteen days following the accident, Gary underwent four major surgical procedures: exploratory laparotomy, craniotomy, open reduction of the fractured right leg, and drainage of fluid from the infected skull injury. On the twentieth day of his hospitalization, Gary was transferred to pediatrics on the basis of the apparent stabilization of his medical condition. Although he remained comatose, Mrs. L interpreted his departure from the ICU as indicative of the start of Gary's recovery. The limits of his stabilization became apparent, however, during the following week when Gary's frail, weakened body was subjected to a fifth and sixth surgical operation. The fifth was brain surgery to determine the verity of what appeared to be cerebral hemorrhaging, while the sixth was to reset a bone in his fractured right arm.

Middle Phase
Medical condition

Fifteen days after meeting Mrs. L, I met Gary's father. Mr. L was a verbal man and we had little difficulty in establishing a mutually satisfying relationship. He related several of his concerns, including: his low earnings and the financial hardship this caused for his family; the travel time and expense involved in the 180 mile round-trip between the hospital and the L home; the ability of his 1964 model automobile to make these trips; the cohesion of his family and the help of his other children at home while their mother was with Gary; and his confidence in God that his son would eventually recover. I supported and encouraged Mr. and Mrs. L's coping abilities and their mutual reliance and I acknowledged the fortitude and endurance they had shown throughout their very trying ordeal.

Family membership group
Expression of doubt in ability to solve problems

Expression of respect of client integrity and ability

During this and subsequent weeks, my developing relationship with Mrs. L coalesced into one based on mutual trust, honesty, and respect. We spent much time dealing with the

Deepening engagement in process

Impact of setting

Right to privacy
Help for client to
continue and to
accept responsibility
while affirming
client's worth and
ability

incessant medical crises and setbacks which exacerbated Mrs. L's physical, emotional, and psychological exhaustion. Her physical fatigue was, in turn, increased by a relentless flow of curious visitors, even strangers who "came to see the little boy in Room 280." Mrs. L found it tedious to have to repeat time and time again the circumstances surrounding Gary's admission and treatment. I suggested various tactful ways of dealing with this flow of visitors, while simultaneously asserting Mrs. L's right to more privacy should she find this alternative more desirable. During the following month, our relationship was beset by a series of events which made it the most difficult and emotionally draining period of the entire helping process, for both of us. These events occurred on a variety of levels. Since I had not previously worked with a family with such a complicated sociomedical situation, I supplanted my efforts frequently through supervisory conferences and through consultation with other staff in the Pediatrics Unit.

*Intervention on
behalf of client*

Due to the nature of the accident and the family situation, an integral part of my services revolved around the procurement of tangible resources to help cover the enormous expenses the L family was incurring because of Gary's extended hospital stay and numerous surgical procedures. Possible resources included the Bureau of Crippled Children (BCC), Supplemental Security Income (SSI), County Social Services (CSS), and the City Welfare Department (CWD). Two weeks after my initial inquiry and referral, a public health medical evaluation was completed by the Health Department and forwarded to the BCC. Three weeks later, a BCC evaluation was completed, only to end in a denial of assistance due to Gary's poor rehabilitative potential.

Collaboration

Use of new content

*Use of hospital
resources and policy*

At this point, a relative of another patient gave Mrs. L the name of a local lawyer and suggested that he might be of help in the L family's attempt to obtain financial reparation from the owner of the truck that hit Gary. At Mrs. L's request, I contacted the local bar association to determine the lawyer's credibility and then contacted the lawyer for a description of his services. After checking with the hospital's legal advisor about the soundness of the lawyer's verbal contract and fee level, I arranged an interview with him for Gary's parents.

Mr. and Mrs. L asked that I be present at their meeting with the lawyer to lend support to the family and to interpret their concerns to the lawyer. During the meeting the legal situation was explored and the lawyer's services were clarified. A formal contract between the lawyer and Mr. and Mrs. L was signed, thus relieving the L's concern about an appropriate legal course of action.

Because she was living in the city five days each week, Mrs. L had been unable to apply for Medicaid in person at the County Social Services office. Mrs. L, therefore, agreed to try to apply in the city. Following the initial contact with the lawyer, therefore, Mrs. L and I walked to the local SSI office and to the City Welfare Department. This walk was one of our most meaningful interactions. In addition to getting her away from the hospital for a couple of hours, this interviewing technique enabled Mrs. L and I to share together the frustration of the application process.

Mutuality of the clinical process

At the SSI office, we were told cordially that Gary could not qualify for payments unless he was physically residing at home. We then proceeded to the CWD, where we learned that interdistrict applications were rare, but possible. We obtained the necessary forms and I later confirmed with the county office that under the circumstances, a mail application would be "allowed." It was another two weeks before the 14 pages of application forms were completed and mailed.

During our walk, Mrs. L and I, for the first time, discussed at length Gary's continued unresponsiveness and the possibility of his death in the near future. We both now realized the slim chance for recovery he had and much of our communication was nonverbal. By now, our relationship had grown into one of mutual trust. During this phase, I used a great deal of empathy and attention to concrete details as a means of strengthening Mrs. L's already enormous capacity to function under intense stress.

Expression of need for reassurance and encouragement

Help for client to continue to accept responsibility for her part in the process

The following day, Gary underwent his seventh operation to draw infected fluid from his head wound and to insert a permanent drainage tube. Gary survived the procedure and was listed in satisfactory condition.

Medical condition

Ever since Gary's transfer to pediatrics, Mrs. L had been actively involved in providing basic nursing care to her son, including position changes, washing, powdering, changing diapers, and so on. Her skills had increased to the point where she was able, under supervision, to administer her son's nasogastric tube feedings every four hours around the clock. Following Gary's most recent skull surgery, he required fresh sterile dressings for his head wound and Mrs. L helped the nurses with this task to the extent that her skills permitted.

Deepened involvement in the process

Eleven weeks after Gary's accident and admission to the hospital, Mrs. L made her first extended visit home. She stayed at home for five days. These days away from Gary and the hospital were a welcome break for Mrs. L who, during the previous week, had had the disheartening experience of watching her deteriorating son lie comatose on his tenth birthday.

Respect for client integrity, ability, and worth

Upon her return to the hospital, Mrs. L and I had a lengthy interview which represented our most in-depth exploration thus far of Gary's poor prognosis. Previously, she had avoided any lengthy discussion of his deteriorating condition and probable death. Partly to sustain her ability to function, I had respected her avoidance by not probing. Instead, I had waited for, and then responded to, the opportunity as it arose that day when Mrs. L felt confident enough to share these charged feelings and thoughts with me. Later, in retrospect, I realized that Mrs. L's first, and then progressively longer visits home, actually represented her gradual separation from Gary in preparation for his physical absence after his death.

Medical condition

Intervention on behalf of client

Beginning expression of readiness to end

Through all of this month and into the next, Gary's condition remained virtually unchanged. Intermittent medical intervention was geared to basic maintenance. During this time, I conducted a fruitless search for a long-term care facility that would accept Gary for placement. Mrs. L spent longer periods of time at home, checking with the hospital staff on Gary's condition daily by telephone. This indicated: (1) her increasing need to separate from Gary prior to his impending death; (2) her need to devote more attention to her other children and husband; and (3) her increased faith in the nursing staff's ability to care properly for her son in her absence.

Expression of anger, discouragement, and frustration

Early in the fifth month of Gary's hospitalization, Mrs. L's frustration reached a breaking point. During our interview one day, Mrs. L freely expressed her pent-up anger and sorrow over the injustice of her son's accident and injuries, the endless paperwork for various assistance applications, and the seemingly sluggish process toward a legal settlement. I supported and encouraged this emotional ventilation by Mrs. L. Following this explosion, Mrs. L became more composed and called the lawyer to arrange for a meeting to clarify the legal intricacies of his work on the family's behalf.

The following week, when I arrived on the unit, I was met by Mr. L, who informed me that he had been called to the hospital that morning from work because Gary had "taken a bad turn." We proceeded to Gary's room, whereupon a joint interview was held regarding his vomiting and high fever, possible indications that he would not survive the night. The L's expressed their faith in God and that they had placed the fate of their son in His hands. I supported this healthy adaptive mechanism, which enabled these two exhausted parents to cope with the impending final crisis. Before leaving, I left my home telephone number with the L's and urged them to call if they felt a need for my presence during the night.

Respect for clients

Mutuality of clinical process

The next morning, I learned that Gary had died at 1:00 A.M. Since the L's had already left the hospital to return home by the time I arrived, I telephoned them. Mrs. L expressed relief at the final ending of Gary's suffering and was thankful for the hospital staff's support throughout her ordeal. We agreed to speak the following week about the time and place of Gary's funeral.

As it turned out, Gary's funeral was held on a weekend, three days after his death. In all the confusion, Mrs. L lost her wallet, with my telephone number in it, and was unable to contact me. She apologized for this profusely, especially since the funeral was held three days earlier than originally planned. Mrs. L described to me, in detail, a gratifying funeral conducted by the same preacher who had officiated at her marriage to Mr. L.

Mutuality of concern

For four months following Gary's death, the L family and I maintained regular telephone contact, as I attempted to help them, as much as possible, with the reordering of their lives in the absence of one young family member. During this time, I was also involved with the L's lawyer regarding numerous communications and documents to complete the legal settlement. Since Medicaid, Mr. L's group health insurance, Gary's life insurance, and the truck driver's liability insurance were all components to be untangled for the reconciliation of hospital costs, a lengthy process ensued to determine which resource would cover which services.

Ending Phase

Intervention on behalf of the client

My ongoing contacts with the L family included a home visit. I accompanied the lawyer to the L's home so that: legal matters could be settled; I could assess the status of the L family's coping abilities; I could determine if Mr. and Mrs. L were ready to end our clinical relationship. We spent about two hours together, during which we went to the county courthouse to name Mrs. L executrix of Gary's estate and to Mr. L's previous employer to obtain insurance records. Mr. L had been laid off on a semipermanent basis due to a production slowdown. I also accompanied Mr. and Mrs. L on a visit to Gary's gravesite behind a small country church.

Affirmation of client
ability to begin again

Expression of readi-
ness to end

Although I was personally devastated by the abject poverty in which the L family was forced to live, I was impressed by their apparently functional adaptation to the loss of their son. As we reviewed the course of our work together over the last nine months, and the tragic circumstances that had brought us together, Mr. and Mrs. L expressed readiness to continue on their own and belief in their mutual ability to begin again. As we said goodbye, we agreed that the time had come to end our relationship.

Retrospective
Review of the
Clinical Process
and Its Outcomes

Mrs. L's emotional reaction to Gary's accident naturally varied during different stages of his hospitalization. At the outset, she was a mother who, under severe and strenuous conditions, was in a state of emotional shock and unable to grasp the full implications of Gary's injuries. Every day was a crisis for the first four weeks of Gary's hospitalization and much of our work together was "here and now" oriented, as both Mrs. L and I strove to deal with the immense burden of reconciling such a tragic occurrence with some degree of hope and ability to go on.

Following stabilization of Gary's medical condition, Mrs. L was able to deal better with the financial and legal aspects of the situation. This occurred concurrently with Mrs. L's growing understanding that Gary was unresponsive because he was in a coma caused by irreparable brain damage. When Gary seemed, finally, to be out of physical danger, we were able to deal with many of the long-term implications of his condition. Mrs. L's expectations for Gary's recovery steadily lowered. In our initial contacts, Mrs. L expressed her anxiousness to see Gary walk again, even if he required mechanical assistance. As Gary's condition worsened, Mrs. L's hopes were that he would at least speak to her sometime, even if he had to remain in a wheelchair. Her later hopes were influenced by the realization that Gary would never again walk or talk and that nasogastric tube feedings would be his nutritive sustenance for the rest of his life, which probably would not be a long one.

It was emotionally discouraging for me to actually observe and share these progressively lowered expectations. When I contemplated the emotional stress Gary's medical condition and prognosis aroused in me, I was able to gain a small degree of empathic understanding of the devastating crisis which the entire L family was experiencing. I was not reluctant to share my own emotional responses with Mrs. L, when appropriate, and within the context of the mutuality of our clinical relationship.

My own growth as a medical social worker, and my knowledge and skill grew and expanded as a result of my work with Gary's family. With regard to interdisciplinary collaboration, I experienced a shift in my relationship to the L's lawyer. During initial contract formulation, I remained skeptical of the lawyer's vested financial interest in arranging for a quick legal settlement. My doubt, however, was transformed into trust, and later into a sense of collegiality, as I observed how the lawyer conveyed a sincere desire to work out a settlement with the family's best interests guiding his work. As a medical social worker, I refined my ability to work effectively within a task-centered framework of service delivery by addressing my interventions to those stressful areas identified by Mrs. L throughout our contacts. Constant informal renegotiation of our mutual and different tasks took place as we focused on reality-based problems of continued living under the most stressful circumstances.

The total experience of having lived with the L's through the multiple events that arose from their son's injuries has had a profound impact on me. Through sharing knowledge and self, I became intimately involved in a basic human struggle—the search for meaning in death. The specific example of Mrs. L's struggle to reconcile the death of her own child with her religious faith was an example of life's ongoing nature—a forward moving process of change and growth, despite the occurrence of highly stressful crises. In this respect, the L family continually dealt with emerging, new, yet everpresent problems in daily living—such as Mr. L's unemployment, the illness of other children, and an ongoing battle to maintain financial subsistence—while simultaneously maintaining some degree of psychosocial integration in the face of Gary's deteriorating physical condition and eventual death. Thus, the L family demonstrated the ability to continue and to begin again. In retrospect, our work together resulted in mutual learning and growth—for the L's and for me.*

The case of Gary provides an overview of clinical social work process in a health setting which dramatically explicates the nature of clinician-client interaction. Frequent reference is made to the relationship which the clinician and Mr. and Mrs. L established as Gary's accident and subsequent physical deterioration and death brought them together in a

*Source: Marcel O. Charpentier, A.C.S.W., Director of Social Service, The Memorial Hospital, Pawtucket, Rhode Island 02860.

particular membership configuration. It is to aspects of the clinical relationship, its nature and qualities, that we now turn.

Relationship: The Connection and Quality of Clinical Membership

The concept of relationship was first introduced into social work literature and thought by Virginia Robinson (1978) who, in order to better understand it and its place in social casework practice, as that practice was then understood, sought to "lift the fact of relationship out of its settings and consider it afresh" (pp. 104–105). Stimulated by Robinson's consideration of the concept, social caseworkers came to regard relationship as central to, if not a precondition for, effective social casework practice. As a consequence, the development of relationship as a concept is most extensive in social casework theory and practice.

Despite its centrality in most formulations of social casework, however, the concept of relationship itself has proven difficult to define. Four tendencies found in most definitions of the term lend support to this conclusion. The first is a tendency to describe relationship as a process, rather than to define it as a concept in its own right. The second tendency is to emphasize the psychological elements of process. The third is an almost exclusive association of the concept with social casework. The fourth tendency derives from the third and is focused on the concept of relationship as characterized in one-to-one social casework formulations.

These tendencies are particularly apparent in the earlier definitions of relationship which make use of such descriptive phrases as: "the interplay of [caseworker and client] personalities" (American Association of Social Workers, 1929, pp. 29–30); "transfer . . . an emotional relationship to the client" (Taft, 1924, p. 143); "the mental and emotional natures" of interviewer and interviewee (Young, 1935, p. 2); and "the dynamic interaction . . . between [the] personality trends and drives" of "two individuals" (Aptekar, 1941, pp. 48–49).

As social work's knowledge base grew, however, understanding of relationship expanded to incorporate elements of process other than purely psychological ones. Lyndon (1948), for example, moved the notion of relationship beyond the limits of strict psychological process, but maintained the process focus and the one-to-one emphasis.

> The relationship is the sum total of all that happens between the participants— all the words exchanged, the feelings, attitudes, actions, and thoughts expressed; everything, in fact, that the client and worker do whether open and overt or devious and hidden. (p. 16)

While these and other descriptive definitions contributed to social work's understanding of relationship, some did so in distinctive ways that are significant to its development as a social work concept. Young and Aptekar, for example, added dimensions that anticipate the notion of membership. Young noted that whatever the words used to describe the process of relationship, the objective is "to establish a bridge" whereby the caseworker and client can become "we," thereby "winning across the void which separates man from man and gaining a feeling of kinship" (p. 353). Likewise, Aptekar followed his reference to "personality trends and drives" with a note of caution that suggests other dimensions of relationship and prefigures the notion of membership.

> What happens depends upon the two individuals who, it should be remembered, are participating simultaneously in other relationships. In addition, much depends upon the situation in which people get together. (pp. 48–49)

Hamilton (1951) added dimensions to the definition of relationship that emphasized its nature as a social work concept.

> . . . the professional relationship involves a mutual process of shared responsibilities, recognitions of the other's rights, acceptance of difference, with the goal, not of isolation, but of socialized attitudes and behavior stimulating growth through interaction. (p. 27)

Hamilton's inclusion of mutuality, sharing, recognition, and acceptance as dimensions of relationship denoted more clearly its qualities. In addition, her stress on socialized attitudes and behavior is distinctive and clearly consistent with the profession's concern with social functioning as its central purpose.

All four tendencies were brought together by Biestek (1957) in what is, perhaps, the most penetrating examination of relationship in the literature of social casework. Biestek defines relationship as "the dynamic interaction of attitudes and emotions between the caseworker and the client, with the purpose of helping the client achieve a better adjustment between himself and his environment" (p. 12). He refers to relationship as "the soul of casework" and he describes the interaction as "primarily *internal*," consisting of "feelings and attitudes" which are usually not expressed in words (p. 18).

Biestek followed this definition by dividing relationship conceptually into seven elements, or needs, from which he derived seven corresponding principles. These principles are: individualization, purposeful expression of feelings, controlled emotional involvement, acceptance, nonjudgmental attitude, client self-determination, and confidentiality. He placed these elements in an interactional framework with three directions according to the need of the client, the response of the caseworker, and the awareness of the client (p. 17). In defining the seven principles as principles of action (process), Biestek noted that they are simultaneously qualities and elements—"qualities in the sense that they are necessarily present in every good relationship; elements in the sense that conceptually they are constitutive parts of the relationship" (p. 18).

Thus, Young and Aptekar, while fully within the tradition of interpreting relationship as a form of process, implied that relationship might also denote connection. Lyndon expanded the definition of relationship beyond the limits of psychological elements, and Hamilton brought the concept fully within the purview of social work purpose. Hamilton's definition also suggested some of the qualities inherent in the casework relationship. Finally, Biestek identified the essential elements of the casework relationship as qualities from which principles of action (practice) derive.

All of these contributions, however, maintained the tradition of describing relationship in one-to-one social casework terms. Not until Smalley (1967) defined relationship simply as "helping people to help themselves" was relationship fully freed from the conceptual confines of social casework. In her consideration of relationship as the "essential core" of practice, Smalley provided the conceptual basis necessary to identify relationship as a phenomenon with underpinnings in psychological, process, and social theory generic to all forms of social work and not restricted to social casework or to the interaction of a caseworker and one client (pp. 167-75).

Despite the important contributions these and other definitions of relationship made to social work thought and practice, and despite the fact that relationship was eventually freed from its almost exclusive conceptual association with the psychological elements of process and social casework practice, all of the definitions cited above are fully within the custom of defining relationship as a form of process. Thus, they do not distinguish relationship conceptually from process.

Given the propensity evident in social work literature to use important terms interchangeably, definitions of relationship as process add to, albeit unintentionally, the confusion already inherent in the synonymous definitions of process and method. This may be a consequence of the tendency in social work for theory to follow practice, rather than to lead it.

Relationship Defined

How then can relationship be defined to indicate its distinctiveness as a social work concept? More specifically, how can it be defined with regard to clinical social work? Relationship, as understood here, has two

essential meanings. First, it refers to the state of being related or connected. Second, it denotes the interest, involvement, or concern that
forms the basis for mutual association.

In the first sense, the sense of being related or connected, relationship is
synonymous with membership. As the social worker and the client(s) gain
clinical membership, they become related, significant to one another,
connected. Put another way, the clinical social worker and the client(s)
are related by virtue of their common membership in the clinical group.

In the second sense, relationship denotes the quality of the connection
of the clinical social worker and the client(s). Truax and Carkhuff (1967)
identify the qualities of nonpossessive warmth, accurate empathy, and
positive regard (genuineness/authenticity) as relationship qualities that
are essential if practitioner-client interactions are to be therapeutic for
clients. Other terms used to denote the qualities of the connection between the social worker and client(s) are trust, reciprocity, and acceptance.

Qualities of Clinical Relationship/Membership

Table 3.3 identifies some of the qualities of clinical membership, their
basis in human needs, the principles that derive from them, and the
definition of these principles in practice. The table draws on Biestek's
framework, but terminology and principles are modified to free them
from the social casework context and to bring them into consistency with
the membership formulation. This modification requires additional comment, however, inasmuch as the terms and descriptions in Table 3.3
represent somewhat sharp departures from those traditional in social
work.

The qualities of mutual recognition, treatment, and appreciation are
inherent in the principle of personalization. The term personalization is
used to denote the social nature of each person. It preserves the notion of
each person's need to be recognized, treated, and appreciated as a "me,"
but also recognizes that each person's "me" is a part of others by virtue of
his or her social memberships. This is the case in clinical social work
membership as well as nonsocial work memberships. As members, the
clinical social worker and clients retain their "me" but are also parts of a
new "we."

People need to express more than feeling. As social beings capable of
cognition as well as emotion, they also need to express thoughts and
actions in ways that can be understood by others. To do this, people must
trust one another and not fear condemnation—that is, a sense of trust, of
personal freedom must typify the interactions of members. In clinical
memberships, this sense of freedom and its expression has as its purpose

TABLE 3.3 Relationship Qualities of Clinical Membership and Related Practice Principles

Quality	Basis	Practice Principle	Definition
Mutual recognition and appreciation	The mutual need of people as human beings to be recognized, appreciated, and treated as persons.	Personalization	The recognition and treatment of members to express understanding of their contributions and abilities and their significance as social beings.
Mutual trust; a sense of personal freedom in a social context	The mutual right and need of people to express their feelings, thoughts and actions, both positive and negative, in relation to others.	Purposeful expression of feelings, thoughts and actions	Recognition of the right and agreement that members are free to express thoughts and feelings, even negative ones, and to act without fear or discouragement or condemnation and that such expression is to be encouraged when appropriate.
Mutual understanding	The mutual right and need of people to receive sympathetic and empathetic responses to feelings, thoughts, and actions.	Purposeful involvement	Sensitivity to the feelings, thoughts and actions of members and appropriate responses that indicate understanding and appreciation of them.
Mutual appreciation and concern	The need of people to be recognized by others as social beings of worth, despite positive or negative attributes.	Acceptance	Creation of a sense of safety that allows members to reveal themselves, abandon dysfunctional defenses, and be free to examine themselves and identified problems.
Fairness; non-partiality	The mutual need of people to be treated fairly in relation to others, even if their feelings, thoughts and actions are not approved.	Equity	Not taking sides and exclusion of the assignment of guilt while objectively identifying mutual responsibilities and tasks.

(continued)

68

TABLE 3.3 (continued)

Quality	Basis	Practice Principle	Definition
Choice	The mutual need and right of people to make their own choices and decisions within the context of membership constraints and opportunities.	Social self-determination	Action that denotes recognition of the right of members, as socially responsible beings, to make their own decisions and choose their own courses of action.
Mutual respect; privacy	The need and right of people to maintain privacy and to have personal information kept within the limits they designate.	Confidentiality	The obligation to keep personal information disclosed in the clinical situation private, but with the understanding that it may be shared with other professionals who are similarly bound, the exception being situations bound by legal requirements.

the facilitation of efforts to resolve problems in social functioning. In pursuit of this purpose, clients must be free to express their negative thoughts, their fears and uncertainties, their hatreds, angers, and resentments as well as their positive thoughts and feelings. The principle of purposeful expression of feelings, thoughts, and actions recognizes this need as a manifestation of the relationship quality of trust.

The quality of mutual understanding reflects the reciprocal need to be treated by others with empathy and concern. It is the basis for the principle of purposeful involvement which indicates sensitivity to the feelings, thoughts, and actions of clients as clinical members. This principle is similar to the principle of purposeful expression since the purpose of the involvement is to facilitate problem resolution or change. The phrase *controlled emotional involvement* is sometimes used to express this principle, but the involvement is with more than emotional content. Thoughts and actions are also involved. In addition, the term "controlled" can be interpreted to mean something other than purposeful. It can, for example, be interpreted so as to place the social worker at the center of the relationship. This may be accurate in some respects, as in the clinician's responsibility for managing time. It is not accurate, however, in other respects, as the principle of choice suggests.

The principle of acceptance is one that sometimes causes problems as a result of its interpretation. It inheres in the need of people to be recognized as social beings of worth, whatever positive or negative attributes they may possess. In this sense, it reflects the relationship qualities of mutual appreciation and concern. Acceptance does not, however, imply approval. As Biestek clearly points out, "acceptance does not mean approval of deviant attitudes or behavior. The object of acceptance is not 'the good' but 'the real.' The object is pertinent reality" (p. 72).

The importance placed on justice by social workers has been noted. This value reflects the concept of fairness as a fundamental quality of the relationship between the social worker and clients. This quality is sometimes translated to mean nonjudgment, but nonjudgment, like acceptance, can also be interpreted to connote implied approval. It can also be interpreted as a quality of passivity on the part of the social worker.

Clients, however, are entitled to active participation on the part of the social worker and that activity includes the rendering of judgments based on professional knowledge and expertise that reflect conclusions based on direct observation and the expert interpretation of data and behavior. In this connection, objectivity goes hand-in-hand with sensitivity to the meanings of data and behavior and their interpretation to clients. Nonpartiality is a key variable here, as is avoidance of capricious or arbitrary conclusions and interpretations. Hence, the term equity is used to designate the principle that reflects the quality of fairness and nonpartiality.

Frequent reference is made in social work literature to the concept of self-determination. The belief that people need and have a right to make decisions and choices in the conduct of their lives, and not to have decisions or choices made by others imposed on them, is an integral part of the fabric of human interaction in Western Society. As Regensburg (1978) and others have noted, however, this need and the right that derives from it are not absolute. The decisions and choices of one person have meaning to others, and vice versa. To reflect this reality, the principle of self-determination is modified to become *social* self-determination. Use of the term "social" as a modifier indicates the limits on independent choice that inhere in the social organization of human life and in particular memberships.

An additional comment on choice and the related principle of social self-determination is in order. In clinical memberships, the nature of choice is such that it resides primarily with the clients (Faatz, 1953). It is, after all, the clients who make the decision to seek and to use the help of the social worker. It is also their choice to continue to use that help or to seek help elsewhere or none at all. Thus, in the final analysis, it is the clients who determine the utility of the social worker's service.

Confidentiality, as a practice principle, flows from the relationship quality of respect for privacy that typifies the connection of social worker and clients as clinical members. This quality and its related principle inhere in the need of people to keep personal information private or knowledge of it limited in ways that they designate. Confidentiality itself is limited as a practice principle in two important ways. First, personal information about clients may be shared by the social worker with other professionals if such sharing is deemed appropriate and useful. In such cases, clients should be told what information is to be shared, with whom, and for what reasons. They should also know that the professionals with whom the information is shared are similarly bound by the principle of confidentiality. This is particularly significant in health agencies where a great deal of information may be shared among professionals through charting in the client's record or through team and other forms of collaborative practice.

Legal requirements also constrain the principle of confidentiality under certain conditions. Wilson (1978) has discussed in detail the limits imposed by law on the right to privacy and on the principle of confidentiality in social work practice. The need for clinical social workers to be intimately aware of these constraints is obvious and knowledge of them and their variations is prerequisite for responsible professional practice. In any case, clients should be informed of the limits of confidentiality and any constraints on their right to privacy at the outset.

Table 3.3 and its discussion represent an attempt to build on previous efforts to define relationship in social work thought and practice. In this attempt, relationship qualities are viewed as traits descriptive of the desired connection of social worker and clients as clinical members. As such, they are meant to serve as illustrations and not to be regarded as definitive or exhaustive.

In a similar way, the definition of the practice principles identified in Table 3.3 and discussed here illustrates the basis for some of the techniques used by clinical social workers to express the relationship qualities necessary for positive clinical membership. In this sense, clinical skill lies not so much in the social worker's "use of relationship" as a series of interactive techniques, but in the social worker's ability to create the psychosocial ambience or climate which makes possible a positive, helpful connection among members of the clinical configuration.

Conclusion

Clinical social work in the health field is predicated on the intersection of health problems and social functioning problems. When such intersections occur and require, or are amenable to, social work intervention, the social worker and the client(s) become members of a clinical membership group and engage in a process of problem definition and resolution that reflects a balanced perception of biopsychosocial elements and social work purpose. The process is neither bounded by a single custom, protocol, theory, or etiquette, nor is it dependent on any single method of intervention. It is, however, characterized by several identifiable conditions. Among these are differentiated clinical membership roles, responsibilities, and attributes and the conscious use of time. In addition, as members, the connection of the social worker and the client(s) is typified by identifiable relationship qualities, among which mutuality is primary.

References

American Association of Social Workers. *Social case work: Generic and specific, a report of the Milford conference.* New York, 1929.

Aptekar, Herbert H. *Basic concepts in social case work.* Chapel Hill: University of North Carolina Press, 1941.

Bartlett, Harriett M. *Analyzing social work practice by fields.* New York: National Association of Social Workers, 1961.

Biestek, Felix P. *The casework relationship.* Chicago: Loyola University Press, 1957.

Faatz, Anita J. *The nature of choice in casework process.* Chapel Hill: University of North Carolina Press, 1953.

Hamilton, Gordon. *Theory and practice of social case work.* New York: Columbia University Press, 1951.

Lyndon, Benjamin H. Development and use. In Richard Sterba, Benjamin H. Lyndon, and Anna Katz (Eds.), *Transference in casework.* New York: Family Service Association of America, 1948.

Regensburg, Jeanette. *Toward education for health professions.* New York: Harper & Row, 1978.

Robinson, Virginia P. A changing psychology for social case work. In Virginia P. Robinson, *The development of a professional self: Selected writings, 1930-1968.* New York: AMS Press, 1978. (Originally published by University of North Carolina Press, Chapel Hill, 1930.)

Smalley, Ruth E. *Theory for social work practice.* New York: Columbia University Press, 1967.

Taft, Jessie. Time as the medium of the helping process. In Virginia P. Robinson (Ed.), *Jessie Taft: Therapist and social work educator, a professional biography.* Philadelphia: University of Pennsylvania Press, 1962, pp. 305-324. (Originally published in *Jewish Social Service Quarterly,* December 1949, 26:2, 189.)

Taft, Jessie. The use of the transfer within the limits of the office interview. *The Family,* October 1924, 5:6, 143-146.

Truax, Charles B., & Carkhuff, Robert R. *Toward effective counseling and psychotherapy: Training and practice.* Chicago: Aldine Publishing Company, 1967.

Wilson, Suanna J. *Confidentiality in social work: Issues and principles.* New York: The Free Press, 1978.

Young, Pauline V. *Interviewing in social work.* New York: McGraw-Hill Book Company, 1935.

4 Clinical Social Work Diagnosis in Health Settings

Introduction

In Chapter 3, process and relationship were examined as aspects of clinical social work practice in health settings. In this chapter, focus on the third frame of Bartlett's schema is maintained as attention is directed to clinical social work diagnosis, another aspect of practice in health settings. Three dimensions of clinical social work diagnosis are considered here: (1) the nature of diagnosis in clinical social work; (2) clinical social work diagnosis as process and product; and (3) the aims and characteristics of intervention plans based on clinical social work diagnoses. Methods of clinical social work intervention are explored in Chapter 5.

The Nature of Diagnosis in Clinical Social Work

Over the years, a number of diagnostic formulations have been developed and used in clinical social work practice. To some degree, they reflect different theoretical orientations that yield different definitions of diagnosis and its purpose in clinical social work. In this regard, the long-standing debate over whether diagnosis or assessment is the more appropriate term for this aspect of clinical social work is suggestive of the differences in point of view found in the profession. Perlman (1957) has summarized succinctly the problems social workers have had with diagnosis.

> Probably no process . . . has been as troubling . . . as this one of diagnosis. The symptoms of its problematic character express the range of the case-worker's defensive-adaptive responses—from the relentless pursuit of "complete" diagnostic understanding as though it would magically yield a cure to a

reluctance to come to any conclusion beyond an "impression;" from blocking at case recording to grasping at ready-made labels; from viewing the concept of diagnosis as a credo to holding it to be anathema. (p. 165)

Part of the difficulty social workers have with diagnosis, as a concept and as an activity, stems from the multiple meanings of the term. The close association of social work with medicine and psychiatry, and the meaning of diagnosis in those professions, have also been factors. Three of the meanings of diagnosis are closely associated with medical practice and together they constitute the definition of the term that is, perhaps, most widely understood in American society. Diagnosis, in this sense, refers to three related activities: determination of the identity of a disease or illness by medical examination; ascertaining the cause or nature of a disorder or malfunction from its symptoms; and classification on the basis of scientific examination.

Briar and Miller (1971) note the success of medicine with regard to these three diagnostic activities, which are inherent in the medical model of study, diagnosis, and treatment. Furthermore, the development of scientifically based classification schemes, whereby medical conditions are differentiated according to discrete categories, has made possible the development of successful strategies of medical intervention in many diagnostic categories.

Belief that a diagnostic system comparable to medicine's is necessary for the achievement of a firm scientific foundation, and that such a foundation is necessary for professional recognition, has been present in social work thought for most of this century. In the health field, one of the earliest social work efforts to develop such a scheme was reported in 1927 by Gordon Hamilton. At the request of Hugh Auchincloss, a physician at the New York Presbyterian Hospital, Hamilton analyzed case records to develop a scientific approach and terminology for social diagnosis in the medical field. Hamilton enlisted the cooperation of social workers in other hospitals and together they analyzed literally hundreds of case records. Hamilton's report of this effort and the foreword to it by Auchincloss were optimistic, but Cannon (1952) notes that their efforts to develop social diagnosis as a parallel of medical diagnosis proved futile in the end because the variables involved were too complex and their functions too serendipitous to yield to classification according to discrete categories. Similar efforts throughout the years have had similar results and to date no single diagnostic scheme exists in social work equivalent to medical diagnosis, either in precision or acceptance.

Psychiatry has also attempted to develop diagnostic schemes comparable to those of physical medicine. As Briar and Miller observe, however, the "psychiatric typologies developed thus far cannot be applied reliably and have not led to the development of definitive and clearly successful therapies specific to the categories of these typologies" (p. 141). For social work, the significance of psychiatry's efforts in this regard stems from the absence of a well-defined diagnostic scheme and classification system in social work and lies in the subsequent use of psychiatric typologies by social workers in clinical practice. As Briar and Miller further observe, however, the reliance of clinical social workers on psychiatric typologies is problematic because they have been "developed for the classification of mental illness" and are, therefore, inadequate for the clinical social worker's diagnostic task.

> At most, psychiatric nosology only identifies personality types—the categories are not psychosocial and do not define situations or units larger than the individual, such as the family. When a caseworker classifies his cases within a typology of mental illness, he is reducing the problem these cases present to varieties of mental illness. To say that Mr. Jones, who is unemployed and having problems with his wife and son, has a character disorder is to imply that "character disorder" is the problem, thereby minimizing other salient aspects of the situation that may be more important and/or more amenable to remedy. (p. 142)

Briar and Miller make an additional point that needs to be mentioned in this consideration of efforts by social workers to develop or use diagnostic schemes comparable to those of medicine, which differentiates cases from one another in order to identify the most effective strategy of medical intervention. They assert that "diagnostic efforts are justifiable only insofar as they contribute to the effectiveness of intervention" (p. 144). It follows, therefore, that if the diagnostic system does not do this, or if only one interventive method is available, then the diagnosis is irrelevant.

Diagnosis, however, has a fourth meaning, one which is more amenable to social work definition and purpose. According to its fourth meaning, diagnosis is the process of analyzing or ascertaining the nature of a problem or situation. Perlman's definition of diagnosis is consistent with this fourth meaning of the term. She defines diagnosis both as a process and as a product.

> . . . examining the parts of a problem for the import of their particular nature and organization, for the interrelationships among them, for the relation between them and the means to their solution—this is the *diagnostic process*. The conclusions this process leads to, stating what the trouble seems to be, how it is related to the client's goals, what means the agency, the caseworker, and the client himself can bring to bear upon the trouble—these conclusions are the *diagnostic product*. Diagnosis, if it is to be anything more than an intellectual

exercise, must result in a "design for action." It is the reflective thinking which shapes the problem-solving work. (p. 164)

Perlman's definition of diagnosis as social work activity is one of the most succinct in the profession's literature. Its significance lies in its focus on all of the parts of the problem, the resources available for its resolution, and its call for a plan of action. It is this multifactorial focus of social work diagnosis that has led many social workers to prefer the term assessment. When defined in terms of its fourth meaning, however, as Perlman has defined it, diagnosis is a term that accurately describes this aspect of clinical social work practice.

Clinical Social Work Diagnosis as Process and Product

To be effective and responsive, any clinical social work diagnosis must be a diagnosis "for now," a tentative diagnosis. It is the basis for the joint problem-solving work of the clinician and clients. To serve this purpose, the diagnosis must be shared with the client(s) and, as their work gets underway and proceeds through the various time phases of clinical social work process, the diagnosis must change as the configuration of the elements of the problem change. Thus, clinical social work diagnosis is evolutionary in character and responsive to the changing nature of the condition or problem to which it relates.

Three things are necessary for effective diagnosis in clinical social work in health settings. The first is a balanced perception of the bio-psychosocial elements in the diagnostic process and product. This, as has been noted, is required for the realization of professional purpose. This is not to say, however, that emphasis isn't given to particular elements at different points in the process of problem diagnosis and resolution. At one point, for example, emphasis may be on biological elements. Focus on the physical nature of renal dialysis and its implications for biological life in cases of kidney failure is an example of such an emphasis. At another point, attention may focus on social components, such as the constraints on social, recreational, occupational, and sexual activity inherent in the need for regular dialysis. In still a third instance, focus may be given to the psychological factors inherent in the problem, as, for example, the depression, dependence, and ambivalence about life and death experienced by some people who are dependent on the dialyzer. Maintenance of a balanced perception of all of the components and their interrelationships is, nevertheless, the fulcrum upon which effective diagnostic skill in clinical social work rests.

The second requirement for effective clinical social work diagnosis is a systematic approach which is appropriate and responsive to the problems of central concern to the field in which the practice occurs. While meeting this criterion, the diagnostic scheme must simultaneously meet a third. That is, it must allow for the realization of social work purpose. It is to such a system, developed by Hans S. Falck specifically for clinical social work in health settings, that our attention now turns.

In developing *The Social Status Examination in Health Care*, Falck (1981) had in mind the need of clinical social workers in health settings for "a concise method of gathering and organizing data about health care clients" (p. 1). In responding to this need, Falck developed a diagnostic approach based on the concept of membership, with three parts: the examination items (diagnostic process); formal assessment (diagnostic product); and intervention plan. The system has two distinct advantages. First, it assures the client "a certain level of service that takes into account his/her social situation linked to whatever else brings him/her to the health setting." Second, it enables social workers "to demonstrate quite precisely the areas of social work concern and activity; the how and what social workers think about" (p. 1).

The Diagnostic Process

Part I of the examination consists of fourteen items which, when viewed as a whole, meet the criteria for effective diagnosis explicated above. First, the examination items reflect a balanced perception of pertinent biological, psychological, and social elements. Second, they recognize and respond to the central concerns of the health field, which are physical illness, disease, disability, and injury. Third, since the examination items are based on membership variables, each has biopsychosocial significance, thereby making possible a conceptualization of the problem(s) involved in the situation in terms that recognize social work purpose and make possible its realization. As a consequence, the examination items demonstrate what Perlman refers to as the diagnostic process in terms that are specific to clinical social work in health settings.

Table 4.1 presents the fourteen items of the examination in tabular form. It identifies the major membership variables in the items and summarizes the diagnostic rationale for each.

In some professions, diagnosis is a somewhat solitary undertaking. That is, responsibility for the diagnostic process resides solely with the professional. While the physician, for example, may rely on input from the patient, at least to some extent in the initial phases of medical diagnosis, it is the physician who initiates and administers the diagnostic procedures. The situation is somewhat different in clinical social work, as Falck's stress on the mutuality of the process makes clear.

TABLE 4.1 Items in the Social Status Examination in Health Care

Item	Membership Variable	Examination Content	Explanation
1	Life stage	To what developmental stage in life does the client(s) belong; what developmental level has the client(s) achieved?	The issue is not a client's age per se or whether a client's developmental level is viewed as good or bad or in need of support or modification. Rather, an observational estimate of the client in terms of this item is useful in understanding client strengths and weaknesses in coping with the health condition.
2	Health condition	What is the client's illness/disability (health condition/problem)?	Some health conditions directly modify behavior while in other cases behavior change is an indirect result of the health condition. The client's current behavior needs to be explored in terms of the health condition.
3	Family and other memberships	What family and other membership issues are linked to the health condition and how are they linked?	Adverse health conditions nearly always influence the quality of membership in family and with other important persons.
4	Racial/ethnic membership	Is the client a member of a racial or ethnic group? Do cultural factors influence the social management of the health condition? Are issues of gender or sexual identity involved?	Certain health conditions/problems occur with more frequency among some racial and ethnic groups. Culture, group values and standards, and management of health problems are heavily dependent on group membership. Effective intervention requires respect for such variables.
5	Social class	Estimate the social class membership of the client(s) and its connection with the social management of the health condition.	Class differences between social worker and clients may differ and must be taken into account in evaluations of how clients deal with the health condition/problem.

(continued)

79

TABLE 4.1 (continued)

Item	Membership Variable	Examination Content	Explanation
6	Occupation	How does the health condition/problem influence the client's occupation, i.e., abilities/disabilities, temporary/permanent, limitations on work functioning, etc.	Some estimate of whether or how the client condition/problem affects the client's ability to work is needed. Especially important is an estimation of the physical effect of the condition on the social and psychological meaning of work. For many, work is connected to their view and image of self and modification of their work life can lead to other consequences.
7	Financial condition	How does the client's health condition/problem influence his/her financial condition? What income maintenance efforts are being made? Does the client have savings? Is the client supported by others? By whom?	The intent is to determine the financial condition of the client, family, or other persons important to the client. All that is known about the financial assets and liabilities of the client should be considered.
8	Entitlements	Does the client carry health, accident, disability, life insurance? Is it being used to pay for services connected with the health condition? Who pays? Is the client entitled to veterans' benefits?	This item continues consideration of the financial condition of the client in relation to payment of charges for health care. It should not be assumed that people who have insurance coverage use it when needed. Some do not know what their insurance or veterans' benefits cover, in what amount, or for how long.
9	Transportation	What transportation is available to the client? To relatives or other visitors?	In a society that places a high premium on being able to move about, not being able to command adequate transportation is perceived as a sign of inferior social status. At issue are the mobility of health clients,

(continued)

TABLE 4.1 (continued)

Item	Membership Variable	Examination Content	Explanation
9 (continued)			obtaining out-patient care, agency services that offer transportation for health care of health maintenance, and asking and taking help from relatives, neighbors, or friends.
10	Housing	What kind of housing is available? What is the impact of the health condition on housing and of housing on management of the health condition? Who lives with the client?	Housing is not only a physical variable, but a social one as well. Knowledge about the client's housing can lead to more extensive knowledge of the client's life style and its meaning in relation to his/her health condition.
11	Mental functioning	Describe the client's mental functioning. Is the client aware of time, place, person? Can the client participate knowledgeably in decision making in regard to his/her future?	Questions about the client's mental functioning should be made with care and sharp discrimination and not to "prove" the client's incapacities. Decreased ability to participate in decision making may indicate mental illness, anxiety, or neurological problems. Consideration of the client's mental status may identify others who can assist with decisions about the client's future or, in some cases, lead to legal considerations.
12	Cognition	Does the client understand the nature of his/her health condition. How does the client express concern over the condition?	Client knowledge and understanding of his/her health condition is important from the standpoint of what the client is told and what he/she thinks it means. The psychosocial issues involved are complex, i.e., defending against knowledge too overwhelming or threatening to consider; the nature and extent

(continued)

81

TABLE 4.1 (continued)

Item	Membership Variable	Examination Content	Explanation
12 (continued)			of the involvement of the family and others in knowing and discussing what is wrong with the client.
13	Cognition	Can the client follow medication and other self-care instructions? Who can assist clients in this regard? Upon whom is the client dependent?	At issue is the ability of the client to follow instructions and whether the life circumstances of the client are such as to encourage it. Involved are the client's willingness and ability to plan, to keep medication schedules, obey frequency and dosage instruction... Others may be involved, i.e. diets, weight reduction, management of the consequences of the health condition. The nature of these issues is primarily social since others are usually involved and communication demands are complex.
14	Psychosocial elements	How ready or reluctant is the client in asking for help? Or in using it when offered? How well does the client work with the social worker or other health care personnel?	At issue is how the client(s) use help, whether they wish help, under what conditions, and what it means to them to ask for or refuse it.

Adapted from Hans S. Falck. *The Social Status Examination in Health Care.* Richmond: School of Social Work, Department of Continuing Education, Virginia Commonwealth University, 1981, pp. 4–18.

The term examination as I intend and understand it is to describe the mutual effort by social worker and client to gain as complete a picture as seems needed to identify the desirability and practicality of social work help. (p. 2)

Mutuality presupposes client action as well as clinician action. This point requires emphasis, if only to differentiate clinical social work diagnosis from diagnostic schemes developed for nonsocial work purposes which posit diagnosis as the exclusive province of the professional practitioner.

Since mutuality is a stipulation for the effective use of the examination, it follows that the examination items are not intended for use as a simple checklist, nor do they constitute a test of some kind. Indeed, as Falck asserts, the examination "is not something to be passed or failed" and "its successful use does not depend on asking questions of the client" (pp. 2–3).

Successful use of the items in the examination for diagnostic purposes requires interviewing skill, mastery of which is an essential component of the common base of social work practice. Specialized practice rests on this base. In this connection, Kadushin's (1972) definition of an interview serves as an apt reminder of the complex dimensions of skilled interviewing.

The simplest definition of an interview is a conversation with a deliberate purpose, a purpose mutually accepted by the participants. An interview resembles a conversation in many ways. Both involve verbal and nonverbal communication between people during which ideas, attitudes, and feelings are exchanged. Both are usually face-to-face interactions, aside from the telephone interview or conversation. As in a conversation, participants in the interview reciprocally influence each other . . . The crucial characteristic which distinguishes an interview from a conversation is that the interaction is designed to achieve a consciously selected purpose. (p. 8)

The Diagnostic Product

Part II of *The Social Status Examination in Health Care* yields the diagnostic product. It is in this phase of Falck's diagnostic approach that the clinician analyzes the data that flows from the diagnostic process, draws inferences from them, and reaches conclusions logically based on them. The results constitute the diagnostic product or the diagnosis.

Table 4.2 presents the three essential steps in this phase of the diagnostic scheme in tabular form. The content of the steps and the activity associated with each is summarized and briefly explained in the table.

This part of the examination, which Falck refers to as the formal assessment, is the social worker's responsibility. That is, it is the social worker who summarizes the information gained from the diagnostic

TABLE 4.2 Steps in Formulating the Diagnostic Product of the Social Status Examination in Health Care

Step	Content	Explanation
1	Develop a formal assessment of the client's social status based on information gained from the fourteen Examination items.	The aim of this step is to describe the client as a person who is part of others. It is based on the information and impressions gained in the interview(s) with the client(s). The intent is to formulate as precise a picture as possible of the client and those people who are important in his/her life, with emphasis on the client's health condition.
2	On the basis of the information and impressions of the client's social status, draw inferences as to the meaning of the information provided by the client(s) in the interview(s).	The information and impressions that are the building blocks of the diagnostic formulation come from the interview(s) with the client(s) and are identified as such. Inferences appear as professional judgements and are legitimate provided they are identified as inferences by the social worker.
3	On the basis of Steps 1 and 2, draw conclusions about the client's social status, with particular focus on the client's health condition.	Conclusions are the ending statements that summarize the assessment of and inferences about the client(s). They are to be identified as conclusions and, as conclusions of the social worker, constitute the diagnostic product. Conclusions, as diagnostic products, are the basis for clinical intervention, but are subject to constant change as more information and inferences become available.

Adapted from Hans S. Falck, *The Social Status Examination in Health Care.* Richmond: School of Social Work, Department of Continuing Education, Virginia Commonwealth University, 1981, p. 19.

process, draws inferences, and reaches conclusions logically derived from an analysis of this information. The successful accomplishment of the tasks involved in each step requires knowledge pertinent to the particular client(s), the particular medical or health problem or condition involved, and diagnostic expertise. In this sense, diagnosis is the personalized configuration of knowledge and skill that clients expect from the clinical social worker, and to which they are entitled. The social worker's diagnosis—the conclusion(s) reached—however, is not only based on client input, but is shared with the client(s) for use by the client(s). Hence, the mutuality characteristic of clinical diagnosis in social work is preserved in this phase of Falck's diagnostic scheme.

In this regard, Smalley (1967) identifies four factors deemed essential for effective social work diagnosis, all of which are embodied in Falck's formulation. These four factors are: (1) the diagnosis is related to the use of social work service; (2) it is developed with the engagement and participation of the client(s); (3) it is recognized as being subject to continuous modification as the helping process unfolds and develops; and (4) it is made available by the social worker to the client(s) for use in the course of their mutual activity (p. 134). In this way, the clinical diagnosis in social work is not a diagnosis *of* the client(s), but a diagnosis *for* the client(s).

Once the diagnostic process yields the diagnostic product, it is possible for the clinician and client(s) to move to the third phase of *The Social Status Examination in Health Care*, the phase Falck refers to as "the intervention plan."

The Clinical Intervention Plan: Aims and Characteristics

If clinical intervention on the part of the social worker is to be helpful to the client(s), it must be meaningful to them. Part III of the examination, therefore, calls for the development of an intervention plan derived logically from the diagnosis of the client's social status in relation to a health problem or condition. Table 4.3 summarizes the aims and characteristics of such an intervention plan.

The fact that clinical social work diagnosis and intervention are intimately connected, that the latter must evolve logically from the former if it is to be helpful and meaningful to the client(s), may appear to be an obvious point to the experienced social work clinician. Since it involves an issue that has been problematic in the past, however, it merits some reiteration.

If the social worker relies on a diagnostic approach or classification system developed for nonsocial work purposes, it is likely that the diag-

TABLE 4.3 The Aims and Characteristics of Intervention Plans Based on the Social Status Examination in Health Care

Aims	Characteristics
To develop a plan for clinical intervention that is derived logically from the Examination (diagnostic process) and Formal Assessment (diagnostic product).	The intervention plan partializes the needs of the client(s) into manageable parts.
	The intervention plan helps the social worker and the client(s) gain a sense of priorities in terms of the complexity and urgency of the help needed.
To develop a plan for clinical intervention capable of modification as new needs become apparent, new information comes to light, and as the client(s) gain new and different insights into his/her situation.	
	The intervention plan is logical in terms of the time available for social worker/client(s) activity, financial resources and entitlements, etc.
	The intervention plan is logically based on evidence—information given by the client(s) and the inferences of the worker—and on data.
	The intervention plan permits joint social worker/client(s) monitoring of the helping process, i.e. what has been accomplished; what remains to be done.
	The intervention plan changes as the diagnostic formulation changes.

Adapted from Hans S. Falck, *The Social Status Examination in Health Care.* Richmond: School of Social Work, Department of Continuing Education, Virginia Commonwealth University, 1981, p. 20.

nosis will have little relationship either to social work purpose or to the clinician's actual intervention. Such diagnostic procedures run the risk of being inappropriate, or of having little meaning in terms of the client's perception of his social situation and/or needs, and, therefore, will be of little consequence to the client. In this connection, as in other phases of clinical social work activity, it is helpful to remember that the nature of choice in clinical social work resides, ultimately, with the client(s).

The intervention plan indicates what is to be done, why it is to be done, how it will be done, and who will do what. Like the diagnostic process, the intervention plan is the joint activity of the clinician and the client(s). Like the diagnostic product, it is tentative and subject to revision. These two points are made clear by Falck.

The intent is that an intervention plan be formulated—to the maximum extent possible—by the social worker and the client together. It is subject to change as new needs become apparent, as new information comes to light, and most particularly as the client gains more and different insights into his/her situation. This will, and in fact ought to, change the diagnostic formulation and the intervention plan. (p. 20)

An Illustration from Practice

The following case material illustrates the use of *The Social Status Examination in Health Care* in clinical social work with an older woman whose diagnosis of breast cancer has necessitated a radical mastectomy. In this case, the client's medical/health condition and its treatment has exacerbated problems in her ability to manage her social memberships.

This example from practice touches upon multidisciplinary practice as a dynamic in the health field, and it illustrates the fact that social work assessments and diagnoses must sometimes be made rapidly, and on the basis of incomplete data. All items of Falck's examination items are touched on in this illustration, with one exception. That exception is item #9, transportation. It can be assumed, however, from other aspects of the case that the client has driven prior to her present situation and that she will be able to do so again once she has fully recovered. In the meantime, it can be assumed further that relatives will take care of her transportation needs or that, given her financial situation, she will be able to use other forms of transportation should the need arise.

One further introductory comment is necessary. Examination item #4, race or ethnic membership, is not a factor in this case. Religious membership, however, is. The clinician in this case might have dealt with the client's religious membership under examination item #3, family and other memberships. Instead, it is dealt with under item #4 to highlight the importance of the client's religious membership to her.

The Case of Mrs. A

Mrs. A was referred for social work services by her physician following a radical mastectomy subsequent to a diagnosis of breast cancer. The surgery was reportedly successful, but the physician had some concern about the healing of the incision and the client's potential range of motion. An extended hospital stay was anticipated in order to monitor this situation and social work assistance was requested to help the client adjust to the mastectomy and to plan for her future.

Medical Status and Social Work Referral

Diagnostic Process
First interview

Following a review of her chart, a brief introductory meeting with the client took place. Mrs. A was an attractive, thin woman in her early sixties who was currently separated from her husband. She was warm and outgoing and some-what talkative, but her affect betrayed an element of sadness and uncertainty. I explained that I would be available to her to discuss any questions or concerns she might have about the mastectomy and that we would work together on plans for her discharge from the hospital. Mrs. A appeared amenable to this suggestion and said that she could use some help at this time to sort through a number of problems in her life. We then agreed to meet regularly during her hospital stay to discuss her concerns. Our next meeting time was set and after leaving Mrs. A, I noted our appointment on her chart to avoid possible conflicting appointments or tests.

Clinician's Assessment

Life stage (#1)

On the basis of this beginning, I was able to organize my assessment along a number of dimensions. Mrs. A's chrono-logical age suggested she should be somewhere between Erikson's (1964) developmental stages of generativity vs. self-absorption and integrity vs. despair. That is, she should be somewhere between the continuum of preoccupation with the fate of future generations and personal needs and com-forts and the development of a sense of her life as a whole. Data on which to base a tentative conclusion about Mrs. A's life stage was insufficient in this interview and it remains an area for further exploration.

Health condition (#2)

With regard to her health condition, Mrs. A's affect and non-verbal behavior suggest that she might be dealing with two separate but related issues. First, she might be concerned about the actual diagnosis and the outcome of the surgery. Since a diagnosis of cancer is equated with impending death by many people, Mrs. A might be uncertain as to whether the operation was, in fact, successful. If this is the case, Mrs. A may be vacillating between hope that she is "cured," ac-ceptance of the diagnosis as terminal, and denial of the diagnosis. Various degrees of anger, bargaining, and depres-sion may be involved. Second, Mrs. A may be concerned about her self-identity and self-image as a result of the sur-gery. Mrs. A faces the task of adjusting positively to an altered body image, while anticipating an uncertain future. Such tasks can result in contradictory demands on the adaptive capacity of the ego and may produce thoughts and behavior that are confusing or alarming. If this is the case, Mrs. A will need help in her efforts to maintain a normative and functional affective response to the biopsychosocial assaults stemming from her changed health status, rather than a dysfunctional, static one.

Mrs. A appears willing to work with me and to use the social work services offered to her. The meaning and/or impact of the possibility of clinical social work services on Mrs. A, however, requires further clarification.

Psychosocial status (#14)

During this meeting, Mrs. A said several things were bothering her. She ʰegan by discussing the background of her "worries," but said the first thing she wanted to work out was her living arrangements after she left the hospital.

Diagnostic Process
Second interview

Mrs. A explained that she had separated from her husband of 31 years several months before she discovered she had breast cancer and the subsequent mastectomy. She stated that she and her husband had no children and that their marriage had suffered, and until recently survived, a number of separations. Most of these had been initiated by her husband. The present separation, unlike the others, was a legal one and was also the longest. Mrs. A related that the present separation was not precipitated by any specific crisis or event. Rather, she had decided that after all her years of marriage, she needed a life of her own and to see if she could manage to care for herself on her own. Mrs. A did not give any further details of her marriage, or the reasons for the separation, except to say that she had found the separation to be a positive experience. No plans for a divorce were mentioned.

Family (marital) membership (#3)

Mrs. A said she had been living with a widowed cousin in another part of the community. She said she had been able to meet her financial obligations fairly well with the income she earns as a secretary and by keeping her expenses minimal. She added that she has a steady social group of friends and finds her church and personal devotional life very supportive.

Housing (#10)
Occupation (#6)

Mrs. A said that the threat of cancer, and now the limitations she expected because of the surgery, were jeopardizing all of her plans and her new start. She said the cancer diagnosis had been like a dark cloud over her ever since the doctor had first mentioned it as a possibility. She also expressed concern about the possibility of a limited range of motion, and not being able to lift or carry. Though she said her pastor had been very helpful, she was still confused and uncertain about what to do. She said her greatest fear was being left alone. From the tone of Mrs. A's voice and her facial expression, it was clear that this fear is very real to her.

Cognition (#12)

Religious membership (#4)

Mrs. A also expressed her fear of being left alone in terms of her preoccupation with what she would do and where she would go after leaving the hospital. On the one hand, she said she could return home to her husband who, she admitted, had faithfully attended her when she was ill in the past. She

Family membership (#3)
Housing (#10)

was obviously attracted to this option, but also ambivalent about it. As she said, it offered security, care, and familiarity, but, she also said, she was fairly certain she wanted "to leave that situation behind." Mrs. A related that in his last visit, she felt as if her husband was using her uncertainty about her plans to pressure her into returning home, where he would "never leave again and would care for her every minute of the day." Mrs. A said the separation had been good for her, but she was afraid that if she didn't return home now, she was cutting off all possibility of ever going back to her husband. She said she wasn't sure she wanted to do that.

The alternative was to ask her cousin Mrs. T and her two daughters to "nurse" her after she left the hospital. Mrs. A said that her cousin had graciously invited Mrs. A to stay in her home, but added that her cousin was "constantly on the go, very active, hardly at home long enough to change her shoes." Mrs. A was both afraid of being a burden to her cousin and her cousin's daughters, with whom she had not been very close until recently, and afraid that they would go off and leave her without any help and without realizing how *Financial condition* much help she really needed. Mrs. A said she wanted to hire *(#7)* a nurse or homemaker, but she knew that she wouldn't be able to afford one, especially since it would be some time before she could return to work. Mrs. A said she was really torn by this problem and very upset.

Entitlements (#8) Recognizing Mrs. A's concern about her future after she leaves the hospital, and seeing it as the center of a wheel of related problems and concerns, I reassured her that we would work out a satisfactory arrangement together and that I would look into the possibility of financial benefits to which she might be entitled. I then asked Mrs. A when her family would next visit her and suggested that we meet as a group to find out more about the possible alternatives she has for living arrangements after she leaves the hospital. Mrs. A thought this was a good plan and we set a meeting for the following evening.

Clinician's Assessment During the course of this interview, it appeared that several variables were interacting in ways which the group meeting with Mrs. A, her husband, her cousin, and her cousin's daughters might help to clarify.

Family membership (#3)

Mental functioning (#11) Mrs. A's description of her present "needs," both in terms of recovering from the mastectomy and planning for the future, appear to be influenced to a considerable extent by her wish "not to be left alone." While such a response is valid, given

Mrs. A's biomedical status, it conflicts with her desire to maintain her "independent life" and her legal separation from her husband. Her apparent ambivalence and anxiety seem to prevent Mrs. A from integrating the need to be taken care of while recovering from the mastectomy with her wish to be independent, thereby frustrating her attempts to reach a decision regarding her living arrangements after discharge from the hospital. Mrs. A may need help, therefore, to participate knowledgeably with her husband and cousins in clarification of her options. She may also need support in reality-testing the consequences of her options.

Family membership (#3)

There appears to be some discrepancy between Mrs. A's actual psychosocial level and the life stage that is age-appropriate for her. Was, for example, Mrs. A's intent in separating from her husband a reaction to his having left her in the past, or did it enable her to express a sense of self that she had previously been unable to express? Is her desire to be independent in conflict with her fear of being abandoned, or is the separation an indication that she has resolved the tasks inherent in the generativity vs. self-absorption stage through preoccupation with her own needs and comforts?

Life stage (#1)

The family group interview should also help to clarify if Mrs. A really has one, two, or no options in terms of living with family members after hospital discharge. If her husband and her cousin are indeed willing to have her stay with them and are willing to meet her needs during recovery from the surgery, then Mrs. A does, in fact, have two options to choose from. If, however, neither is serious about their invitations and willingness, then other options must be identified and explored.

Housing (#10)

Assuming such help is needed, even if she stays with her husband or her cousin, clarification of Mrs. A's ability to pay for home health care is needed. It may be that her financial resources are sufficient to cover such care or it may be that she is eligible for benefits that would do so. If the two identified options, living with her husband or her cousin, are not real ones, these factors will assume even greater importance.

Financial condition (#7)

Entitlements (#8)

To clarify some issues, Mrs. A and I met together prior to the arrival of Mr. A and the other family members. I asked Mrs. A how she and her husband had met. Mrs. A explained that they met through mutual friends while she was in college. Her father, a minister, had not approved of the marriage because Mrs. A did not complete her education after she married, and her husband had not gone to college. Mrs. A said that her father had placed great value on education.

Diagnostic Process
Third (family) interview
Social class (#5)

Family (marital)
membership (#3)

Mrs. A, in response to my question, described her marriage as one characterized by affection and traditional norms which, she said, were their "form of love." She said her husband was a generous provider who made possible a "comfortable lifestyle." She added that she had been a pleasant wife who made no demands. When asked why she and Mr. A had separated so often during their marriage, she gave his extramarital relationships as the reason, but claimed she was not a jealous wife. Mr. A continued to provide for her during these separations and would eventually return. She said she had been satisfied with this arrangement for the most part. Mrs. A

Occupation (#6)
Social class (#5)

explained that she had started working more than ten years ago, and that even though she was working, "women just didn't leave their husbands," and neither did she. Besides, she added, "I wasn't unhappy."

Entitlements (#8)

Mrs. A said that when she decided, finally, to leave her husband, it was "to try it on my own, to have my own independent life to manage." She added that Mr. A was not supporting her financially at the present time, but that her hospital bills would be taken care of under his health insurance. She added that she had checked that before her admission.

Cognition (#12)

I asked Mrs. A how she felt about her surgery and how she thought she was adjusting to her overall health status. She replied that she was grateful the doctor had operated when he did. She added that since she had started working with the nurses and the occupational therapist and was learning more about self-care, she was much more aware of the mastectomy. She said she wasn't too concerned about her appearance at this point, but much more concerned about what it

Cognition (#13)

represented. She was worried about whether all of the cancer had been removed and what she would do when she left the hospital.

Family
membership (#3)

At this point, Mrs. A's cousin, Mrs. T, and one of her daughters arrived. After we were introduced, Mrs. T turned her full attention to Mrs. A and began what appeared to be an established pattern of questioning her about assorted details of her progress. Mrs. T appeared to shift her position without waiting for Mrs. A to answer her questions. Her manner toward Mrs. A was authoritative and maternal, which surprised me as I had expected a more distant and formal relationship from Mrs. A's description of their relationship. Mrs. A's initial response to Mrs. T was passive and yielding, but after a time, Mrs. A suddenly scolded her cousin for trying to "mother" her.

This reaction caught Mrs. T, her daughter, and me by surprise. I decided to use this interruption to discuss the possibility of Mrs. A returning to Mrs. T's home after her discharge from the hospital. Without hesitation, Mrs. T stated that she and her daughters were planning on this and had begun to prepare for Mrs. A's return to their home. Mrs. A appeared to be completely surprised by this statement and quickly remarked that Mrs. T had forgotten about her busy schedule and didn't realize how much help she would need and how much she wasn't able to do. Mrs. T replied that they would just work around her schedule and that she would just "have to cut down on a few meetings for awhile." Mrs. A's facial expression and nonverbal behavior continued to reflect surprise. I noted that it wasn't necessary to make final plans at this point and that Mrs. A and I would continue to discuss her situation and options. Mrs. T added that Mrs. A knew she was welcome to return to her home at any time and all she had to do was to let her know.

Mr. A did not arrive, as he said he would, and after waiting for some time, Mrs. T and her daughter, who had said little during the meeting, left. Mrs. A and I agreed to meet the following day to begin to clarify her options and to move toward an initial decision regarding her posthospital plans.

Despite the fact that Mr. A had failed to appear at the scheduled meeting, the interaction of Mrs. A and Mrs. T, together with the data and impressions gleaned from my two interviews with Mrs. A, provided enough information to formulate an initial diagnostic assessment of Mrs. A's social status in relation to her health condition.

Diagnostic Product

Mrs. A's current health condition, stemming from a diagnosis of cancer and a radical mastectomy, has had a direct impact on her ability to function socially. Her emotional reaction, both to the diagnosis of cancer and the temporary disability caused by surgical intervention, has forced a choice of discharge alternatives that appear to represent conflicting options for the client, whose social situation was already precarious because of her recent separation from her husband.

Health condition (#2)

Mental functioning (#11)

Mrs. A's current task of deciding between returning to her home and husband, or to her cousin's home, is hampered by her fear of being left alone—fear of being left unattended and fear of being abandoned in her illness. Mrs. A is preoccupied with her immediate welfare and what will happen to her when she is discharged, but she is beginning to express some

Housing (#10)

concerns about the efficacy of the mastectomy and its effect. It can be expected that as immediate problems are resolved, these latter issues will become more significant to her.

Family membership (#3)

Assessment of Mrs. A's family memberships indicate that her extended family, Mrs. T, and her two daughters, are supportive of the client. However, since their relationship was only recently renewed, following Mrs. A's separation from Mr. A, it is not clear as to whether Mrs. A will avail herself of their offer to help. Mrs. A's relationship with her estranged husband needs to be clarified, both in terms of Mrs. A's social status and as a realistic discharge planning alternative. What can be deduced from the scarce information and confusing impressions about the nature of their current relationship is that it remains significant enough to the client to give some consideration to her husband's offer to return home for her convalescence.

Religious membership (#4)

Mrs. A's religious membership is significant to her. Further information is needed to determine if a referral to or perhaps collaboration with pastoral care would be of use to the client.

Social class (#5)

Mrs. A appears comfortable and at ease with her middle-class status. This is reflected in her attitude toward work, which is positive, her valuing of independence and self-care, and her social activities, including her church activities.

Occupation (#6)
Financial condition (#7)
Entitlements (#8)

There appear to be no serious occupational difficulties or financial constraints confronting Mrs. A, other than the present limitations on her range of motion which preclude her immediate return to work. Insurance coverage is intact and adequate. Financial savings and help from her family will support the client until she is able to return to work and regain her regular income.

Cognition (#12)

Initial concern about Mrs. A's decision-making ability, given certain aspects of her behavior, proved to be unfounded. Interaction with Mrs. A suggests that she does have the ability to discriminate between choices and to plan for her future in light of her health condition.

Life stage (#1)

Mrs. A's apparent ambivalence about whether or not to maintain the separation from her husband and her unrealistic and somewhat childlike concern about whether someone will be available to nurse her after she leaves the hospital suggest the need for marital counseling to resolve her position regarding her marriage.

Psychosocial (#14)

Mrs. A's ability to engage in and make positive use of a helping relationship is attested to by her work with the nursing staff and the occupational therapists with respect to self-care and recovery from the temporary disability caused by her surgery, and by her willingness to work with me and her significant others to resolve psychosocial dilemmas and plan *Cognitive (#13)* for her future. During the remainder of her hospitalization, it is anticipated that Mrs. A will continue to be interested in and capable of participating in her own care and recovery. Though beset by several issues related to her marital situation, Mrs. A is appropriately concerned about her health condition and her convalescence. It also appears that Mrs. A will use the various offers of help from her family members in constructive ways that will enhance her physical and psychosocial recovery.

Following discussion with Mrs. A, and dependent upon her **Tentative Plan** agreement, it is tentatively planned to work with Mrs. A in five areas. First, clinical services will be provided to help Mrs. A make a positive psychosocial adjustment to her medical diagnosis and the physical assault on her body caused by the radical mastectomy. These services will support her functional coping with the tasks inherent in full biopsychosocial recovery. In this connection, collaboration with pastoral care will be explored, if Mrs. A thinks such joint intervention will be of help to her.

Second, discharge alternatives will be explored and clarified with the goal of helping Mrs. A to discern and understand the consequences of each for her future, and to choose realistically and appropriately among the alternatives.

Third, interdisciplinary meetings will be arranged for Mrs. A, the family member(s) with whom Mrs. A decides to live after discharge, Mrs. A's occupational therapist and nurse, and myself to learn about the physical care and exercise Mrs. A will need after discharge. These meetings will also be used to clarify what can be anticipated in terms of Mrs. A's physical abilities and limitations.

Fourth, the possibility of a referral to a local homemaker service or home health program will be explored, depending on the assessment of Mrs. A's medical needs and psychosocial situation at the time of discharge.

Fifth, clinical social work services will be offered to help Mrs. A to resolve her ambivalence about her marriage while she is hospitalized. If needed, or required, a referral for ongoing marital casework will be made at the time of actual discharge from the hospital.*

*Source: Amanda Cummings, M.S.W., North Charles General Hospital, Baltimore, Maryland.

One final comment about *The Social Status Examination in Health Care* needs to be made. Falck's formulation stipulates that both the diagnostic product (formal assessment) and the intervention plan be developed in written form. The written diagnosis is based on a written summary of the information made available from the examination itself. It identifies the inferences and conclusions made by the clinician as such, and explicates their bases.

Definite advantages accrue from developing the diagnosis and intervention plan in written form. First, in written form they are immediately accessible to both the clinician and client(s). Thus, they are tangible, something that can be taken hold of and used. They serve as reference points for the clinician and client(s) in their mutual efforts to clarify and monitor the helping process, and as base points for their revision and modification of problem definitions. Second, a written diagnosis and intervention plan provide the clinical social worker with a baseline for developing, expanding, and refining practice expertise.

Conclusion

In summary, diagnostic procedure in clinical social work in health settings is based on mutuality and is endorsed by the clinician and the client(s) as the basis for their joint work. This procedure begins with an examination of a problem or problems in social functioning related to a health problem or condition. This exploration constitutes the diagnostic process and it yields the diagnostic product which, in turn, is related intimately to the subsequent plan for intervention. Falck's *The Social Status Examination in Health Care* meets the criteria for effective social work diagnosis. Its three parts—examination items (diagnostic process), formal assessment (diagnostic product), and intervention plan—constitute a rational diagnostic system for clinical social work in health settings.

References

Briar, Scott & Miller, Henry. *Problems and issues in social casework*. New York: Columbia University Press, 1971.

Cannon, Ida M. *On the social frontier of medicine: Pioneering in medical social service*. Cambridge: Harvard University Press, 1952.

Erikson, Erik. *Childhood and society*. New York: W. W. Norton & Co., 1964.

Falck, Hans S. *The social status examination in health care*. Richmond: Department of Continuing Education, School of Social Work, Virginia Commonwealth University, 1981.

Hamilton, Gordon. A medical social terminology: Preliminary report of a study in classification and terminology for case work in hospitals and clinics. Foreword by Hugh Auchincloss, *Hospital Social Service*, Vol. 15 (1927), pp. 199-233.

Kadushin, Alfred. *The social work interview*. New York: Columbia University Press, 1972.

Perlman, Helen Harris. *Social casework: A problem-solving process*. Chicago: University of Chicago Press, 1957.

Smalley, Ruth E. *Theory for social work practice*. New York: Columbia University, 1967.

5 Methods of Clinical Social Work Intervention in Health Settings

Introduction

In the two preceeding chapters, process, relationship, diagnosis, and intervention planning were considered from a membership perspective as aspects of Bartlett's third frame of reference—social work practice in a particular field. That focus continues in this chapter as the methods of clinical social work are considered.

Discussion of clinical social work methods in the health field is complicated by several factors: (1) the breadth of the health field itself and its problem of central concern, the definition of which shifts according to level of care, type of setting, and particular program; (2) the inconsistent definition and use of the term *method* in social work; and (3) the apparent redefinition of the terms *case* and *casework* by health social workers. These factors are considered briefly in this chapter as prefatory to an examination of clinical social work methods and techniques within the membership framework.

The Variety of Clinical Social Work in the Health Field

The variety of medical, social, and other services provided in the health field is enormous. Service emphasis and focus shifts from prevention, to treatment, to restoration, to continuing service according to level of care. At all levels, and in all sectors, the purpose of clinical social work remains the same, namely helping people to manage their social memberships when their ability to do so is affected by actual or potential physical illness, disability, or injury. As definition of the problem of central concern to the health field shifts within its various sectors, however, so do the focus and content of clinical social work, which ranges from prevention and education, to adjustment to drastically changed living conditions and circumstances, to helping people deal with major changes in social roles, future expectations, and life goals precipitated by a changed medical condition or health status, to preparation for death and separation.

In addtion, clinical social workers throughout the health field work with clients in various membership configurations and employ a variety of techniques in doing so. They may, for example, work with one client in one instance, a family in another, a nonkinship group in a third, or some combination of these in a fourth. The key here, as always, is consistency with social work values, maintenance of biopsychosocial balance, and the realization of social work purpose. Finally, the clinician must be mindful of the time frame of the clinical process which may vary within and across level, setting, and program of service.

Figure 5.1 summarizes the relationship of social work's common base to the specialized practice of clinical social work in the health field according to units of intervention and levels of care. In this figure, units of intervention refers to the particular client configurations with whom clinical social workers interact, thereby suggesting the interventive methods employed in the process.

In preventive and primary care, focus is on education, prevention, early detection, and routine care. Settings at this level include family planning clinics, well-baby clinics, neighborhood health centers, health maintenance organizations, genetic counseling services, and office based —solo or group—medical practice. Clinical social work at this level may be short-term or serial in nature. In a venereal disease clinic, for example, the clinical social worker may help a client or a couple in one session or in a nonkinship group that meets only once or twice. Emphasis in such practice is usually on education and casefinding. In family planning and genetic counseling clinics, service emphasis may include educational matters, but the clinician also helps clients with complex problems in membership management. Work in such instances is often intensive and may last longer. In other settings at this level, work with clients may be serial in nature, as in the case of clients who use public clinics to meet routine and episodic health care needs.

In secondary, acute care, the problems of central concern include emergency treatment and critical care and, depending on sector, early detection. At this level, services are delivered in hospital emergency rooms, in-patient and out-patient clinics, intensive care units, general medical and surgical care units, and in newborn nurseries and postpartum care units. Secondary level settings include general, community, and teaching hospitals. Care is often episodic and, since the average length of patient stay at this level is usually less than a week, clinical social work services are usually short-term and intensive. In certain instances, how-

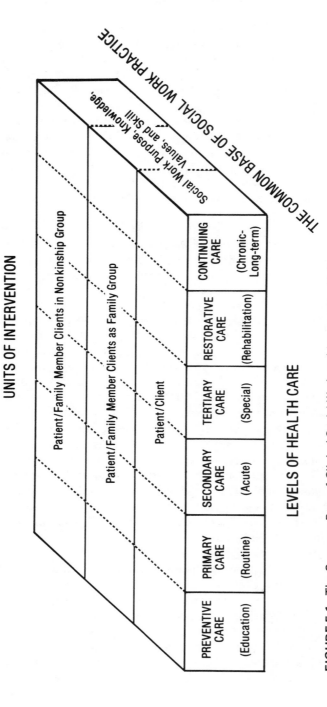

FIGURE 5.1 The Common Base of Clinical Social Work and Interventive Units According to Levels of Health Care

ever, the time frame may be longer or serial. The focus of clinical social work at this level is often on helping people to cope with catastrophic medical conditions precipitating dramatic changes in their lives. Services may include crisis intervention; helping clients adjust to changed circumstances and conditions; helping clients make plans for hospital discharge, posthospital care, and the future; and helping clients prepare for death and separation.

Tertiary level care is highly specialized and is often organized to cover large geographic areas. Services may be offered in the specialized, technical departments of teaching hospitals, or in specialty hospitals. These may be organized according to particular kinds of health conditions or on the basis of particular population groups. The time frame of the service process at this level is usually longer than that of primary and secondary care. Clinical social work service may be offered to help clients cope with highly charged emotional reactions and responses to medical conditions; modify their physical environments to accommodate new demands posed by the patient/client's medical or health status; move out of customary family and/or social roles and into new ones; and develop new life goals and expectations in light of changed biological circumstances.

Restorative care also covers a range of services and settings, including: routine postsurgical care; routine medical care; rehabilitation; and home health care. Restorative services are provided in nursing homes, inpatient facilities for substances abusers, rehabilitation hospitals, specialized services for the physically disabled, and through home health agencies and hospital home care units. Service may be progressive, extended, or rehabilitative in nature. The time frame for care is longer, but the medical diagnosis and prognosis tend to be positive. Clinical social work services at this level are akin to those at the tertiary level.

In continuing care, the medical diagnosis and prognosis may be less positive. Focus at this level is on long-term and chronic care, and services are made available in nursing homes, domicilaries, and chronic care facilities, such as dialysis centers and units, and in hospices. The time frame is often long-term, but the focus and content of clinical social work services may vary at different points in any given case. Services may be offered, for example, to help clients in nursing homes or other long-term care facilities to deal with the separation and loss attendant to giving up their homes. At another point, socialization services may be offered to help such clients become meaningful resident members. At still another point, clinical services are offered to families of clients who often feel guilty about, and need help in maintaining a positive relationship to the relative or friend whose changed health circumstances have placed him or her in a new living situation. Family social work is common at this level, as it is at the others. Sudden changes or new circumstances may require rapid intervention to help clients deal with unanticipated crises. Helping clients and those significant to them prepare for death and separation is another common focus of clinical social work at this level of care.

In summary, the problem or problems of central concern to the health field shift according to the level of care. While the purpose of clinical social work in the health field remains constant at all levels, its focus and content also shift according to the level of care. At all levels, the clinical social worker helps people in various membership configurations: the patient/client alone; the family group with its patient/client member present; the family group without its patient/client member present, if the latter is medically unable to participate; or the patient/client and/or family members as members of a nonkinship group.

Finally, the concept of time must be considered, for it governs the clinical process regardless of the clinical method used. As noted in Chapter 3, all social work processes are characterized by identifiable time phases which denote the beginning, middle, and end of clinician/client interaction. The length of service in a particular instance will depend on level of care, setting, program of service, and client need. Even in single clinical encounters, where the entire process is completed in one meeting, the phases of initiating, sustaining, and terminating the process are present and can be observed. In instances where the process consists of multiple meetings, these time phases characterize both the process as a whole and each meeting within it. Thus, time expands and contracts in clinical social work depending on circumstances and needs, and the skillful use of time governs the clinician's intervention.

A Definition of Method and Technique

Throughout most of social work history, the definition and use of the term method have been loose. Method is often used interchangeably with such terms as process, modality, and technique. Three observable trends in the development of social work practice have mitigated efforts to separate method from other concepts and to define it in its own right. The first consists of the ways the profession's traditional discrete methods—social casework, social group work, and community organization—have evolved, expanded, and been refined. The second is the evolution of what Roberts and Northen (1976) refer to as "integrated theory that directs intervention with individuals, families, and formed groups" (p. xi). The third is the tendency to use nonsocial work terms to describe social work methods.

The discrete method notion hinges on the position that each social worker can only be, and should only be expected to be, skilled in the use of one of the traditional social work methods. From this point of view, professional expertise is defined as skill in the use of the one method. Social casework and social group work are generally regarded as clinical methods because they require the face-to-face interaction of the social worker and clients and are designed to help particular clients with particular problems in social functioning, or as defined here, in membership management. Community organization, on the other hand, aims to bring about change at a broader level in order to enhance social conditions that permit the optimal social functioning of all. Although it is generally agreed that clinical social workers use some aspects of community organization in their clinical work, these aspects have not been particularly well-conceptualized or articulated in clinical social work theory.

The integrated theory approach is based on the position that skill in one discrete method of social work is insufficient to meet the demands of professional social work practice. In integrated theory models, modality is often used in place of method as a key concept. Modality is defined by the number of clients with whom the clinician works at a given time and professional expertise is defined as competence to engage in multiple modalities of intervention. Proponents of the discrete method position tend to emphasize the importance of "practice skill" in their arguments, whereas proponents of the integrated approach tend to emphasize the importance of "professional competence." These positions are not really antithetical, however, since competence requires skill and the clinician without skill is not competent.

While social work practice can be viewed historically in terms of the evolution of the discrete and integrated method streams, it would be an error to conclude that there are, in fact, three discrete methods and one integrated approach. This is because a variety of discrete and integrated method models have been developed. Each model is based on selected theories of human behavior and these theories differ in fundamental ways. These differences, in turn, lead to markedly different definitions of focus, client, practitioner, and intervention. Thus one cannot accurately say that *the* social casework method, *the* social group work method, or *the* integrated method is used in a given instance of clinical social work. What is used is one of the *models* of social casework, social group work, or integrated method.

Finally, in considering both the discrete and integrated method models, it is apparent that each involves a definition of method that includes some form of assessment or diagnosis, a cluster of knowledge about human behavior, a defined way of working with people, and some definition of social work values and purpose (Bartlett, 1970, p. 35). Thus, the discrete methods, as traditionally defined, and integrated methods, as presently defined, are more than methods and may more accurately be regarded as processes.

The tendency to use nonsocial work terms to describe clinical social work and its methods has compounded the confusion. Chief among these nonsocial work terms are: counseling, psychotherapy, therapy, and treatment. Counseling literally means to advise, to give an opinion or instruction, to direct the judgment or conduct of another with regard to a particular course of action. Synonyms for counseling include recommending, suggesting, admonishing, educating, and warning. As a professional method, counseling is associated primarily with education and educational psychology. Within social work, it is a technique used by the clinical social worker to further some aspect of work with clients. Thus, counseling does not define clinical social work, nor does it define social work methods. It is only a technique, an aspect of clinical social work methods.

In contrast to counseling, psychotherapy is a method for curing psychological abnormalities and disorders by psychological techniques. It is sometimes defined as treatment of the ego. Psychotherapy is a method that evolved outside of social work and it is used by a number of professions and disciplines. Although some social workers do work as psychotherapists, the focus and purpose of psychotherapy are too narrow to allow for the realization of social work purpose and it cannot be properly regarded as a social work method.

The terms therapy and treatment are of a different order. They are associated primarily with medicine, although their definitions have been generalized to cover the nonmedical activities of other professions, including social work. Each is too vague to describe clinical social work methods. In addition, unless they are substantively qualified, they are too general to describe clinical social work process.

It seems clear that method needs to be defined separately from process and technique if the terms are to be used consistently in clinical social work and understood by others. The concept of process was discussed in some detail in Chapter 3 and that discussion will not be repeated here. It should be remembered, however, that clinical social work process includes all aspects of the clinician/client interaction, from start to finish, from intake to termination.

With these comments as introduction, the following definitions of method and technique, as they are understood within the membership framework, are offered:

Method is an orderly, logical, and systematic mode of procedure employed within the clinical social work process. It derives from the particular clinician/client configuration and directs how they work together. The use of a particular social work method is based on a clinical diagnosis and a specified plan, and requires professional competence and technical skill.

Technique refers to a specific behavior or action of the clinical social worker to implement and/or further the use of the method so that agreed-upon objectives are attained. Techniques cut across methods and are generally used in various clusters or combinations. They come into play as use of the method unfolds and progresses. A technique is what the clinician uses to further the clinical work at a given point.

Thus, process, method, and technique are separate, albeit related concepts. Techniques implement the method which is used within the clinical social work process. These definitions form the basis of the discussion of clinical social work methods and techniques explicated later in this chapter. For the moment, the following outline of clinical social work process in health settings illustrates the place of methods and techniques in the overall scheme.

I. *Intake or Referral*
   A. Source
      1. Client application
      2. Referral by other health professional
      3. High-risk screening for social work services; social work case-finding
   B. Presenting problem(s)
      1. Medical/health condition and status
      2. Membership management problem(s) related to the medical/health condition or status
      3. Other problems
   C. Services requested or offered
      1. Social work services
      2. Collaborative services
      3. Health team services

II. *Exploration (Diagnostic Process)*
   Mutual and/or parallel efforts by the clinical social worker, client(s), and/or other health professionals, including:
   A. Information gathering
   B. Examination of data and separation of facts from feelings
   C. Perception of the problem(s) by clinician, client(s), and/or other health professionals involved
   D. Contributing factors (medical/health status and prognosis, psychosocial factors, including cultural, ethnic, racial, religious, socioeconomic, and other membership variables) as seen by clinician, client(s), and other health professionals involved

III. Clinical Social Work Assessment (Diagnostic Product)

Assessment (diagnosis) encompasses:

A. The clinical social worker's analysis of the data gathered, including an estimate of the client's coping strengths and limitations at the present time and the interrelationships of medical/health status and pertinent membership variables

B. The clinician's estimate of the problem, shared with the client(s) and other health professionals involved and tested against the client(s) own expectations and view of the problem(s), taking into account areas of agreement and differences among all participants

IV. Contract (Intervention Plan)

Based upon the exploration and assessment of data that has been analyzed and evaluated,

A. Mutual goals are set

B. Immediate next steps are defined

   1. Specific clinician, client, and/or other health professional tasks are identified

   2. The relationships of tasks to goal achievement are clarified

   3. Intermediate objectives are determined

V. Intervention (Implementation of the Plan)

A. Method selection

   1. Related to the plan and its goals

   2. Embodies social work values and biopsychosocial balance

   3. Makes possible the realization of social work purpose

B. Method implementation

   1. Use of clinical social work techniques

   2. Viewed in the context of method and the overall context of the clinical social work plan, including collaboration with other health professionals where appropriate

C. Continued engagement (use of method)

   1. Ongoing interaction of clinician, client(s) and/or other health professionals aimed toward goal achievement

   2. Ongoing assessment, and reassessment, by clinician, client(s), and other health professionals, separately and together, of problem(s), procedures, and goals

VI. Termination and Evaluation

Before proceeding to a discussion of methods and techniques, it is first necessary to consider the terms *case* and *casework* as they are currently used by clinical social workers in the health field. Like process, method, and technique, clarity about the definition of case and casework is important for consistency and understanding.

A Redefinition of Case and Casework

Observations of current practice suggest that the terms *case* and *casework* are no longer used by health social workers to refer to the discrete method of social casework. Rather, their meanings are more general and they are used to refer simply to the work of the clinical social worker with particular clients. In this respect, current usage represents a return to earlier definitions, rather than a true redefinition of the terms.

Both terms originated as social work terms in the charity organization societies that dominated philanthropic activity in the United States at the end of the nineteenth century. Case referred to a particular instance of service, usually a poor family. Casework referred to work with these families on a case-by-case basis. The growth of social work as a profession and the movement of social workers into new areas of service led to a new definition of the two terms.

> During the first two decades of the twentieth century, the method spread from the COS's (soon to be known as family agencies) to hospital social service departments, child-placing agencies, the school social work field, court clinics, and state mental hospitals. (Germain and Gitterman, 1980, p. 351)

As members of the emerging social work profession moved into new agencies and service sectors, they realized that the case-by-case approach could also be used to help one client at a time, as well as one family at a time. The original family focus of the approach was expanded accordingly, or contracted, depending on point of view. Simultaneous efforts to place philanthropy on a scientific basis, and to professionalize services and those who provided them, accelerated the transformation of the case-by-case approach into what became known as the social casework method. The publication of Richmond's *Social Diagnosis* in 1917 had the effect of centering efforts to professionalize social work on the expansion and refinement of social casework as a discrete method of practice. In developing her model, Richmond incorporated the medical model and drew on the concepts of diagnosis in medicine and social evidence in law. As the transformation of casework from approach to method progressed, focus on the individual became dominant and the terms case and casework came to mean those instances where the social worker used the discrete social casework method, usually, but not always, with one client. Similarly, the term caseworker came to mean the practitioner who was skilled in use of the social casework method.

These definitions dominated social work as a profession well into the 1960s and were mirrored in the evolution of medical social work where the discrete method definitions of case, casework, and caseworker were central to theory and practice. By the end of the 1960s, however, it was clear that the discrete method definitions of these terms were no longer dominant in the health field. "Social work functions are no longer limited to casework . . . but have expanded to include efforts to help people in groups, advocacy activity, community action, and community planning" (Society for Hospital Social Work Directors, 1971, p. i).

Today, the terms case and casework have more general meaning in the health field. Their definitions are more akin to those of the past. The term case refers to the particular client configuration with whom the clinician works in a specific instance. Casework simply means working with health social work clients on a case-by-case basis. Neither term is restricted to instances in which the discrete method of social casework is used. The complicating factor here is that the terms now have multiple meanings. On the one hand, they are defined in general terms akin to their definition in the early days of social work. On the other hand, they continue to be used in terms of their discrete method definitions. With these points in mind, attention now turns to a consideration of the methods of intervention available to clinical social workers in health settings, as defined within the membership framework.

Methods of Clinical Social Work Intervention

The membership perspective is within the mainstream of social work thought and practice. It evolves from concepts deemed essential to the definition of social work as a profession and it accords primary importance to social functioning and social stress as central concepts. The perspective derives from a synthesis of object relations theory and symbolic interaction theory. The person is viewed as a social being who is simultaneously psychological and social by definition. People are not perceived, therefore, in terms of separate psychological and social components, but only in terms of the single psychological-social continuum that defines human nature.

Membership in social groups is seen as fundamental to human life. Successful social functioning is determined by the ability of people to manage their memberships: (1) in ways that are mutually satisfactory to them and to those with whom membership is shared; and (2) in ways that make possible community life in an organized society. Helping people to manage their memberships when they are confronted by various forms of stress, including actual or potential physical illness, disabilty, or injury, is deemed to be the purpose of social work. It follows, therefore, that since people cannot be divided into psychological and social parts, or separated from their social memberships, clinical social work cannot be divided into psychological and "concrete" services, nor can clinical work *with* clients be separated from clinical work *on behalf of* clients.

Accordingly, the membership approach proceeds from the common base of social work and draws selectively on concepts common to a number of social work theories and method models. These concepts are redefined in membership terms and the test for their selection and use is congruence and consistency in fit. Among these concepts are: process, structure, function, the meaningful use of time, relationship, problem, problem solving, task, member, membership, the disciplined use of self, and the notion of the person-group whole.

Agreement to engage in clinical social work process confers membership on both the social worker and the client(s). The interaction of clinician and client(s) is face-to-face and essentially nonintimate in the primary membership sense. That is, practitioner and client(s) share secondary membership. Clinical social work process, the membership connection of the clinician and client(s), and the quality of clinical membership, have been discussed in Chapter 3. The roles of the clinician and client(s) in diagnosis and planning have been explicated in Chapter 4. The key word in these aspects of clinical social work is mutuality. Clinical social work methods and techniques, however, are the tools of the social worker. They are the means by which the practitioner intervenes and makes assistance in the management of membership available to clients.

There are three basic methods which the clinical social worker uses to help clients. They are: the one-client method; the family group method; and the nonkinship group method. These three methods are sometimes denoted as one-to-one casework, family casework, and social group work respectively. Given the theoretical base and perspective of membership, however, all three of these methods are regarded as group methods by definition. This is so even for the one-client method since use of the method requires the presence of one clinician and one client, the smallest clinical social work membership configuration and the minimum number required for a group. The definition of the three methods as group methods also derives from the fact of the client's seen and unseen group memberships.

Whether the client sees the worker in an actual face-to-face group or whether the client comes to the worker as one person alone . . . the client . . . brings his groups with him. So does the social worker. When several people interact with each other under the guidance of the worker, we can speak of a "seen" group. When, as in some situations, the only people in the room are the client and the worker, we still speak of "seen" but also of "unseen" groups, i.e. those meaningful others all of us know about even when absent. Regardless of the size of any "seen" group, each client and worker carries a myriad of previous experiences in groups other than the one in the clinical situation. All members bring with them their unseen groups: family, work, friends, church. (Falck, 1981a, pp. 1-2)

With respect to self, others, and situation, clients in all three methods carry three important roles: reporter, re-enactor, and planner (Falck, 1981a). Despite these commonalities, however, the three methods do differ in their particulars.

The One-Client Method

In the one-client method, for example, the client's "unseen" group memberships take on a special significance since they are not physically present with the client and the clinician. As a consequence, the client's roles as reporter, re-enactor, and planner are particularly vivid since the work done in the clinical interaction depends on them to a greater extent than is true in the family group and nonkinship group methods. The following outline of selected factors to be considered in the one-client method dramatizes this difference.

I. *Content and Focus*
   A. Use of the method
      1. In relation to the clinical social work diagnosis
      2. In relation to the intervention plan
      3. In relation to the medical situation
      4. In relation to other health professionals
   B. The client's "unseen" membership groups
      1. Primary memberships
         a. Family
         b. Friends
         c. Others
      2. Secondary memberships
         a. Occupation
         b. Religion
         c. Other
      3. Tertiary memberships
         a. Culture/ethnicity
         b. Race
         c. Socioeconomic
         d. Other
   C. The determination of clinical tasks, by:
      1. The health setting, including other health professionals
         a. Medical/health related tasks
         b. General/social tasks

      2. The client
      3. The clinical social worker

II. *Client Member Roles*
  A. The client as reporter
      1. Of self
         a. Who he/she is
         b. How he/she thinks
         c. How he/she feels
      2. Of "unseen" group memberships
         a. Family and family roles
         b. Social and economic roles
         c. Other membership roles
      3. Of goals and expectations
         a. Dreams/hopes for the future before the present medical/
            social situation
         b. Impact of the medical/social situation on dreams/hopes in
            the present and for the future
  B. The client as re-enactor
      1. Projection on the clinician
         a. Of past experiences and relationships
         b. Of present experiences and relationships, including those
            with family, friends, other health professionals
      2. Expression of need in relation to medical/social situation
         a. To validate self in terms of past experiences and relation-
            ships
         b. To be accepted in the present; to belong
         c. To manage his/her memberships
      3. Interpretation
         a. Of self
         b. Of group memberships
         c. Of medical/social situation
  C. The client as planner
      1. Ability to assess
         a. Present medical/social situation
         b. The future
         c. The past, for use in the present, to plan for the future
      2. Ability to define
         a. Present medical/social problems and tasks
         b. Present and future objectives
         c. Necessary behavior to achieve objectives
      3. Ability to use clinical social work membership
         a. To exploit the present moment
         b. To enhance problem solving (coping) ability and skill

     c. To better manage his/her memberships, taking into account
       the medical/social situation

III. The Clinician's Roles
   A. In relation to the health setting
     1. As agency/department representative
     2. As health team member
   B. In relation to the client
     1. As clinical member
     2. As enabler, facilitator, etc.
   C. In relation to the social work profession
     1. As representative of the profession
     2. As health professional

In general, the clinical social worker helps the client to select and use previous experiences and relationships in the present. Focus is on the reality of the present moment and the meaning of the medical/social situation in the present and for the future. The clinician holds himself and the client(s) accountable for their behavior as clinical members and for planning in the present for the future.

Because the client's outside reality is not immediately available in the clinical situation when the one-client method is used, that reality must be reported and re-enacted by the client. As a consequence, the client's outside reality tends to take on a somewhat more abstract and more symbolic quality in the one-client method. When the family and non-kinship group methods are used, the outside reality of the client's membership groups are present in the clinical interaction, at least to some degree. This is so because of the physical presence of the family membership group in the clinical situation in the family group method and the physical presence of aspects of various outside client memberships in the non-kinship group method.

The Family Group Method

In the family group method, the reality of family membership is immediately available in the clinical situation. Emphasis is on helping the family group, *as a primary membership group*, to manage itself in relation to the medical situation of its patient member and the social problems attendant to that situation, including changes or tasks imposed by it on the family. Variations in the method stem primarily from two variables. The first is whether the patient member's medical condition permits his or her participation in the clinical interaction of the social worker and the family. In instances where the patient member is an infant, in intensive care, is comatose, has suffered a cerebrovascular accident, or is otherwise constrained by his or her health status, participation in the clinical work is not possible. In such instances, the patient member is an "unseen" member of the clinical group, an "unseen" participant in clinical interaction. The second variable is how the family defines itself.

When using the family group method, the clinical social worker's role is not to solve the family's dilemmas personally, but to assist the family in managing itself effectively in a way that is mutually satisfactory to its members in the context of the reality of its medical/social situation. Since the clinical social worker is primarily responsible for the use and direction of the family group method, a number of rules required by the method are generally stipulated at the outset. These rules structure the interaction of members within the method, and agreement to them is a precondition for the effective use of the method. Such agreement is usually reached at the time the intervention plan is determined. Nonagreement to the rules might preclude use of the method and/or modify certain other options at the planning stage.

The following outline includes the group method rules and other selected factors that must be considered when the family group method is used.

I. *Family Group Method Rules*
   A. Family group sessions
      1. Number of sessions
      2. Length of sessions
   B. Family group attendance
      1. Requirements for attendance
      2. Consequences of nonattendance
   C. Family group interaction
      1. Expression by all members of opinions, ideas, thoughts, and feelings
      2. Examination of all comments by family and clinician as clinical members

II. *Family Composition and Definition*
   A. As a primary membership group
      1. Marital roles
      2. Parental roles
      3. Offspring roles
      4. Sibling roles
   B. The family's "unseen" members
      1. Primary members
         a. Patient member, if unable to participate
         b. Close relatives
         c. "Honorary" relatives, e.g., godparents

        d. Intimate friends
    2. Secondary members
        a. Peer group memberships
        b. Church membership
        c. Employment group memberships
    3. Tertiary memberships
        a. Religious affiliation
        b. Ethnic/racial membership
        c. Socioeconomic membership

III. Family Group's Perception of the Medical/Social Situation
  A. As the patient member's problem
    1. Patient member's ability to fulfill family/social roles
    2. Imposition of patient member's family/social roles on other family members
  B. As a family group problem
    1. Effect on the present functioning of the family as a group
    2. Effect on the future functioning of the family as a group
  C. Degree of problem consensus
    1. Areas of agreement
    2. Areas of disagreement

IV. The Family Group's Culture
  A. Family norms and standards
    1. Role definition and authority
        a. Traditional
        b. Nontraditional
        c. Mixed
    2. Family decisions
        a. Decision-making authority and patterns
        b. Degree of disagreement permitted
        c. Modes of conflict expression
        d. Methods of conflict resolution
    3. Family interaction
        a. Expression of feeling and sentiment
           (1) Modes and patterns of expression
           (2) Restrictions on expression
        b. Family member alliances
           (1) Isolating certain members
           (2) Scapegoating certain members
           (3) Blaming certain members
        c. Family cohesion
           (1) Individuation of family members
           (2) Sense of belonging, support, respect, love

V. *Family Group and Family Member Activities*
   A. Prior to present medical/social situation
      1. Within the family group
      2. In the community and community groups
   B. Subsequent to medical/social situation
      1. Impact on family activities as a group
      2. Impact on family member activities in the community and community groups

VI. *Clinical Membership Roles of the Family*
   A. Reporting
   B. Re-enacting
   C. Planning

VII. *Clinical Membership Roles of the Social Worker*
   A. In relation to the health setting
   B. In relation to the family as client
   C. In relation to the social work profession

The one-client and family group methods have predominated in clinical social work in the health field since social workers first began to practice in the field. These methods were first "borrowed" from the charity organization societies and adapted for use in hospital out-patient departments and clinics. As social work in the health field grew and expanded, however, these methods took on certain characteristics derived from the synthesis of social work and health field knowledge.

The Nonkinship Group Method

Use of the nonkinship group method by clinical social workers in health settings is more recent. Despite the extensive use of group approaches by other health professionals throughout the field, clinical social workers have been slower to use them and sometimes reluctant to do so. Interest in the nonkinship group method has grown slowly but steadily, however, since the middle 1950s.

The nonkinship group method has distinct advantages. First, use of the method makes it possible for one social worker to help more clients than is possible with the one-client and family group methods. Second, the method makes it possible for clients with similar medical/social problems to help one another, as well as to be helped by the clinical social worker. Third, the client's ability to deal with the medical/social situation and to simultaneously manage his or her memberships is enhanced since help is given and taken within a context that approximates the outside reality of the client's memberships.

Falck (1981b) has developed a seven-part frame of reference for the nonkinship group method. It is characterized by the clinician's perception of: (1) all that transpires in the group as "here and now" phenomena; (2) all group interactions as cross-sectional statements of each member's and the group's behavior patterns; (3) the group as an entity, in the sense that a family is an entity; (4) the group as an action system; (5) clients and clinician as group members; (6) all member behavior as reflective of internalized experiences of other memberships that are carried in symbolic form by members in the present group; and (7) interactions of client members as peers (pp. 5-6).

In the health field, the nonkinship group method is particularly useful when clients facing similar medical/social situations need to learn something about the medical condition; how to do something in relation to the medical condition; and how to deal with the psychosocial implications of the medical condition. The criterion for the method's use in any given instance is whether it will maximize the client's ability to manage his or her memberships, given the opportunities and constraints imposed by the medical/social situation.

Given this condition, clients who are medical patients and clients who are not medical patients can benefit from the nonkinship group method. Such factors as age, sex, place in the family, and so on may be important variables for some groups, but the common denominator is the similarity of the medical/social situation of clients in the nonkinship group. As is true of the other two methods, clarity about the rules required for use of the nonkinship group method is important at the outset. The following outline includes selected factors to consider when the nonkinship group method is used.

I. *Health Program or Setting*
   A. The relationship of the group to the problem of central concern to the health setting in which it is embedded
   B. The influence of the organizational structure on the group

II. *Group Characteristics*
   A. Purpose and goals
      1. The group's defined and agreed-upon purpose and goals
      2. The medical/social problem(s) to which the purpose and goals of the group relate
      3. The relationship of the group's purpose and goals to those of the health setting
   B. Program related
      1. Kind or type of group; one-time, open-ended
      2. Criteria for group membership
      3. Relationship of the group to social work service

    C. Group related
      1. Type of membership; open or closed
      2. Group composition and size
      3. Group activities

III. *Group Culture*
    A. Quality of group interaction
      1. Patterns of verbal and nonverbal behavior
      2. Group membership roles
      3. Degree of group cohesion
    B. Norms and standards
      1. Institutionalization and use of authority
      2. Limitations on group activity and interaction
      3. Decision-making patterns
      4. Effects of norms and standards on group behavior
    C. Sentiment and feeling
      1. Modes of expressing sentiment and feelings
      2. Modes of expressing and resolving conflict
      3. Degree of group morale
      4. Effects of sentiment and feeling on group behavior

IV. *Group Activity*
    A. General activities
      1. Types of regular group activities
      2. Achievement and maintenance of balanced participation by group members
    B. Program activities
      1. Planning and use of program media
      2. Group purpose served by use of program media

V. *Clinical Roles of Client Members of the Group*
    A. Reporters
    B. Re-enactors
    C. Planners

VI. *Clinical Roles of Social Worker Member of the Group*
    A. Contextual roles
      1. Representative of social work purpose
      2. Representative of health setting
      3. Representative of the nonkinship group
    B. Group roles
      1. Professional expert
      2. Enabler, facilitator, etc.
      3. Liaison to the health setting and social work department

The methods of clinical social work discussed above are clinician directed. The clinical social worker, as professional expert, therefore, carries responsibility for their use. The selection of any one of the three methods depends on the clinician's assessment of the client situation. All three methods make use of a number of clinical social work techniques. These techniques have a generic quality and are discussed in the following section.

Clinical Social Work Techniques

Among the techniques commonly used by clinical social workers are authority, clarification, confrontation, counseling, decision making, exploration, facilitation, interpretation, options identification, support, and the use of structure. Table 5.1 summarizes the definition, purpose, and focus of some of these techniques.

In general, *authority*, as a clinical social work technique, inheres in the knowledge, training, and expertise of the clinician. It validates the clinician as a source of information and lends credence to the clinician's advice. The clinical social worker uses authority judiciously when rendering professional judgments and in supporting or not supporting certain client behavior. While the use of authority dramatizes the clinician's opinions or position, it is used most frequently to cut through client inaction and resistance. Authority is almost always used in combination with other techniques. It is always tempered by the client's right to social self-determination and by the nature of choice in clinical social work.

Clarification is a technique used to enhance the client member's ability to perceive himself in relation to others, and in relation to the medical/social situation. It is often used in combination with the techniques of exploration and options identification. When skillfully used in combination, these techniques enhance the psychosocial functioning of clients by facilitating changes in the ways they regard themselves, others, and the medical/social situation. Their function is to facilitate task accomplishment and goal attainment by focusing on the client's ability to manage the membership problems deriving from or impacted by the medical/social situation.

Confrontation challenges client behavior in a direct way. Often used in combination with interpretation, the behavior confronted may take a variety of forms, including denial of the situation and its inherent problems and tasks, rationalization of the constraints imposed by the patient/client's medical status, or socially unacceptable behavior. The general function of confrontation is to withdraw support for such behavior.

Counseling is used to provide clients with a rational justification for

TABLE 5.1 Selected Clinical Social Work Techniques

Technique	Definition	Purpose	Focus
Authority	Expertise on a subject.	To render a professional judgment or opinion.	On the clinician's professional knowledge and expertise.
	Accepted source of information and advice.	To support positive member behavior.	
	Power to determine.	To stop unacceptable member behavior.	
Clarification	To make understandable.	To enhance client member's awareness of self, of others, of situation.	On client member abilities to cope with feelings, thoughts, behavior, situation, problem, task.
	To achieve insight.		
Confrontation	To face reality.	To withdraw support for negative client behavior.	On client member feelings, behavior, common experience, situation, problem, task.
Counseling	To educate, inform.	To provide client members with new knowledge or understanding.	On abilities of client members to make decisions, to discriminate among alternatives and consequences of decisions.
	To reinforce knowledge or understanding.	To facilitate development of skill in coping with membership problems and situations.	
	To recommend.		
Exploration	To bring facts, opinions, and feelings into the open.	To understand membership situation and variables.	On client member feelings, experiences, behavior, and situation.

(continued)

119

TABLE 5.1 (continued)

Technique	Definition	Purpose	Focus
Facilitation	To move forward an action or process.	To help client members to maximize their use of clinical social work membership.	On the meaningful interaction of clients and clinician.
	To assist the progress of a person or process.		
Support	To sustain; keep steady.	To clarify and examine client member feelings, and situation.	On abilities and constructive defenses of client members.
	To express faith and confidence.		On client member efforts to cope, to accomplish tasks, and to achieve goals.
	To give realistic approval.		
Use of structure	To provide direction for clinical interaction.	To create a climate for clinical work and problem solving.	On agency policies, procedures, and services.
			On the use of space, furnishings, amenities.

changing their behavior and their attitudes. Its function is to demonstrate congruence or incongruence in the degree or kind of changes required of clients by the medical/social situation and their own interests and objectives relative to successful membership management. The ability to counsel inheres in the clinical social worker's expertise and authority. It usually takes the form of educating, informing, recommending, advising, and reinforcing client knowledge and understanding.

Decision making, as a technique, is used by the clinician in the context of his or her membership with the client(s), and often in combination with options identification. It frequently takes the form of a professional judgment. Social workers are sometimes hesitant about rendering professional judgments. It should be remembered, however, that rendering professional judgments is not synonymous with being judgmental, and that clients are entitled to the professional opinions and conclusions of the clinical social worker with whom they share clinical membership.

Facilitation, as a clinical social work technique, is used to modify negative interactions in a positive direction and to affirm positive progress. Its use promotes and enhances membership connections and guides member interaction toward task accomplishment and goal attainment. Facilitation often takes the form of feedback from the practitioner to the client(s) and it is reflective of the clinician's ongoing assessment of the differences and similarities underlying the clinical interaction. When skillfully used, facilitation enables clients to move within the process toward personal growth and positive change.

Support is a technique used by the clinician to reduce client anxiety and to enhance client self-esteem. It often takes the form of an expression of faith or confidence or the realistic approval of client behavior or action. Support also facilitates goal attainment.

The use of *structure* takes two basic forms. On the one hand, it is used to clarify and set limits and boundaries that flow from the policies, procedures, and service programs of the health setting. Structure, in this sense, inheres in agency function and is the variable against which clients test their ability to control and direct themselves. On the other hand, the technique relates to the clinician's use of space, furnishings, basic amenities, and other aspects of the physical setting in working with clients.

The use of clinical social work techniques are overtly oral in nature. Specific phrases spoken by the social worker generally signal their implementation. Table 5.2 gives examples of such phrases for selected techniques. It should be borne in mind, however, that these phrases are usually accompanied by nonverbal clinician behavior which dramatizes their meaning.

A few words about technical skill are in order before this discussion is brought to a close. In some quarters of social work, technical skill is

TABLE 5.2 Techniques for the Management of Membership in Clinical Social Work

Technique	Clinician's Expression
Clarification	"What is going on between you?"
	"What is going on between us?"
Confrontation	"This is what you do to yourself."
	"This is what you do in relation to others."
Interpretation	"This is what your behavior means."
	"This is what our behavior means."
Options identification	"What are the possibilities in your situation?"
	"What are the possibilities for changing?"
	"What are the possibilities in our situation?"
Decision making	"This is the best thing to do at the present moment."

Adapted from Hans S. Falck. "Membership." School of Social Work, Virginia Commonwealth University, 1981c. (Mimeographed.)

looked at askance. The implication is that conceptual expertise is more important than, if not preferable to, technical skill and that the two notions are dichotomous and polar. The view taken here is that dichotomies in social work thought and practice, including this one, are seldom helpful. While the professional practitioner must operate from the basis of a conceptual framework, that framework alone is not enough to render professional help to social work clients. Help is given inevitably through some method. In clinical social work, methods derive from the particular configuration of clients with whom the practitioner works. Moreover, the effective use of method requires technical skill. For the clinical social worker, professional competence lies in the skillful use of the specific methods and techniques that together constitute the profession's specialized body of clinical procedures so as to achieve results that are consistent with client need, agency function, and professional purpose.

Conclusion

Clinical social work services are offered to clients in the health field whose lives have been impacted by a change, or potential change, in medical or health status. Although the focus and content of the services rendered shift throughout the field as the definition of the problem of central concern to the health field shifts within its various sectors, the purpose of clinical social work remains constant—the lessening of social stress experienced by clients and the enhancement of their social functioning by assisting them in the management of their social memberships.

Clinical help is rendered through the connection of clinician and client within the context of clinical social work process. This process makes use of one or more specific methods which derive from the particular client configurations with whom the clinician works. The clinician, as the person responsible for directing and using the method, employs a variety of techniques to implement the method. The use of specific techniques is dictated by client behavior in relation to a specified purpose and goal.

References

Bartlett, Harriett M. *The common base of social work practice.* Washington, DC: National Association of Social Workers, 1970.

Falck, Hans S. *The "seen" and the "unseen" group in clinical social work practice.* Richmond: The Virginia Organization of Health Care Social Workers, Monograph #3 in the Health Social Work Practice Series, 1981. (a)

Falck, Hans S. *Guidelines for group work.* Virginia Commonwealth University, School of Social Work, 1981. (b)

Falck, Hans S. Membership. School of Social Work, Virginia Commonwealth University, 1981. (c) Mimeographed.

Germain, Carel B. & Gitterman, Alex. *The life model of social work practice.* New York: Columbia University Press, 1980.

Richmond, Mary. *Social diagnosis.* New York: Russell Sage Foundation, 1971.

Roberts, Robert W. & Northen, Helen (Eds.). *Theories of social work with groups.* New York: Columbia University Press, 1976.

Society for Hospital Social Work Directors of The American Hospital Association. Proposal to prepare a position statement on education for the practice of social work in health settings. Chicago, 1971.

6   Clinical Social Work in Collaborative Health Care Practice

Introduction

In the health field, people representing many professions and disciplines direct their efforts toward problems of health maintenance and care of the ill, disabled, and injured. Sometimes the work proceeds in parallel fashion. There is little or no face-to-face interaction among practitioners working with the patient/client and each relies on written records for the input of others. At other times, consultation among different practitioners takes place on a case-by-case basis. At still other times, service is coordinated and offered through a formal team approach. From even a cursory review of the literature, it is clear that collaboration is a basic characteristic of the delivery of health and medical services.

Despite its importance as a mode of service delivery, however, there has been little study of the effectiveness of collaboration among health practitioners or of the various forms it takes. In discussing health teams, for example, Ducanis and Golin (1979) point out that to date the team approach "has generated more rhetoric than research and an adequate theory of teams has yet to be formulated" (p. 1). They note further that much of the team literature is anecdotal and experiential in nature and that it borrows freely from the social sciences and professions, particularly from "theories concerning organizational, group, and individual behavior," with little regard for congruence (p. ix). Ducanis and Golin, and Kane (1975a) represent efforts to develop a more coherent basis for the formal team approach. Their criticisms, however, can also be applied to other forms of collaboration. Indeed, as the indiscriminate use of terms to denote all forms of collaborative practice suggests, a systematic framework for collaboration in the health field is still evolving.

In this chapter, attention is directed to selected aspects of collaboration which practice wisdom suggests should be included in a systematic frame-

124

work for collaborative practice, regardless of the form it takes. Focus is on prerequisites for, and constraints to, effective collaboration and on generic components of the collaborative process. A social work perspective is stressed with emphasis on clarity of terms and the need for professional integrity in collaborative practice.

Clinical Social Work in Collaborative Practice

Among the professionals who, in collaboration with others, offer services to people seeking help in health settings are clinical social workers. Indeed, health social work itself was established initially through the collaborative efforts of a physician, a social worker, and a nurse. Like all health professionals, clinical social workers are nearly always engaged in some form of collaborative practice. In fact, one of the most distinctive attributes of health social work derives from the fact that health social workers not only have to synthesize the common social work base with the complex characteristics of the health field, but that they must do so while in almost constant interaction with other health care providers. Conway (1979/80) states it succinctly:

> In delivering service the social worker must always remember, in addition to the fact that the patient did not come asking for social work that he, the social worker, is not the only one who is responsible for service delivery and not the only one who cares about the patients. Sometimes he has the major responsibility, sometimes others have this responsibility, but more often than not it is a shared one. I personally believe that collaboration is a primary process for the social worker in this kind of setting no matter what his role, function, or purpose is. Therefore, no social worker can practice as an independent even though he must practice and uphold all of the values, knowledge, and skills of his profession. (p. 43)

Social workers have been collaborating with other practitioners in the health field for most of this century and a substantial body of literature has developed with respect to these efforts. While much of this literature addresses either generic aspects of collaborative practice (Cabot, 1909; Cannon, 1923; Cockerill, 1951; Dana, 1983) or the formal team approach (Kane, 1975b; Lonsdale, Webb and Briggs, 1980; Stein, 1955), a good deal focuses on collaboration in such specialties within the field as cancer (Johnson and Stark, 1980), cardiology (Goldston, 1952), chronic pain (Berns, 1978), discharge planning (Collier, Hast and Delbauve, 1955), pediatrics (Terry, 1981), and rehabilitation (Conway, 1976). In addition, health social workers have a long tradition of contributing to the professional education of other health care providers (Bartlett, 1939; Rehr, 1974; Reynolds, 1977; Rice, 1953), and a growing literature on social work consultation attests to the use of this form of collaboration in health settings (Mercer and Garner, 1981; Watkins, Holland and Ritvo, 1976; Unger, 1978).

Given social work's long history of collaboration with others in the health field, it is, perhaps, surprising that a more comprehensive social work framework for collaboration has not evolved. The fact that it hasn't, however, is not unique to social work. Indeed, this situation is common to all of the health disciplines, as the indiscriminate use of terms coined by them to define and describe their collaborative efforts indicates. Some attention to these terms is, therefore, necessary prior to defining collaboration and considering some of the factors that, from a social work perspective, are indispensable for effective collaboration.

Unravelling Collaboration Terms

In the health field, those who provide services represent professions and disciplines with differing knowledge, values, skills, and purpose. A number of terms have been coined to describe both their joint work and the differences among them. These terms include: *multidisciplinary* and *multiprofessional*; *transdisciplinary* and *transprofessional*; *intradisciplinary* and *intraprofessional*; *interdisciplinary* and *interprofessional*.

The root word of these terms is either *discipline* or *profession*. Of the two, *discipline* is the more inclusive since it refers to a field of study and is not restricted to one kind of practitioner within the field. *Profession*, on the other hand, refers to a calling that requires specialized knowledge and often long academic preparation. Neither term is wholly satisfactory for all instances of collaboration, however, since both disciplines and professions may well be involved in the collaborative process in some cases but not in others. In any case, the terms are used interchangeably and will likely continue to be so used until such time as a unified theory of collaboration develops and is accepted throughout the field.

More problematic than the root words are the prefixes used to modify them. *Multi*, for example, means "many" or "multiple." The term multidisciplinary, therefore, refers simply to representatives of more than one discipline directing their efforts toward a common problem. It does not indicate anything in particular about their work together. *Trans*, on the other hand, means "across," "beyond," or "through." *Transdisciplinary*, therefore, suggests work that either cuts across disciplines or variables that are common to all of them. *Multi* and *trans* retain their meanings whether the root word they modify is discipline or profession. As modifiers, they add little that clarifies the notion of collaboration.

The prefix *intra* suggests a different set of circumstances. The meaning of *intra* is "within." *Intradisciplinary*, therefore, means within a discipline, whereas *intraprofessional* means within a profession. When applied to social work, for example, *intradisciplinary practice* refers to the joint work of people of varying preparation and function within the discipline of social work, for example, a professional social worker, a social work technician, and a social work aide. In contrast, *intraprofessional practice* refers to the joint activities of two or more professionally trained social workers.

The prefix *inter* more accurately describes the kind of activity health practitioners usually have in mind when they refer to collaboration. *Inter* means "between," "among," or "together." Like the other prefixes discussed above, *inter* does not change the essential meaning of the root words *discipline* and *profession*.

In addition to the root words and prefixes noted above, some attention needs to be directed to the notion of collaboration itself since collaboration can take a variety of forms. Primary among these are: case-by-case collaboration; consultation; education; and team practice.

Forms of Collaborative Practice

Case-by-case collaboration occurs when practitioners of different disciplines share diagnostic information and intervention plans for a particular patient/client or programatic problem. This is the oldest form of collaborative social work practice and in many settings is the prevailing form of collaboration. Most typically, it involves exchanges between the nurse, physician, and social worker regarding an individual patient/client with whom they are working at the moment. Case-by-case collaboration can be quite formal, as in postclinical conferences. It can also be quite informal and can occur over coffee, in parking lots, or in stairwells. Dana has noted the strengths and weaknesses of this form of collaboration.

> As a way of influencing the scope and quality of health care services, this mode has the advantage of tailoring the interpretation of both social health need and social work service to the level of understanding and knowledge of the individual nonsocial work colleague. It does not, however, provide the opportunity for the institutionalization of social services as an integral component of patient care and or institutional planning and management that are described as the major advantage of the team concept. Nor does it allow for the same control of social work rights and responsibilities that the more structured models of collaborative practice make possible. (p. 211)

Consultation literally means "to give expert advice," and the dictionary defines a consultant as one who "gives expert professional or technical

advice regarding matters in hi° field of special knowledge or training"
(Kadushin, 1977, p. 27). As a foi m of collaborative practice, consultation
predates modern medicine and health care. As Dana notes, health practitioners have sought the advice and counsel of colleagues since ancient
times "as a means of enhancing their own capacities for assessing and
dealing with problems" (p. 215). Although consultation has been defined
in numerous ways, Caplan's (1970) definition probably best expresses its
meaning and use in the health field.

> Consultation is the process of interaction between two professional persons—
> the consultant who is a specialist and the consultee who invokes the consultant's
> help in regard to current work problems with which he is having some diffi-
> culty and which he has decided are within the other's area of specialized
> competence. (p. 219)

The advantage of consultation, from a social work point of view, is that
when skillfully used it can rapidly enhance the psychosocial knowledge
and understanding of other health practitioners. Its disadvantages are
inherent in its nature as a form of collaborative practice. Consultation is
freely sought by the consultee, but with no assurance or commitment to
the consultant that the advice and counsel given will be followed.

Education, as a form of collaborative practice, involves the social
worker in the training of other health care providers. Dana defines it as a
means to broaden and deepen in nonsocial work colleagues an understanding "of the influence of social and psychological factors in the
prevention, treatment, and control of health problems" (p. 207). Educational collaboration can occur informally on a day-to-day basis as health
practitioners interact with one another and learn from one another about
their differing knowledge, values, purpose, and skills. It also occurs
formally when social workers serve as faculty in the schools and training
programs of other health care providers. The social worker serving formally in the collaborative education of nonsocial work colleagues needs
three fundamental kinds of knowledge: (1) of social work purpose, values,
and skills; (2) of the purpose, values, skills, and educational process of the
other disciplines involved; and (3) of learning theory and educational
methods, including didactic and experiential methods.

The team approach, as a form of collaboration, involves a number of
people with different roles and functions who are associated in common
work or in common activity. In the health field, however, the word *team*
is used in two distinct ways. On the one hand, it refers in a general way to
the people who are employed in a particular setting, such as a hospital,
public health clinic, or rehabilitation center. In this sense, the meaning of
team is somewhat abstract and philosophical. It is broad enough and

vague enough to include all forms of collaboration, but doesn't necessarily imply any of them.

On the other hand, *team* also denotes specific groups of people who work together in a formal, structured way to deliver services. The composition of the formal team is usually determined by the particular needs of patients, or is mandated by enabling legislation or agency policy. A team might include a nurse, a physician, a social worker, and various therapists and technicians who work together in a planned way. In this sense, *team* refers to a specific form of collaborative practice. Like its composition, however, the function of the formal team varies according to circumstances. A team may have a restorative function when working with stroke victims in a rehabilitation center or cancer victims in a hospital, or a preventive function in a public health clinic, or a diagnostic function in a child development center. Whatever its composition or function, however, the basic purpose of the team approach, as collaborative practice, is to organize and integrate the work of practitioners from more than one discipline in order to coordinate the specialized services of the team's members and to integrate them for the benefit of the patient/client.

Given the various forms collaborative practice takes in the health field, the variety of terms used to describe collaboration, and the differences in meaning and interpretation these terms suggest, some agreement about terminology is necessary for understanding. It is to a generic definition of collaboration in the health field that attention now turns.

Collaboration Defined

Of the possible combinations of root words and the prefixes that modify them, observation suggests that *interdisciplinary* is gaining ground as the preferred term for describing the various forms of collaborative practice in the health field. Collaboration, therefore, is defined in this chapter as *interdisciplinary practice* by two or more practitioners from two or more fields of learning and activity, who fill distinct roles, perform specialized tasks, and work in an interdependent relationship toward the achievement of a common purpose. The prefix *inter* makes clear that representatives from more than one discipline are involved and work together; *discipline* is broad enough to include professionals, but is not limited to them; and *practice* avoids limiting the definition to any one form of collaboration, such as the formal health care team.

With this definition in place, it is now possible to proceed with a discussion of some of the generic dimensions of collaboration as interdisciplinary practice. Accordingly, prerequisites for collaboration are considered in the section that follows.

Prerequisites for Effective Collaboration

Aspects of the particular kind of membership shared by clinical social workers and clients in health settings have been explored in preceeding chapters. That the notion of membership extends to and includes other practitioners in health settings becomes clear when consideration is given to Falck's (1977) contention that there is only one test that interdisciplinary practice needs to meet: "that it be of advantage to clients" (p. 35). In developing this idea, Falck notes that: (1) clients benefit from a wide variety of knowledge and method; (2) knowledge and skills useful to clients often cannot be known or exercised by any one practitioner or profession; and (3) certain knowledge and skills are common to the helping professions. Given these assumptions, Falck lists four prerequisite attitudes for successful interdisciplinary practice: (1) thorough commitment to the values and ethics of one's own profession and belief in its usefulness; (2) belief in an holistic approach to client problems; (3) recognition of the interdependency of practice; and (4) recognition of the expertise of colleagues and others (p. 36).

Commitment to One's Own Profession

To collaborate effectively with members of other disciplines, the clinical social worker must be well-grounded in social work. Dana asserts that "a firm hold on the values as well as the knowledge and skills of social work is a prerequisite for working jointly with others" as this is "the protection that the profession affords against collaboration as . . . capitulation" to the norms and procedures of others (p. 182). This theme has been sounded throughout the chapters of this book as emphasis has been given to the critical function of social work values in determining the appropriateness of knowledge to be integrated, and procedures to be incorporated, into the health social worker's practice base from nonsocial work sources. That values are of no less importance when the clinical social worker's practice is extended to interdisciplinary practice has long been recognized by health social workers. Cockerill (1951), for example, pointed out that social workers bring to the collaborative process a social philosophy that is characteristic of the social work profession. Included in this philosophy is the value accorded to the person as a social being of dignity and worth who does not surrender his or her basic human rights by virtue of becoming a health or medical care client.

When the protection afforded by commitment to the profession weakens, or is surrendered by the clinical social worker's capitulation to the knowledge, ethics, or procedures of other disciplines, confusion of purpose and a devaluing of the social work contribution to the joint under-taking may result. In her discussion of the need for clarity of purpose, Cockerill cited Coleman (1950) who, in distinguishing between social casework and psychotherapy, called attention to the fact that casework renders its most distinguished service when the caseworker's focus of concern is on the "*relatedness* aspects of personal problems" (p. 384). Cockerill also cited Rockmore (1951) to support her claim that many social workers fail to demonstrate sufficient conviction about the useful-ness of social work in their collaborative work. Rockmore's criticisms include behaviors that express this lack of conviction: excessive modesty; constant stress on the tentativeness of conclusions and the need to learn more; and undue emphasis on the profession's youth. To counteract these and similar behaviors, Rockmore suggests full appreciation of the corner-stones upon which the profession's practice rests: the dynamic significance of full client participation in the process; the emotional implications inherent in recognition of the client as a person who can make choices and decisions; and the therapeutic potential in helping clients to engage in meaningful and productive activity.

In the context of interdisciplinary conferences, Conway (1979/80) relates an example from her own experience that aptly illustrates commit-ment to social work and belief in its usefulness while simultaneously recognizing and respecting the contributions of other practitioners.

At one of these conferences [the] physician asked me rather definitely to order a wheel chair for a patient whom I felt could not use it. In my most frank, honest, and straightforward manner I said I could not do that. Dead silence covered the room and it was obvious that I needed to respond. I could not tell him, a physician, what to do and neither could I say whether or not the patient needed the wheel chair medically. I could say, however, from my standpoint as a social worker that she could not use it from a social standpoint. She was severely disabled with arthritis and needed help in all that she did including getting to and from the bed or chair or toilet to the wheel chair and there was no one to help her do this. Her husband was past seventy-five, a severe cardiac himself, and somewhat senile. She had no other human supports. She also had little if any financial supports available. I told him again that I could not tell him what to do as a physician but that I could not use the patient's or the community's money for an item [that] in my best judgement . . . I knew would not be useful. . . . he agreed with me and we began to consider alternative plans for the patient. (pp. 45–46)

Conway points out that the concepts of risk, trust, process, spontaneity, continuity, demonstration of role, function and purpose, and choice were used in this instance of collaboration. She elaborates on the application of these basic social work notions to collaborative practice by noting that risk and trust are reflective of an evolving relationship that builds continuously from one experience to another and involves choices, in this case by the physician and the social worker. Conway emphasizes the importance of credibility and relationship as central concepts which lead to understanding and respect, and adds: "I really thought his plan was terrible but if I had told him that, I would have embarrassed him, made him angry and gotten into a will struggle" (p. 46).

Belief in a Holistic Approach

The view of the person as a being who is simultaneously biological, psychological, and social is basic to all social work activity. So basic is this view, in fact, that social workers in other fields easily recognized it in the early medical social work descriptions of patients and problems in medical care. Cannon (1954), for example, draws attention to addresses to the American Hospital Association by Jane Addams and Julia Lathrop in 1907 as instances where leaders of the profession, whose own practice experience was outside the medical social work field, clearly perceived both the need to treat the patient as a person and the general failure of hospitals to do so.

The establishment of the first medical social work department at the Massachusetts General Hospital in 1905 is significant not only because it marks the formal beginnings of health social work in this country, but also because it constituted formal recognition by an institution of medical care that the patient is indeed more than a medical diagnosis. While it can, perhaps, be argued that the holistic view was primarily associated with social work during the first half of the century, it is evident that it has gained wide acceptance in the last (Pelletier, 1979; Schoenberg, et al., 1972). The current emphasis on an holistic approach in nursing and in the therapies confirms this conclusion.

In the context of his or her total life situation, the holistic approach considers every aspect of the person as related to all other aspects. A change or problem in one aspect, therefore, affects the others. As a consequence, all dimensions must be considered, not just the presenting problem, if the treatment is to be effective. Since no single practitioner or discipline can possess all the knowledge and skill that may be required, the holistic approach is best implemented in the health field through interdisciplinary practice which takes advantage of the range of knowledge and skill various specialists bring to the problem-solving process. Thus, the holistic approach requires a balance of the differential assessments of patient/client needs made by various health practitioners. This interdisciplinary diagnosis then makes it possible to integrate the services rendered by the different specialists into a coherent treatment plan to meet those needs.

The holistic view is observable in clinical social work services directed toward problem identification and intervention predicated on an assessment of the interrelationships of health and social factors and their impact on the patient/client and his or her significant others. The association of social work with the holistic approach is particularly apparent in rehabilitation centers where clinical social workers are often assigned pivotal roles in facilitating and maintaining it (Browne, Kirlin and Watt, 1981; Conway, 1976). In interdisciplinary contacts, the clinical social worker: (1) identifies sources of stress to the patient/client, both within the health setting and external to it; (2) analyzes how these sources of stress interact and influence, for good or ill, the patient/client's behavior with respect to health maintenance, recovery from illness, or restoration from a disabling condition or injury; and (3) promotes the coordination and integration of services to help the patient/client achieve the optimal levels of health and social functioning possible under the circumstances.

Recognition of the Interdependence of Practice

Collaboration in health settings rests on the belief that the full range of knowledge and skills required by the holistic approach cannot be commanded by one single practitioner or discipline. Recognition of the interdependence of the health disciplines is, therefore, inherent in the holistic approach and is a prerequisite for effective health and illness care. Given these assumptions, it follows that both the similarities *and* the differences among those providing services must be understood, emphasized, and respected if the holistic approach is to be realized and collaboration successful.

Recognition of the expertise of colleagues requires understanding of the disciplinary or professional purpose of each participant in the collaborative process and how that purpose defines and shapes the expertise of each. At the same time, there must be recognition that the helping professions and disciplines draw on common sources for their basic science base. Among these sources are anthropology, biology, economics, psychology, and sociology. No single discipline or profession can claim exclusive dominion over the knowledge that study and learning in these sciences yields. Rather, disciplinary difference and expertise derive from the ways each discipline incorporates and uses knowledge from these basic sciences in pursuit of its own purpose.

In his consideration of differences in disciplinary activity, Bowers (1950) concluded that:

> the specific differences of any art, distinguishing it from all others, are to be found in its subject matter, its end or purpose and the means or instruments it uses to achieve that end; the *what*, the *why* and the *how*. It is not necessary that each of these components in a specific art differ from the corresponding components in other arts, but, at least, the combination must be unique or there could be no differentiation. One body of subject matter may be shared by many arts, while each has its own intrinsic end or its own particular means. (p. 125)

When the participants in the collaborative process act consistently in terms of the *what*, *why*, and *how* of their own disciplines, the purpose of each becomes clear to the others. This clarity, in turn, illuminates the distinct practice roles, functions, and services germane to each discipline and tends to facilitate the development of the mutual respect and appreciation that the interdependent nature of health and medical care requires. In this connection, Purtillo (1978), a physical therapist writing generically about education for the health professions, notes that "professional goals can be realized only when [students] learn to combine their skills with those of their professional allies, and when, together, they effectively interact with the person needing their skills—the patient" (p. vii).

Recognition of the Expertise of Colleagues

Clients do not generally come to hospitals and other health facilities for social work services. Rather, they come to prevent, deal with, or recover from some form of physical stress. It follows, then, that in addition to a firm commitment to the purpose of social work and skill in the delivery of social work services, the clinical social worker in health settings must also understand the myriad health problems or medical conditions that bring clients to the setting and ultimately to the social worker.

In Chapter 2, attention was drawn to the need of the social work clinician for biomedical knowledge in order to work intelligently and appropriately with patient/clients. Such knowledge leads to recognition of the expertise of colleagues and thereby facilitates intelligent collaboration with others who serve clients in health settings and for whom such knowledge is central to purpose and function. In discussing the interaction of medical social workers and residents in a large hospital, Savard (1952) made the case for such knowledge in terms that ring true more than a quarter of a century later.

The social worker must be able to produce on a sound, realistic basis. Included as a prerequisite is the necessity for him to know the various diseases with which he is dealing as a *medical* social worker. It is impossible to ask the resident pertinent questions unless one has a working knowledge of the patient's disease. It is not enough for the social worker to have a general knowledge of the limitations of the disease, how long the patient will be incapacitated and his prognosis. One must be able to fit these generalizations to the illness in question. The resident is very apt to become irritated if all of these same questions are asked week after week about each patient considered, when in some cases they are totally irrelevant. The medical social implications of an appendectomy as compared to a myocardial infarct is an example of two very different problems. One cannot ask intelligent questions about something of which one knows nothing. (pp. 25-26)

Savard also points out that a working knowledge of medicine is important in another respect. It strengthens interdisciplinary collaboration because it enables the participants to recognize one another's difficulties and to support one another. In cases of physician-social worker-nurse collaboration, for example, biomedical knowledge enables the social worker to recognize the difficulties involved in the practice of medicine and to support the physician and nurse when the results of medical treatment are indefinite or when treatment fails to arrest the patient's problem.

To grasp their full importance, the prerequisite attitudes for effective collaboration need to be considered with reference to variables that influence them in negative directions. In the section that follows, some of these variables are briefly considered.

Constraints to Effective Collaboration

In addition to the four prerequisite attitudes, Falck identifies variables that serve as major obstacles to effective interdisciplinary practice: (1) role blurring; (2) extreme role specialization; (3) professional expansionism; and (4) the wish for indispensability and enhancement of status. These obstacles can separately or collectively constrain any and all of the attitudes deemed necessary if interdisciplinary collaboration is to be of use to clients.

Role blurring is an indication of surrender to norms and procedures other than those of one's own profession, and often of professional purpose. Professional identity and commitment are surrendered, for example, when health practitioners adopt the stance that they should not only be knowledgeable about one another's purpose and methods, but should also be able to take one another's place. In essence, this stance holds that when one or more practitioners are not present, others can represent their point of view and discharge their functions. Role blurring, as a form of détente, often occurs as a result of ill-conceived efforts to lessen or eliminate interdisciplinary conflict. It may also result from poorly conceived attempts to gain acceptance.

In such cases, the surrender of professional identity and commitment are usually masked by benign intentions. Whatever the reason, however, role blurring negates the fundamental reason for interdisciplinary practice by denying that the disciplines involved differ from one another in important ways and that each renders a specialized service to clients.

As noted, the holistic approach requires an appropriate balance of differential assessments and the integration of specialized services as dimensions of a coherent plan to meet the patient/client's needs. Extreme role specialization can upset that balance and integration. This is apparent in instances where clinical social work is conceptually fractured into the so-called psychological and concrete services. Such conceptualizations tend to ignore the fundamental biopsychosocial unity inherent in the social work view of the person and to deny that each has meaning for the other. Overdetermined social work roles deprive both other providers of service and clients of the consistent, integrated contribution expected of clinical social workers.

Role blurring and extreme role specialization can lead to other problems. In the former, interdisciplinary commonalities are overemphasized while differences are deemphasized. In the latter, the reverse is true and differences between the disciplines are stressed while the commonalities they share are played down. Both can create a sense of lost purpose and identity which, in turn, can lead to the outbreak or renewal of conflict among the disciplines. To counteract a sense of purposelessness and lost identity, for example, practitioners may embark on a series of attempts to increase their status and prestige or to attain total control and indispensability.

Such efforts may involve attempts to extend roles and functions beyond disciplinary boundaries. Most health practitioners have experienced, for example, the frustration of trying to work with the chaplain who refuses to deal with religious content and insists on engaging the patient in psychological counseling, the nurse intent upon restructuring the hospital patient's entire family rather than on providing appropriate nursing care, the social worker bent on substituting the purpose and procedures of psychiatry for those of social work, and the physician determined to maintain control over every facet of biopsychosocial diagnosis and treatment from admission through discharge. The results of such behavior are territorial squabbles and interdisciplinary competition.

In such instances, the representatives of the disciplines involved have usually lost their grasp on the purpose of their discipline and their understanding of how each complements the others. The clinical social worker involved in or part of such situations is well advised to bear in mind the stance taken by Cockerill more than 30 years ago.

> To a large degree, the emphasis on the part of the other disciplines is upon the *psychobiological* sources and manifestations of stress. The delineation of the *psychosocial* sources and manifestations of stress is definitely enhanced by what the social worker is prepared to bring to this process. . . . The salient factor in the purpose of the social worker is that it seeks to bring the capacities of the individual and the resources within his community into direct relationship with each other so that the potentials within both are released and made available for the achievement of equilibrium within the individual and meaningful and productive social living. (pp. 27–28)

Thus, although the interdependence of practice is generally recognized in the health field, the actual behavior of service providers does not always reflect this recognition. The reasons for this situation are many. Two important ones are that interdisciplinary practice receives relatively little attention in the educational programs of the health professions and disciplines, and that attempts to deal with the demands of interdisciplinary practice can have unanticipated consequences.

Generic Components of Collaboration

Collaboration, like all forms of intervention, is essentially a problem-solving process. Like other forms of problem solving, it follows a systematic procedure that begins with problem identification and definition and proceeds through evaluation of outcomes. The distinctive feature of collaboration as problem solving is the fact that people representing different disciplines work together to solve the problem. Brill (1976), in discussing teamwork, defines the problem-solving process in terms of problem, purpose, goals, tasks, roles, intervention, and evaluation and revision (p. 122). With only minor modification, these steps can be generalized to apply to forms of collaboration other than teamwork. Table 6.1 summarizes their reconceptualization as generic components of collaborative process.

Problem specification is the starting point and determines if collaboration is required. The presenting problem of most health clients is some form of physical stress that requires health or medical intervention. Rarely, however, do such problems occur in isolation. Almost invariably, they precipitate or are related to other problems. A biological problem, for

TABLE 6.1 Generic Components of Collaborative Process

Components	Content and Activity
1. Problem specification	Specification of the patient/client's bio-psychosocial condition and problem(s) that require interdisciplinary collaboration.
	Identification of the specialized knowledge and interventive skills needed to solve the patient/client's biopsychosocial problem(s).
2. Statement of the collaborative purpose	Definition of the collaborative purpose.
	Identification of the interdisciplinary services and the form of collaboration needed to solve the problem(s).
	Designation of the service providers.
3. Goal specification	Specification of objectives, the attainment of which represent progressive steps toward the realization of the collaborative purpose.
4. Task identification	Identification of specific activities derived from the specified goals and leading to the provision of identified services and/or the coordination of services.
5. Role designation and intervention	Designation of specific responsibilities for each specialist.
	Enactment of roles through the undertaking of specific activities by each specialist leading to goal achievement, realization of purpose, and problem resolution or mitigation.
6. Evaluation and revision	Continuous assessment of each component of the collaborative process and revision, if required, at any point in the process, including return to the beginning.

example, may spread or trigger other biological problems. At other times, the biological problem may cause psychological and social stress, thereby creating other kinds of problems. In still other instances, it may be psychosocial stress that triggers the presenting biological problem. In any case, the client usually experiences an interrelated group of problems that require the services of different specialists.

The kind and scope of the client's problems determine which specialists are needed for their resolution. If the problems attendant to the physical problem are minor, they may not require the services of other specialists. At other times, they may. How the client's problem is identified and defined may also be determined or influenced by such factors as legislative mandates, organizational policy, practice protocols, and case-finding procedures.

Interdisciplinary practice, however, cannot solve all patient/client problems. Identified problems, therefore, must be defined in terms that realistically consider both the client's condition and the resources available.

The *purpose of collaboration* is derived from the specification of the problem. Included in the statement of purpose is identification of the kinds of interdisciplinary services needed, specification of the form collaboration will take, and designation of the service providers. A physician, for example, may sense that something beyond the patient's physical condition is affecting treatment and recovery. Consultation with the nurse may confirm this suspicion. The nurse may suggest that the physician request consultation from a social worker to determine if nonbiological variables are impeding the patient's ability to use treatment and recover. Following an interview, or interviews, with the patient/client, the social worker may inform the physician and nurse that psychosocial problems are interacting with the biological problem and may recommend that they take certain joint actions. If the physician and nurse agree with the social worker's assessment and recommendation, they may agree to coordinate their work to help resolve the psychosocial problems and free the patient/client to make use of the medical treatment to recover physically. The purpose in this case is to coordinate medical, nursing, and social services to facilitate patient/client recovery. It arises from the specification of the problem in biopsychosocial terms. The forms of interdisciplinary practice involved are consultation and case-by-case collaboration.

Goal specification, in turn, derives from the purpose of the collaboration and requires the formulation of objectives. These objectives represent progressive steps which lead to the realization of the collaborative purpose. To be most effective, objectives should be stated in specific terms and should be prioritized. Suppose that in the above case, for example, the patient/client is experiencing emotional stress as a result of fear that the treatment will not be successful. In addition, the patient/client is worried about a son who is having learning difficulties at school, about the maintenance of the family members at home during the hospitalization period, and how expenses attendant to medical care, such as the supervision of preschool children, will be paid. Goals, therefore, might well be to eliminate the patient/client's fears about treatment and recovery, and to lessen or eliminate the problems causing psychosocial stress.

Task identification follows the formulation of goals. That is, each objective implies certain tasks upon which goal attainment depends. In the case illustration, for example, the first goal entails explaining the medical diagnosis to the patient/client, discussing the treatment regimen, and providing reassurance regarding the prognosis for recovery. The second goal involves other tasks, such as exploration of the son's learning problem and identification of resources to help him with it, determination of how the family is functioning and whether support is needed to help it maintain itself during the patient/client's hospitalization, discussion of child care with members of the extended family, and investigation of financial resources. Once the tasks have been identified, they can be clustered and their coordination planned.

Role designation follows the identification and clustering of tasks. In essence, role designation deals with the "who will do what" issues and how each participant will be kept abreast of developments. Some tasks may be shared by more than one participant in which case role overlaps, unlike role blurring, are complementary. In the case situation under discussion, the tasks related to medical diagnosis, treatment, and prognosis might be shared by all three participants. The physician would explain the diagnosis to the patient/client, indicating its dimensions, medical implications, and how it is to be treated. This explanation would involve discussion of the degree of recovery to be expected if treatment requirements are followed, and the consequences of noncompliance. The nurse, in turn, would explain the particulars of treatment to the patient/client as it proceeds. This would include a discussion of medications, for example, why they are required, how they work, their effects on the medical condition, and any side effects that might be anticipated. The social worker would ascertain the degree to which the patient/client understands and accepts the explanations given. Support and reassurance might also be given to help allay any lingering fears the patient/client may have as the process moves toward recovery and discharge from the hospital. Thus, role designation involves the assignment of specific responsibilities for task accomplishment and leads directly to each participant's *intervention*.

Evaluation is the determination of collaborative outcomes. It not only occurs at the end of collaborative activity, but also at each step in the collaborative process. That is, as intervention to accomplish tasks leading to goal attainment occurs, each participant's work is assessed separately and jointly. If the outcomes of service are not those envisioned, or if new problems are discovered, *revision* may occur. Purpose may be redefined, the form of collaboration changed, new goals specified, tasks modified, added, or eliminated, and roles reassigned.

Effective collaboration requires that each participant understand clearly what is expected of him or her and of the others. Roles, decision-making authority, communication patterns, and responsibility for coordination must be clarified and accepted by all. Throughout the process, each practitioner keeps the others informed of the services he or she renders in pursuit of collaborative goals and overall purpose. When these matters are attended to and each component of the collaborative process is addressed systematically, collaboration can be a richly rewarding undertaking for the representatives of the disciplines involved and of significant benefit to the patient/client.

Social Work Advocacy

There is another social work responsibility that has meaning for collaboration and cannot be overlooked. That is the responsibility inherent in the profession's purpose to advocate for changes in policy and procedure whenever such changes are appropriate and will yield socially beneficial outcomes.

Through collaboration, the clinical social worker acquires a direct voice in issues of policy and procedure beyond those pertaining to the organization of health social work services and their delivery to clients. Collaboration among physicians, nurses, social workers, and other health practitioners makes possible joint thinking, action, and recommendations that expand the possibilities otherwise imposed by the limits of one's own specialization.

The point that the clinical social worker needs to bear in mind is that meaningful changes of benefit to clients and practitioners alike can be pursued, and abstract objectives can become realities, through meaningful advocacy within the confines of the health setting itself. Most social work clinicians are familiar, for example, with the negative outcomes for clients in procedures that require that clients wait outside the conference room door for the interdisciplinary verdict. Most are also aware of the benefits that ensue when this and like procedures are modified or eliminated. Thus, justice and equity are not just abstractions or objectives to be pursued only through lobbying and political action in the legislative arena. Justice and equity are immediate concerns for every clinical social worker.

Conclusion

The usefulness of social work in health settings derives from its purpose which, as defined and discussed in this book, is embodied in the idea of social membership and includes social functioning and social stress as central concepts. To collaborate effectively with others, the clinical social worker draws fully and appropriately on the common base of the profession. Use of social work purpose, knowledge, values, and skills is apparent in what Dana (1983) calls the "time-honored social work behavior" necessary for interdisciplinary practice:

1. Acceptance of the need to begin where one's colleagues are.
2. Respect for differences in values, knowledge, and problem-solving styles and capacities.
3. Willingness to share one's own knowledge, values, and skills even when they may conflict with the knowledge, values, and skills that others hold to.
4. Willingness to work through, rather than avoid conflicts.
5. Willingness to change or modify the definition of the problem to be addressed, or the means of addressing it, on the basis of new insights derived from the perceptions and interpretations that other practitioners hold of both the problem and ways of dealing with it (p. 190).
6. Ability to use group process as a means for meeting the salient demands of collaborative practice, for distinguishing between the performance of the collaborative role by social workers and its performance by collaborators from other professions and disciplines, and for transmitting social work knowledge (p. 193).

As Dana notes, social work accepts the need to collaborate with other professions and disciplines as a basic requirement if social work is to be an effective instrument of health and medical care. She also cautions, however, that "there is no inherent virtue in collaboration for collaboration's sake." Rather, the virtue of collaboration lies in "the relevance of social work values, knowledge, and skills to the determination of the objectives and or implementation of the particular task or responsibility at hand" (pp. 181–182).

As to the usefulness of social work purpose, knowledge, values, and skills, Cannon (1933) long ago made the case for social work in the health field.

> Whenever the making of the diagnosis is dependent on facts about the environment of the patient, such as exposure to the detrimental hazards in his work or at home; whenever successful treatment of disease depends on participation of the patient in the plan for treatment, social service may be needed. Expert medical diagnosis is not always enough. To get its full significance it should be a medical social diagnosis. (p. 5)

References

Bartlett, Harriett M. *The participation of medical social workers in the teaching of medical students.* Chicago: American Association of Medical Social Workers, 1939.

Berns, Jacqueline. Team approach to chronic pain. *Health and Social Work*, May 1978, 3:2, 43-55.

Bowers, Swithun. The nature and definition of social casework. In Cora Kasius (Ed.), *Principles and techniques in social casework: Selected articles, 1940-1950*. New York: Family Service Association of America, 1950, pp. 92-127.

Brill, Naomi I. *Teamwork: Working together in the human services*. New York: J. B. Lippincott Company, 1976.

Browne, J. A.; Kirlin, Betty A.; & Watt, Susan. *Rehabilitation services and the social work role: Challenge for change*. Baltimore: Williams & Wilkins, 1981.

Cabot, Richard C. *Social service and the art of healing*. New York: Moffat, Yard & Co., 1909.

Cannon, Ida M. *Social work in hospitals: A contribution to progressive medicine*, rev. ed. New York: Russell Sage Foundation, 1923. (Originally published, 1913.)

Cannon, Ida M. The functions of medical social services in the United States. *Hospital Social Service*, January 1933, 27:1, 1-16.

Cannon, Ida M. Lay participation in hospital service from the point of view of a medical social worker. In Dora Goldstine (Ed.), *Readings in the theory and practice of medical social work*. Chicago: University of Chicago Press, 1954, pp. 57-66.

Caplan, Gerald. *The theory and practice of mental health consultation*. New York: Basic Books, 1970.

Cockerill, Eleanor. The contributions of medical social work to the team of the health professions. *Medical Social Work*, September 1951, 1:1, 18-30.

Coleman, Jules. Distinguishing between psychotherapy and social casework. In Cora Kasius (Ed.), *Principles and techniques of social casework: Selected articles, 1940-1950*. New York: Family Service Association of America, 1950, pp. 380-392.

Collier, G. Miriam; Hart, Elinor G.; & Delbauve, Helen. Teamwork planning for patient's discharge. *Medical Social Work*, January 1955, 4:1, 27-40.

Conway, Joan Bonner. *The social worker in the collaborative process: An analysis of the roles and tasks of the social worker in the collaborative process in a comprehensive medically-oriented rehabilitation center*. (Doctoral dissertation, University of Pennsylvania, 1976. *Dissertation Abstracts International*, 1976, 37:5, p. 3182-A. (University Microfilms No. 76-24-976).

Conway, Joan Bonner. The why and how of relationship for the social worker in a health care setting. *Journal of the Otto Rank Association*, Winter 1979/80, 14:2, 40-49.

Dana, Bess. The collaborative process. In Rosalind S. Miller and Helen Rehr (Eds.), *Social work issues in health care*. Englewood Cliffs, NJ: Prentice-Hall, 1983, pp. 181-220.

Ducanis, Alex J. & Golin, Anne K. *The interdisciplinary health care team*. Germantown, Maryland: Aspen Systems Corp., 1979.

Falck, Hans S. Interdisciplinary education and implications for social work practice. *Journal of Education for Social Work*, Spring 1977, 13:2, 30-37.

Goldston, Elaine C. The medical social worker in a clinical team for the occupational evaluation of cardiacs. *Medical Social Work*, May 1952, 1:2, 1-8.

Johnson, Edith M. & Stark, Doretta E. A group program for cancer patients and their family members in an acute care teaching hospital. *Social Work in Health Care*, Summer 1980, 5:4, 335-350.

Kadushin, Alfred. *Consultation in social work*. New York: Columbia University Press, 1977.

Kane, Rosalie A. *Interprofessional teamwork*. Syracuse, NY: Syracuse University School of Social Work, Manpower Monograph #8, 1975. (a)

Kane, Rosalie A. The interdisciplinary team as a small group. *Social Work in Health Care*, Fall 1975, 1:1, 19-32. (b)

Lonsdale, Susan; Webb, Adrian; & Briggs, Thomas L., eds. *Teamwork in the personal social services and health care*. Syracuse, NY: Syracuse University School of Social Work, Manpower Monograph #14, 1980.

Mercer, Susan O. & Garner, J. Dianne. Social work consultation in long-term facilities. *Health and Social Work*, May 1981, 6:2, 5-13.

Pelletier, Kenneth R. *Holistic medicine: From stress to optimal health*. New York: Delacorte Press/Seymour Lawrence, 1979.

Purtillo, Ruth. *Health professional/patient interaction*, 2nd ed. Philadelphia: W. B. Saunders Company, 1978.

Rehr, Helen, ed. *Medicine and social work: An exploration in interprofessionalism*. New York: Prodist, 1974.

Reynolds, Mildred M. The role of social workers in medical education: An historical perspective. *Social Work in Health Care*, Winter 1977, 3:2, 187-198.

Rice, Elizabeth P. Teaching of social aspects in schools of public health. *Medical Social Work*, October 1953, 2:4, 148-159.

Rockmore, Myron John. Case work today in a psychiatric setting. A paper read before the National Conference on Social Work. Atlantic City, New Jersey, May 14, 1951.

Savard, Robert J. The social worker's participation in medical social ward rounds. *Medical Social Work*, October 1952, 1:3, 21-33.

Schoenberg, Bernard; Carr, Arthur C.; Peretz, David; & Kutscher, Austin H., eds. *Psychosocial aspects of terminal care*. New York: Columbia University Press, 1972.

Stein, Florence. How can the professions work together in service to individuals? *Medical Social Work*, September 1955, 4:4, 160-170.

Terry, Polly Orr. Clinical social work roles in an integrated, interdisciplinary team: Enhancing parental compliance. *Social Work in Health Care*, Summer 1981, 6:4, 1-15.

Unger, Judith M. Consultation: Capitalizing on hospital social work resources. *Social Work in Health Care*, Fall 1978, 4:1, 31-42.

Watkins, Elizabeth L.; Holland, Thomas P.; & Ritvo, Roger A. Improving the effectiveness of program consultation. *Social Work in Health Care*, Fall 1976, 2:1, 43-55.

7   The Clinical Social Work Role in the Health Field

Introduction

In the first chapter of this book, clinical social work in the health field was placed in historical context and some of the major concepts that shape its practice were examined. Variables that inform clinical social work in health settings and provide structure for its practice were explored in other chapters. A synthesis of knowledge from social work's common base and knowledge from the health field was deemed a prerequisite for effective clinical intervention with health clients, and emphasis was given to the centrality of social work purpose in the clinician's work with and on behalf of clients.

In this final chapter, clinical social work in health settings is once again placed in context, with focus this time on components of the clinical role and functions discharged by the health social worker in that role. Emphasis is given to research as a component of the clinical social work role and its importance for the future.

Role Components and Functions

It is often useful to take something apart in order to examine its parts and to determine how they relate to one another. In social work, this procedure has been helpful in identifying various roles carried by members of the profession and in determining how each role relates to the achievement of social work goals. Such analysis is also helpful in defining the functions inherent in each role and in factoring out the knowledge and skills required to discharge those functions effectively. A danger lies, however, in the tendency to define roles in terms of discrete functions and to classify social work practice accordingly.

145

While it may be possible, in some settings, to identify social workers who assume roles defined in terms of only one function, difficulties can arise if it is assumed that professional practice is generally defined according to discrete functions. In most health settings, roles are seldom defined this way. Rather, functions merge and flow as the needs and goals of clients, institutions, and professional practice in the health field dictate. Consistent with this reality, such activities in health social work as planning, consulting, evaluating, advocating, educating, enabling, and research are not defined here as discrete roles, but rather as components of the clinical role. As such, they indicate functions inherent in the clinical role and are professional membership attributes of the social work clinician.

The purpose of this book has been to examine, in some detail, selected aspects of the clinical social worker's practice with and on behalf of clients on a case-by-case basis. Not all of the social work clinician's practice in the health field is defined on this basis, however. Indeed, a committee on staffing patterns of the Society for Hospital Social Work Directors identified 19 functions discharged by hospital social workers in the clinical role. These functions are summarized in Table 7.1. They suggest the breadth of the clinical role in the health field and can be generalized to apply to settings other than the hospital. For purposes of clarity, and with only slight modification, however, they are presented in the table as they were reported by the Society's Committee on Staffing Patterns.

Many of the functions listed in Table 7.1 have been considered in preceeding chapters; others have not. Those that have been considered can properly be regarded as "the heart" of the clinician's practice. These functions include those directly related to work with particular clients, such as psychosocial evaluation and intervention, case consultation to hospital staff, and facilitation of the use of services by clients. Other functions, such as program consultation to hospital staff and community agencies, community service and community health planning, require further clarification and conceptualization as components of the clinician's practice. The attainment of such clarity and conceptualization remains part of health social work's unfinished business.

In addition, it seems that the particular constellation of functions, their relative importance, and how they are discharged may vary from one health setting to another. In acute care hospitals, for example, where the length of service is often very short, where the one-client method may predominate, and where only one face-to-face client/clinician interaction may be the norm, the information and referral function may be of greater importance than it is in other settings where the length of service is longer and the nature of the client/clinician interaction is different. Such differ-

TABLE 7.1 Components of the Clinical Role in Hospital Social Work

Function	Description
Case finding or social risk screening	Identification of patients potentially in need of social work services through a structured, ongoing, outreach program; arrangement for the provision of those services.
Preadmission planning	Exploration of and help with patient/family problems directly related to planning and arranging for hospital admission.
Psychosocial evaluation	The gathering of information about the patient/family's social, psychological, cultural, financial, and other membership situations and utilizing this data for a psychosocial assessment and treatment plan or formal report.
Psychosocial intervention	Helping the patient/family to deal with their situation more effectively, as their situation relates to health and medical care.
Financial assistance	Identification of the need for, and facilitation of the use by the patient/family of financial or other tangible aid provided directly by the hospital social work department, e.g., transportation assistance, medications, prosthetic devices.
Case consultation to hospital staff	Use of structured meetings, on an individual or team basis, to provide specialized knowledge to other health care personnel about the patient/family's psychosocial situation, difficulties with institutional procedures, or problems in using services.
Facilitating use of hospital services	Assumption of an advocacy role within the hospital in behalf of the patient/family with all pertinent departments and hospital personnel.
Health education	The enhancement of patient/family knowledge through a structured program designed to provide factual knowledge to patients and families, e.g. family planning, birth control, sickle cell anemia, alcoholism.

(continued)

147

TABLE 7.1 (continued)

Function	Description
Discharge planning	Exploration of patient/family problems directly related to post hospital care and planning and arranging for that care in order to consolidate gains made during hospitalization.
Information and referral	The provision of information to the patient/family about the types of community resources available; connection of the patient/family with pertinent resources.
Facilitation of community agency referrals	Assistance beyond information to ensure patient/family access to appropriate resources, e.g. completion of applications on behalf of the patient/family; conferences and visits to community agencies on behalf of or with the patient/family; representation of the patient/family to community agencies; escorting the patient/family to the community agency.
Case consultation to community agencies	Use of structured meetings to provide specialized knowledge to the health care personnel of an outside agency regarding the psychosocial situation and problems of a patient/family active with the outside agency.
Utilization review	Participation in the formal concurrent review process of the hospital related to Professional Standards Review Organization requirements.
Research	Study of the psychosocial factors of patient/family care and needs; use of a structured system of review of the clinican's own practice, the quality of services provided by the social work department as part of the hospital's and the department's patient care evaluation and peer review program.
Program consultation to hospital staff	Assessment of patient/client population to determine unmet needs; investigation and channeling of information about patient/client care problems to appropriate departments; identification and recommendation

(continued)

TABLE 7.1 (continued)

Function	Description
	of needed changes in hospital policy and procedure as related to patient/family rights.
Hospital planning	Involvement in the structured activities and mechanisms of the institution related to short- and long-term planning and program development, including outreach and community services.
Program consultation to community agencies	Use of structured meetings to provide specialized knowledge to community institutions.
Community service	Representation of the hospital to the community on matters pertaining to social work; participation in community groups in carrying out appropriate programs.
Community Health Planning	Working in the community with its agencies to develop needed programs and to identify community resources to meet patient/family needs.

Adapted from George Krell, Gary Rosenberg, Robert Spano, and Robert Stepanek. *Staffing Patterns Committee Final Report.* Chicago: Society for Hospital Social Work Directors of the American Hospital Association, 1981, pp. 4–8.

ences require further specification and their implications for refinement of the clinical role in particular health settings require further exploration.

It will be noted that Table 7.1 does not include functions of the administrative social work role. Clinical and administrative roles are generally conceptualized separately in health settings, although in some instances the same person may fill both roles. In small hospitals, for example, it is not uncommon for the director of social work to also provide clinical services to patients/clients. In large hospitals, on the other hand, clinical social workers often carry responsibility for supervising others. Moreover, clinical social workers in the health field are frequently promoted to administrative positions. Thus, although the clinical and administrative roles are conceptually distinct, their relationship is both intimate and immediate. Historically, however, the health social work administrator has received far less attention than has the health social work clinician, and the components of health social work administrative practice, its knowledge base, and skill requirements, await further explication and refinement.

Clinical social work in the health field is dynamic and multidirectional. It includes a number of functions, not all of which are defined by the direct delivery of services to clients on a case-by-case basis. This point is made clearly in Table 7.1 which places the clinical social work role in the health field fully within the mainstream of professional social work practice.

We Build on Firm Foundations

In relating the history of health social work's emergence and development, Cannon (1952) noted that the early leaders in the field built their practice "on firm foundations." For more than three quarters of a century, health social workers have labored to strengthen and expand those foundations. The fruits of their labors can be discerned in the ever-widening range of health and medical settings where social workers practice and in the dramatic increase in the number of professional social workers employed in the field. In these efforts, health social workers have been distinguished by their use of statistical analysis and scientific methods of study.

Cannon's first book (1913) on hospital social service suggests the use early hospital social workers made of statistical data in many phases of their practice. In 1922, only four years after its formation, the American Association of Medical Social Workers established a Committee on Functions to "find out what the facts of practice were" (Stites, 1955, p. 68). Another indicator of early efforts to generate knowledge through systematic study occurred in 1927 when Hamilton reported the results of a study to classify social casework in hospitals and clinics.

It was the Association's Committee on Functions, however, that provided the major impetus for the scientific examination of health social work practice during these early years. Under the Committee's auspices, a series of studies were planned and implemented which not only advanced knowledge for health social work, but ultimately contributed to the knowledge base of the whole profession (Committee on Functions, 1930; Bartlett, 1934, 1940; Thornton, 1937).

Not all of the Association's efforts were focused on large-scale research projects. Through case competitions, the Association also encouraged its members to study and record their own practice in a systematic way. Some of the winning records of these competitions were published (Breckenridge, 1928), in part to provide teaching materials, but also to facilitate the examination, comparison, and criticism of "agreed upon methods used with satisfactory results" (p. viii).

While the Association undertook no subsequent studies comparable in depth and scope to those of the 1920s and 1930s, the work continued into the 1940s. Elledge (1948), for example, used Association findings as the basis for her work on patient rehabilitation.

In these early research efforts, focus was on social casework as the primary interventive method. Beginning in the 1950s, however, and continuing for a time into the 1960s, attention turned to the potential use of social group work in the health field (Frey, 1966). This broadening focus followed the formation of the National Association of Social Workers in 1955 and reflected its search for a common base to unify the discrete methods and fields of practice. The study of health social work was an important programmatic aspect of the National Association during its first years (Regional Institute Program, 1966).

Although the passage of time, the proliferation of knowledge, and the advance of technology have rendered the findings from these past studies outdated in many instances, their importance transcends their limitations. These studies reflect the dedication of those who undertook them to the study of practice, the generation of knowledge, and the refinement of practice skill. The professional commitment of the health social workers of the past provides today's practitioners with role models worth emulating, with standards worth attaining, and with a tradition of scientific inquiry worth pursuing. Lest it be said that the tasks before the health social workers of yesteryear were less complex than those faced by health social workers today, it should be remembered that they developed their roles and pursued their tasks without the array of research methods, statistical packages, and technological apparatuses at the disposal of today's practitioners.

That health social workers continue to build on the work of their predecessors can be discerned in several ways. In 1980, for example, the Editorial Committee of *Health and Social Work* undertook a "project to illuminate the infinite variation of social work practice within the health specialization" (Kane, 1981). The New England Regional Study of social work in the medical and surgical units of acute care general hospitals (Berkman, 1977; Berkman and Henley, 1981), is another example of ongoing interest in the study of practice.

Much of the current study of social work practice in the health field remains, however, essentially descriptive in nature and localistic in scope (Coulton, 1980). Although such studies are necessary first steps and should not be underestimated, the need to move the study of practice forward is apparent. The emergence of the single-subject research design, with its individual-control/applied analysis strategy (Howe, 1974), combined with traditional group designs (Jayaratne, 1977), offers opportunities for advancing the study of clinical social work practice in the health field. Berkman and Weissman (1983) identify four kinds of research for which the clinical social worker's own cases are particularly well suited: (1) descriptive studies; (2) process studies; (3) client satisfaction studies; and (4) effectiveness and/or outcome studies (p. 223).

Kane (1980, 1981, 1982) suggests that practice be described in reproducible units. This is a step all health social work clinicians can and should take. It involves describing the context and content of interventions used in particular cases in sufficient detail to make possible their replication by others. When practice is described in reproducible units, it is possible to refine approaches and subject them to empirical tests "to determine the extent of their effectiveness" (Kane, 1980, p. 3).

Health social work clinicians bear a professional responsibility to test the theoretical constructs upon which their practice rests and to provide empirical evidence to support the outcomes they claim their practice yields. The key to moving forward in the study of clinical social work practice in the health field lies not so much in the availability of methods and technology for the study of practice as it does in the need to reconceptualize and reaccept the research function as an integral part of the clinician's social work role. This need remains a major item on health social work's agenda of outstanding business.

The Past as Guide to the Future

In this last quarter of the twentieth century, American social welfare has been shaken by fiscal conservatism, program reorganization, and service retrenchment. Yet, this same period has been one of continued growth for clinical social work in the health field. Despite discernible trends in the direction of change, however, the future remains unknown.

As time moves on, old frontiers recede, immediate horizons contract, and distant ones expand. In this century, for example, medical science has succeeded in eliminating, for the most part, the ancient diseases that have disfigured, maimed, and killed human beings throughout history, only to be confronted by new ones. Thus, the past and present can only provide a tentative basis for glimpsing the future and its dim outlines.

On several things health social workers can depend. The future will bring with it changes in the organization of the health field, in health and medical care, and in social work. That physical illness, disabilty, and injury will remain a part of the future seems certain. That such conditions constitute social as well as medical phenomena has been established. That health social work must revitalize and extend its tradition of systematically studying its practice to meet the demands of the future is clear.

Important variables in the study of practice are the purpose of the profession and its view of people and the human condition. These variables are central to the membership perspective which is applied, for the first time, in these pages to a field of social work practice. Rooted in psychoanalytic object relations theory and symbolic interactionism, in practice experience and observation, and more recently in scientific study, the potential contributions of this perspective derive from its capacity for clarifying and underscoring the profession's purpose, from its dynamic view of people as interactive and interdependent beings, and from its promise for unifying the activities of social work. The membership perspective, however, is still emerging and developing. Its application to social work in health and in other fields requires further refinement and testing.

If health social workers in the past sometimes erred in believing that the experience gained from their daily work with clients was a sufficient basis for their practice, they would be in even greater error in the present if they concluded that such experience is of no value. Experience that is examined yields understanding. From such understanding comes practice wisdom. Practice wisdom, in turn, yields the questions and propositions upon which the systematic study of practice and knowledge building depend.

With these thoughts in mind, the words penned by Cannon more than fifty years ago to end the revised edition (1923) of her first book have special relevance and seem particularly appropriate for bringing the last chapter of this section to a close.

> We must not resist changes, new adaptations, new and deeper evidence of our interdependence with hospital administration, with medical progress and with the growth of social work itself, for we have been counselled by many of our wise guides that "in proportion to our relatedness are we strong." (pp. 219-220)

References

Bartlett, Harriett M. *Medical social work: A study of current aims and methods in medical social case work.* Chicago: American Association of Medical Social Workers, 1934.

Bartlett, Harriett M. *Some aspects of social casework in a medical setting.* Chicago: American Association of Medical Social Workers, 1940.

Berkman, Barbara. New England regional study of social work practice. Massachusetts Social Workers Coalition for PSRO, 1977. (Unpublished data.)

Berkman, Barbara & Henley, Barbara. Medical and surgical services in acute-care hospitals. *Health and Social Work*, November 1981, 6:4, Supplement, 22S-27S.

Berkman, Barbara & Weissman, L. Andrew. Applied social work research. In Rosalind S. Miller and Helen Rehr (Eds.), *Social work issues in health care.* Englewood Cliffs, NJ: Prentice-Hall, 1983, pp. 221-251.

Breckenridge, Sophonisba P., ed. *Medical social case records*. Chicago: University of Chicago Press, Social Service Monographs, 1928.

Cannon, Ida M. *Social work in hospitals: A contribution to progressive medicine*, rev. ed. New York: Russell Sage Foundation, 1923. (Originally published, 1913.)

Cannon, Ida M. *On the social frontier of medicine: Pioneering in medical social service*. Cambridge: Harvard University Press, 1952.

Committee on Functions. *The functions of hospital social service*. Chicago: American Association of Medical Social Workers, 1930.

Coulton, Claudia J. Research on social work in health care: Progress and future directions. In David Fanshel (Ed.), *The future of social work research*. Washington, DC: National Association of Social Workers, 1980, pp. 119-138.

Elledge, Caroline. *The rehabilitation of the patient, social case work in rehabilitation*. Philadelphia: J. B. Lippincott Co., 1948.

Frey, Louise, ed. *The use of groups in the health field*. New York: National Association of Social Workers, 1966.

Hamilton, Gordon. A medical social terminology: Preliminary report of a study in classification and terminology for case work in hospitals and clinics. *Hospital Social Service*, 1927, Vol. 15, 199-233.

Howe, Michael W. Casework self-evaluation: A single-subject approach. *Social Service Review*, March 1974, 48:1, 1-23.

Jayaratne, Srinika. Single-subject and group designs in treatment evaluation. *Social Work Research and Abstracts*, Fall 1977, 13:3, 35-42.

Kane, Rosalie A. Let's describe practice in reproducible units. *Health and Social Work*, May 1980, 5:2, 2-3.

Kane, Rosalie A. Social workers in health: Commonalities and differences. *Health and Social Work*, November 1981, 6:4, Supplement, 2S-8S.

Kane, Rosalie A. Lessons for social work from the medical model: A viewpoint for practice. *Social Work*, July 1982, 27:4, 315-321.

Krell, George; Rosenberg, Gary; Spano, Robert; & Stepanek, Robert. *Staffing patterns committee final report*. Chicago: Society for Hospital Social Work Directors of the American Hospital Association, 1981.

Regional Institute Program. *A research approach to social work practice in health programs*. Social work practice in medical care and rehabilitation settings. New York: National Association of Social Workers, Monograph VIII in the Series, 1966.

Stites, Mary A. *History of the American Association of Medical Social Workers*. Washington, DC: American Association of Medical Social Workers, 1955.

Thornton, Janet. *The social component in medical care*. New York: Columbia University Press, 1937.

Exemplars

8 Characteristics and Concepts of Social Work Practice

The two articles selected for this first group of exemplars represent, in different ways, the fundamental unity of purpose which has characterized the definition, conceptual base, and practice of social work in the health field for more than three-quarters of a century. The history of this development is chronicled in the literature of the field. Part of that literature was published by the American Association of Medical Social Workers. Beginning in 1919, the Association issued, on an irregular basis, a publication called *The Bulletin*. From 1928 to 1949, however, it was issued six times each year. Then, in 1951, the Association began publication of a formal journal, *Medical Social Work*.

The lead article in the new journal was written by Harriett M. Bartlett (1951), a distinguished medical social worker whose major works (1934, 1939, 1940, 1957, 1961a, 1961b, 1970, 1976) and numerous articles span more than half a century. In the lead article, Bartlett traced the development of social work in the health field over time. In one direction, she reviewed that development from its very beginnings to midcentury. In the other, she projected into the future the need for continued development based on sound analysis. Bartlett's stress on the importance of a balanced understanding and application of psychological, social, and cultural factors—a characteristic of clinical social work in the health field—rings true today. The same is true of her conclusions regarding the cyclical nature of periods of stability and change and the need to be aware of transition periods that signal the move from one to the other. Her careful distinctions between the concepts of field, process, skill, and function directed attention to the need for precision in social work thinking, a need that was sometimes ignored in the ensuing years. The seeds of the NASW Working Definition of Social Work Practice (1958) can be discerned in this article.

The first issue of *Medical Social Work* also included an article by Grace White, "The Distinguishing Characteristics of Medical Social Work" (A). It is reprinted here because it suggests the ferment in social work during the transition period of the late 1940s and early 1950s, when attention was directed to the pursuit of professional unity that led to the creation of the two present-day organizational arms of the profession: the Council on Social Work Education and the National Association of Social Workers.

White, while endorsing this move, sounded a note of caution. Her concern lay with the superficiality of answers to key questions and in uncertainty about the outcomes of professional education programs that stress only generic content. White's concerns are not unlike those voiced today in the ongoing debate in social work education about the relative importance of generic and specific content and preparation. Indeed, Kerson's (1979) analysis suggests that White's caution was well-founded, for Kerson asserts that after 1955 medical social work was submerged by the attention given to generic social work. This was clearly an unanticipated consequence of the movement toward professional unity and, in 1976, Bartlett once again called for sustained, disciplined thinking and writing to carry on the building of the profession and the study of social work in the health field.

It was not until the middle 1970s, when social work in the health field reemerged as a clearly recognizable social work specialization, that attention was once more directed to the distinguishing characteristics that White identified. In the second exemplar reprinted here, "Social Work in Health Settings" (B), Hans S. Falck focuses on the distinctiveness of social work's specialized practice in the health field. Like White, he distinguishes between the person as a medical patient and the person as a social work client. His emphasis on the social effects of illness, rather than on illness itself, and on the social basis and nature of assessment and intervention, place this article in the mainstream of health social work as it has developed over the last 75 years.

References

Bartlett, Harriett M. *Medical social work: A study of current aims and methods in medical social case work*. Chicago: American Association of Medical Social Workers, 1934.

Bartlett, Harriett M. *The participation of medical social workers in the teaching of medical students*. Chicago: American Association of Medical Social Workers, 1939.

Bartlett, Harriett M. *Some aspects of social casework in a medical setting*. Chicago: American Association of Medical Social Workers, 1940.

Bartlett, Harriett M. Medical social work today and tomorrow, *Medical Social Work*, September 1951, 1:1, 1–18.

Bartlett, Harriett M. *50 years of social work in the medical setting: Past significance, future outlook*. New York: National Association of Social Workers, 1957.

Bartlett, Harriett M. *Analyzing social work practice by fields*. New York: National Association of Social Workers, 1961. (a)

Bartlett, Harriet M. *Social work practice in the health field*. New York: National Association of Social Workers, 1961. (b)

Bartlett, Harriett M. *The common base of social work practice*. Washington, DC: National Association of Social Workers, 1970.

Bartlett, Harriett M. A professional reminiscence, *Health & Social Work*, February 1976, 1:1, 6–10.

Kerson, Toba Schwaber, Sixty years ago: Hospital social work in 1918, *Social Work in Health Care*, Spring 1979, 4:3, 331–343.

National Association of Social Workers Subcommittee on the Working Definition of Social Work Practice for the Commission on Social Work Practice, Working definition of social work practice, *Social Work*, April 1958, 3:2, 5–8.

A   The Distinguishing Characteristics of Medical Social Work

Grace White

Why an Emphasis on Difference

The aim of this article is to stimulate others in the medical social field and in other fields of social work to identify the specific characteristics of a particular practice of social work. This article will have served well if it arouses others to test these ideas and improve the formulations. It is unlikely that agreement prevails as to the value of such efforts, and emphasis on difference may seem contrary to the current stress on the generic aspects of social work.

The author is of the opinion that accurate identification of the specific characteristics of particular practices may in time help to secure:

Medical Social Work, Vol. 1 (1), September 1951, 31–39. American Association of Medical Social Workers. Copyright 1951. Reprinted by permission of the National Association of Social Workers, Inc.

1. Greater clarification of the common elements in all social work practice.
2. Better understanding of the essential content in social work education.
3. More accurate use of the term "specialization" in social work.
4. Better selection, guidance, and placement of personnel and possibly greater mobility of personnel.
5. More appropriate emphases in staff development, supervision, and research in specific fields.

Trends in the practice of social work and in education for social work give rise to questions which plague us to seek satisfying answers. Among them are the following:

1. What is the common core in social work, the essential content in education for social work? What content will assure a sound foundation for the practice of social work?
2. Is any specific field of practice, such as medical social work, a "specialization?" Is case work a "specialization" in social work? Are "specializations" defined by process, by setting, by major problems, by specific knowledge and skills, or by what combination of these? If medical social work is not a "specialization," is it a specific field of practice? Or a practice with a special focus?
3. Can the graduate schools in a two-year program prepare for a specific field of practice? Is there validity in "accrediting" or "approving" sequences or curricula which aim to prepare for a specific field of practice?
4. Is there validity in classifying positions, as in merit systems and job analyses, that identify a specific field of practice presuming special knowledge and skills? If so, is the result in limited mobility of personnel warranted?
5. In consideration of future registration or licensing methods, is there validity in classifying social workers by designations such as "medical social workers"?
6. Is there validity and wisdom in continuing a membership association that promotes a specific practice of social work and serves a specific field?

The writer is not satisfied with the answers commonly given; they are often conflicting, superficial, or without basis in facts. No doubt the "specialized" aspects have been overstressed in the past and the current tendency to deny or underestimate difference is a natural reaction. However, minimizing differences and emphasizing similarities give a blurred picture of social work, the misleading gray seen by the eye when a color chart is whirled. On the other hand, minimizing similarities and emphasizing differences may show up the strong reds, blues, and yellows with equal distortion.

Relation of Generic and Specific

The generic content of social work, that which is common to all or several fields of practice, is the accumulated contribution from the specific fields of practice. As knowledge and skill in these several fields grow, likenesses are identified; principles are distilled which together make up the generic content of social work. The relationship of specific practice to generic social work may be summed up in the following premises:

1. All social workers share common purposes, responsibilities, knowledge, skills, and philosophy; these constitute the generic aspects of social work.
2. All social work practice is specific; there is no practice of "generic social work."
3. In all social work practice there is a focus on some particular cluster of human needs; basic knowledge and skill must be supplemented by knowledge and skill related to the special needs and setting, and to the process used.
4. In social casework practice, there are more likenesses than differences in the practice in specific fields; but the differences are distinct and identifiable and have significance for social work as a whole as well as for any specific field of social work.
5. As knowledge and skills related to special needs, settings, and processes are developed, shared, and found useful in other specific practices, additions are made to the generic content of social work.
6. The enrichment of the generic content represents growth toward professional maturity; but the profession cannot achieve its desired goals of services and problem-solving if it fails to recognize that special knowledge and skills are necessary for responsible practice in any type of social work, nor if it fails to stimulate and provide for growth in the specific as well as in the generic content.

Medical social workers use all the basic processes of social work in carrying out the full range of functions; likewise, they need all the basic knowledge and skills of social work to carry out these functions responsibly. Thus medical social work shares the purposes, concepts, and philosophy of all social work, though it has more in common with social work practice that uses casework as the major process than with practice that is based on one of the other social work processes. There is, therefore, more similarity in family, child, psychiatric, and medical social work than there is similarity in medical social work and social group work, for example. However, as hospital group work develops as a "treatment-centered program," medical social work and social group work will have more in common than is true currently.

In addition, medical social workers not only speak but think in a second language; i.e., the language of medicine. They share, in common with all who practice in the medical field, basic knowledge about disease, disability, and medical care. They share the purposes and philosophy of the medical programs of which they are a part. They understand medical practice and the hospital as an institution. They are as much at home in the clinical setting as in the social agency.

The Distinctive Characteristics

There is a common tendency to think that casework practiced in a medical setting is synonymous with medical social work. The practice of social casework is the primary function, but medical social work embraces five major functions:[*]

1. Practice of social casework.
2. Participation in program planning and policy formulation within the medical institution.
3. Participation in the development of social and health programs in the community.
4. Participation in the educational program for professional personnel.
5. Social research.

The unique features of medical social work might be stated in terms of problem, setting, and process:

1. It is concerned with the social needs and problems related to illness, physical handicap, and medical care.
2. It is practiced in collaboration with other professional personnel, as an integral part of multidiscipline services in medical settings.
3. It serves as liaison in coordinating the medical and social services of a community.

[*]More explicit information regarding functions is given in "A Statement of Standards To Be Met by Social Service Departments in Hospitals, Clinics, and Sanatoria," American Association of Medical Social Workers, 1949.

The application of generic concepts and skills to a particular problem situation in a specific field yields social work practice which is neither wholly generic nor wholly specific. Careful examination of the knowledge, skills, and theory commonly thought of as specific to medical social work reveals that both generic and specific aspects can be identified. For example, a situation commonly met is the separation of a man from his family and work in order that he may undergo surgery in a hospital. This situation might arise in any caseload in any agency. Generic knowledge and skills would be used by any caseworker in learning the problems of this man and his family, in assessing the resources and strengths to meet the problems as well as the need for services, in determining the desire for and capacity to use social services, and in giving social services. It can be assumed that a competent caseworker in any specific practice could obtain considerable understanding of his needs and would be able to give appropriate social services.

Many factors would affect the extent to which a caseworker in a social agency would enter into this problem and would also affect the nature of the services given. The competence of the worker, the purpose and resources of the agency, the aspects of the situation presented to the agency, the worker's relationship to the client and members of the family, the availability of medical information and of contact with the surgeon— all would influence the degree of understanding attained and the completeness of the services given.

The same case situation referred by the surgeon to the caseworker in the hospital would involve the use of specific knowledge and skills in addition to the generic. The medical social aspects of the situation become the focus of attention. The term connotes the relationship of the two factors. Medical social problems exist when either the medical aspects in a case situation impinge on the social, or the social aspects on the medical, or both. The medical social worker's focus is on the interaction of the two more than on the totality of the medical or the social. This focus on the interaction is consonant with the *purpose* of the medical care program which establishes the boundaries of the medical social worker's function. In other words, social treatment is directed toward those social and emotional conditions which bear upon the medical condition or treatment of the patient. This calls for more technical knowledge than is often achieved by persons outside medical social practice.

The specific *knowledge* that is pertinent is too comprehensive to cover in this article, but the following examples of such knowledge are illustrative:

1. The medical social worker has exact knowledge of the disease entity with its implications for a given patient, the somatic and

psychic aspects, the failure of the organism to function and adjust to the disease, the manifestations (such as pain, bleeding), the probable causes and outlook with and without treatment.

2. The medical social worker comes to know the experience of illness for a given patient, and, within the illness, his reactions to the illness, to hospitalization, to medical recommendations and treatment. The emotional and somatic content of the illness is unique for every individual.

3. The medical social worker has a disciplined awareness of the psychosocial aspects of illness for a given patient. Directly or indirectly, these psychosocial factors affect his reaction to his illness, to the doctor, to the hospital; his response to treatment. In turn, his psychosomatic condition affects, directly or indirectly, his reactions to his social situation.

Again returning to the surgical patient, about whom there has been previous discussion, the caseworker must know the specific meaning of the illness and the recommended surgery to this patient and his family. The medical realities and the personality must be considered in determining, for example, whether the patient's anxiety is a normal emotional reaction which will lessen with a favorable outcome of the operation, or by a suitable adjustment of the fees or by provision for income for his family. His anxiety may be severe, possibly because of reactivation of unconscious fears of punishment and mutilation. He may reject the diagnosis as well as the need for surgery; at the same time he may be unable to handle his reaction to authority comfortably and so be guilty over his hostile feeling toward those who are offering a way out of his suffering.

The understanding of emotions, such as anxiety, fear, and ambivalence, is, of course, generic in social work but dealing with the constellation of emotional factors in the medical social situation calls for technical knowledge which is an essential part of the equipment of the medical social worker.

It is not the purpose of this paper to outline a specific medical social counterpart for each generic concept. The given examples of specific knowledge are suggestive of the method by which the specific might be identified. The tracing would need to be carried into the factors in the setting that influence the casework practice, into the skills that are involved in the collaborative process and into the coordination of the medical and social services, both within the medical setting and in the community.

One example of *skill*, that of participation in the medical team, might suggest further the nature of medical social practice. Again, its ramifications are much broader than can be covered in this article. The ability to participate in team work and cooperative services is a basic skill of social workers. In the medical setting, some characteristic situations prevail that are significant for the team work in the medical setting.

The "client" of the social worker is the "patient" of the hospital. He recognizes a need and identifies at least part of his problem as a medical problem. He comes to a medical agency, seeking the service of the medical profession. Whether or not he has or is aware of social problems related, or apparently not related, to his medical problem, this awareness is not often in the foreground when he seeks medical care. The social services are provided because they contribute to the medical care; they must be focused to fulfill the primary purpose of the hospital.

The social worker comes into the situation in the majority of cases on referral from the doctor, to explore the situation and to give services which the exploration with the patient reveals are pertinent to the medical care. The patient is seeking medical rather than social services and often has to be helped to understand why study and treatment of his "medical" problem is shared by a social worker. It is in this configuration that relationship with the patient must be established by the social worker and that the collaborative process is carried on.

The medical social worker must exercise her responsibility as one of the specialists in the team and must also yield to the expertness and responsibility of all the others in the team. She must understand the historic role of the doctor, and the various cultural patterns in the use of medical care. She must accept the leadership of the doctor as the person who takes ultimate responsibility for the patient's life and health. Further, the medical social worker must adjust the timing of the social study and treatment so that a collaborative process can be carried on with the doctor and/or any other personnel involved in the medical care of the patient. The social services are not independently timed and considered.

Especially demanding of the social worker's skill is her cognizance and her appropriate handling of authority as a member of the team. Patients invest the physician with authority. This concept of authority is a complex one, including the recognition of "expertness" in a field and the attitude of patients toward it is affected by the desire not to submit, and/or the desire to be cared for. The classical role of the physician is that of an authority figure. The responsibilities assumed by physicians and by hospitals in saving life, in preventing contagion, and in caring for seriously ill persons give rise to practices and procedures which are authoritarian in nature. The individual patient's concept of authority and his ability to accept it when necessary and be free of it when appropriate are complicating factors with reference to individual patients.

The social worker must find a way to remain related in the mind of the patient to the medical services because social service is part of the medical care. At the same time she must find a way to divest herself of the authority the patient ascribes to the team; she must be nonauthoritarian, in order to let the patient have freedom to use the services of the social worker and to play out his feelings toward the hospital, toward his illness and the treatment he is receiving. She must be able to go the full way in permitting the patient freedom of choice even to reject treatment. The doctor too must be helped to accept the social worker's way of working in this as in other aspects of her role.

Implications for Education and Practice

Any recognition of the distinguishing characteristics of a specific practice of social work leads to questions regarding educational preparation for that specific practice. Quite understandably, administrators in any specific practice yearn for additional personnel who are well prepared to practice in that field. The natural place to look for good preparation is to the schools of social work. The trend toward greater emphasis on basic education for social work appears, however, to be accepted as desirable by persons in practice as well as by those responsible for educational programs. There persists, nevertheless, a common assumption that the basic educational program will embrace sufficient content which is specific to a practice so that the graduate of tomorrow will be better prepared for the responsibilities inherent in that specific practice. This assumption might well be examined.

The two-year curriculum in a school of social work is hard pressed to include the enriched generic content which has developed in the past decade. Educators must constantly evaluate that which is essential to a sound basic program and, disturbing or no, the reduction or even elimination of certain content from a course or curriculum is often necessary. A valid criterion is that the content will be widely useful to practitioners in all fields of practice. Therefore, in the final analysis, it seems evident that rich generic content will win out over rich specific content.

If it is agreed that practice in a specific field calls for use of generic knowledge, skill, and attitudes, then it seems likely that "the better preparation" will come largely in the generic content and that the outlook from the present trend is good. It becomes clear that the graduate of a school must attain a large measure of his specific knowledge and skill through practice in a specific field. Since a student's field work practice is always in a specific field, there is an opportunity in the two-year educational program to attain a "plus" to the generic content through training in the specific agency chosen for field work, through the elective courses, and through the selection of a subject for individual research. It seems unwise to think of this plus as "preparation for a specific field of practice," but as preparation *toward* a specific field of practice and possibly a test of aptitude.

Acceptance of focus on basic professional preparation in a two-year graduate educational program places the burden for development of "competent" workers in specific fields squarely on programs of staff development and training in each specific field of practice. The implications of this for the field of medical social work need further examination. The specifics of a practice can be learned through trial and error, no doubt, but that is an expensive and inefficient method. The content of the induction period, the emphases in the supervisory process, and the possibilities for group training seem to warrant further study as substantial methods of furthering competence to practice in a specific field.

Social Work in Health Settings

Hans S. Falck

ABSTRACT: The distinctiveness of social work in health settings is that people served are clients rather than patients; that the focus of work is on the social effects of illness, not illness; that problem formulation and intervention rests on clear understanding of social cause, social manifestation, and social intervention as group phenomena.

This paper is primarily, yet not exclusively, addressed to health care social workers. Although it is true that such workers' practice is influenced and guided by the setting in which they work—hospital, clinic, community mental health center, and others—the vicissitudes of such work strongly suggest that they need a clear link also to their profession, its methods, theories, assumptions, and values. Beyond the clear advantages morale-wise lies a great need. That need is to spell out how such work is social work, not only attitudinally but also theoretically and, by extension, practically. The work is not automatically social work because social workers do it. More than that is needed.

It stands to reason as common sense that in a health care setting one needs to learn all one can about the illnesses that afflict the patients. No

Social Work in Health Care, Vol. 3(4), Summer 1978, pp. 395–403. © 1978 by The Haworth Press. All rights reserved.

graduate school can teach more than a small portion of that; most of it is acquired in practice, from colleagues and especially from patients. But what cannot be taught by nonsocial work colleagues is the social work aspect of helping clients who are there because they are patients, too. That part must rely on social workers who can conceptualize the social work role, who spell out the logic and the reasoning of social work, as well as the goals and ideologies of the profession. Each worker can then make his/her own adaptations befitting the work, his ideas and preferences, and, above all, the needs of his clients.

The thesis of this paper is that medical social work will play its most effective role to the extent that medical social workers display and confirm their identity by what they know and by what they can do. In the absence of either or both, university credentials as well as professional credentials (ACSW or licenses) work to the detriment of workers and the profession; and most of all to patients; and lastly, in relation to other professions.

What this paper will not do is to berate social workers. This is not the proper occasion to compare social workers with physicians or other occupational groups. All professions display a whole range of qualities; and there is no evidence to the author's knowledge that any one of them distinguishes itself from all others in its achievements and its failures.

The Problem

Medical social workers are expected and are committed to render social services to hospitalized patients. Much of what is being said here also applies to social workers in mental health settings. The term "medical" is convenient but could to some extent be expanded to cover workers in psychiatric settings, inpatient as well as community mental health. Secondly, medical social workers almost always work as part of treatment groups in which they play but one role. They are expected and are committed to perform as such and usually at a level of unspecified quality.

In the first case, the patient treatment level, the usual assumption is that the social worker, as others, is an assistant to the physician who is in charge of the patient. The patient is "his" patient, and, as is true of other ownership processes, he exercises control over who works with the patient, toward what ends, if indeed he does so at all. A great many social workers either accept this situation as it is because they agree with it, or they submit more or less unwillingly and resignedly, or they rebel and leave. Few rebel and stay. Many develop an interpersonal modus vivendi that satisfies them, the physicians, and other members of the treatment group.

A cursory review of social work journals suggests, however, the changes that are taking place in social work. One of these is the increase in research work, another is the increasing sophistication of social workers in terms of their knowledge, still another their increasing political sophistication which makes them much less willing than heretofore to take orders from nonsocial workers, and fourthly, the opportunity to join the widespread disillusionment with physicians, the quality of medical practice, the increasing costs, and the general reduction of confidence in the medical establishment. Unquestioned reliance on things and persons medical is on the decline, and the opportunity for more equal participation by social workers in medical work is on the increase. Yet, for fear of overstating the brightness of the new sun, it is still true that hierarchy and authority play extraordinary roles in the allocation of personnel and services to patients.

Yet all of this is not enough. The insufficiency in our own argument lies in the fact that social workers continue to function by the leave of others, rather than autonomously, and would thus continue to react rather than act. To be sure, there is an important qualitative difference between being "let" to work with the patient and not being so "let." The hierarchy may be benign or venal, but it is still *hierarchy without collegiality*. That, then, is another way of stating the problem before us. Hierarchy alone results in restricted and constricted practice. Its central feature is the inability to serve the patient in ways deemed qualitatively desirable (if not necessary!) by those best qualified to make judgments about it. In medicine that is the physician; in social service it is the social worker. Yet, when the major emphasis in the administration of treatment is on hierarchical considerations, the tendencies are very pronounced to let power rather than expertise rule, and at that power uninformed (if not antagonistic on ideological or other grounds) to that over which it is exercised. The choice before us is not between administrative or clinical power as such; instead it is that *hierarchy when standing by itself is insufficient to achieve the desired result, namely, services of quality.* All professions teach their students that central to responsible practice is the exercise of autonomous judgment. Autonomous judgment in the professions consists of data collection, informed decision making regarding the meaning of the data, plus decisions about interventions. The word "autonomous" can be taken to mean independent, but it need not be. It can also be taken to imply and mean that workers exercise their functions by the light of their own profession while at the same time exercising their responsibility, that is, with due consideration of the needs, the rights, and the knowledge and skills of others. Autonomy can be conceptualized in the context of others' functions and rights, as well as one's own. That, then, is also how I would define collegiality. It rests on the commitment to let the patient have his multiple needs met. It recognizes that colleagues with different interests, skills, as well as attitudes are able to offer help with the enormous complexities of being both alive and sick. That places great responsibilities on all members of the treatment group. A corollary to the thesis with which the paper began is that physicians (as others) will play their most effective role to the extent that they display and confirm their identity by what they know and by what they can do. The mutual recognition of the universal validity of that statement is both the basis for true teamwork and for autonomous practice. *One does not confirm one's competence by attempting to practice what one does not know or by exercising non-collegial control over functions not one's own.*

The Nature of Social Work in Medical Settings

Rather than list all the functions social workers perform in medical settings, it will be more useful (if not more instructive) to talk about the logic of social work. The assumption is that one can identify the underlying logical structure of many activities considered part of social work, and that one can also suggest generalizations that could be studied further to see whether or not they stand the test of experience. The identification of logical structure enables us to find integrative principles which, in turn, make it possible to view the work holistically rather than episodically, or in terms of single events. The systematic application of principles or generalizations also has the virtue of defining what makes for a profession.

Not all structures are logical. For example, it seems illogical to define groups in the language of personality. To cite one example, groups are sometimes said to "feel," or they are said to "resist." Groups are at times described as possessing an unconscious. All these are terms not made to explain collectivities. One author suggests that social workers mediate between clients and society (Schwartz, 1961, 1976). He never explains what he means by the implication of "mediate," that is, to be located "between." How is one to take that when we are not really told? Could one not just as well—and probably more logically—argue that by virtue of people's interdependence all are members of society; and that social problems arise precisely *because* we are all members and yet not treated fairly, or evenly, or justly? Or, for that matter, how can one expect to help professionally if the prerequisite be that one stands not as *part of* but outside (if indeed that were imaginably possible) of the society we wish to change? These considerations are not mere word quibbles; they go to heart of how we think, by what logic, and from where come our claims to goal, competence, function, and method. When we make single cause statements about groups, we fail to understand the complexities of human networks. *When social workers in medical settings conceptualize their clients as patients they imply that they treat illness; but that also prevents them from doing what they ought to be doing, namely, to maximize their functioning abilities in their social situation.* That social situation may be concomitant with illness but it is not the same, so that in one sense people are patients and in the other (social work) they are clients who are ill. The latter, then, is a consequence of the illness (for example, unemployment, loss of pay, compromised self-esteem), but it is not illness treated by social workers.

I said in another context (Falck, 1977) that social workers who can diagnose in a social work way declare their competence by taking responsibility for reasoned judgment, and by devising intervention plans. I believe that this is the heart of the issue for medical social work as for all other social work. The statement is intended to point to the heart of the issue of disciplinary (and therefore interdisciplinary) practice. Thus viewed, interdisciplinary practice is also seen as a variant of disciplinary practice. If one does not know his discipline, he has nothing to be interdisciplinary about!

Disciplinary Social Work

I should like to begin this section with a listing of what I believe to be the essential aspects of social work logic, and therefore social work practice:

1. The problems to which social workers address themselves are social in nature and encompass a high degree of probability that they can be alleviated by changes in social arrangements. *Social* means that their causes have to do with behavior involving more than one person, both present and future. *Arrangement* means action(s) by several persons in relation to each other.
2. The method of problem alleviation and resolution is social, that is, persons acting in relation to each other such that the outcomes are more desirable than the conditions giving rise to the requirement for help. Participants in that process are client(s) and social worker. It should be noted that in a situation that is social there are frequently clients, namely, in group work, in family work, in institutions, *who help each other* and therefore also themselves.
3. The social worker brings the resources available to him, and it is part of his function to make these available to his clients through the way both clients and workers employ them. The following is a list of such resources:

a. Knowledge of human life and development in general terms, that is, what is common to most people.
b. Knowledge about the particular client(s) in the specific situation (problem) under discussion.
c. Specific skills (and techniques) assumed applicable to this situation, and based on past experiences with others.
d. The worker's ability to control the quality of his performance by self-observation in action, related to ongoing awareness of what is happening to the client(s) in the process of being helped.
e. The ability of both client(s) and social worker to evaluate the results of their mutual work.

All these dimensions are descriptive of social work practice. They explain why social workers are necessary in health settings.

I think it is necessary now to say more about the use of the term *social*. It is obvious that the word has become so all-inclusive that it is difficult to render it specific meaning. That becomes clear when one considers that it is used for everything from what happens in any given family or other group to vast problems such as unemployment and poverty, to say nothing of mental illness. From the vantage point of its most general use, everyone and anyone who addresses social concerns would be doing social work. It would include schoolteachers and policemen, welfare workers and top-level government officials. The need exists, therefore, to delimit the use of the term—at least for social work purposes—where it stands somewhat apart from its most general meaning in order to communicate with some degree of precision. This can be accomplished in two ways. The first of these is by problem conceptualization and the second by problem resolution. But even then we will not be totally satisfied, and we will be unconvincing that only social workers deal with social problems and through social work methods. We shall be unable to claim uniqueness (or monopoly) of function even in the doubtful case that this were desirable.

1. A problem is conceptualized as social when by cause or effect more than one person would experience gain or loss by its nature, its consequences, or its resolution.
2. The work is considered social work when methods of problem resolution (or alleviation) are utilized that emphasize *the behaviors of people toward each other* as means toward the achievement of desired results. This includes the reciprocal behavior of workers and clients, as well as clients among themselves.

The fact that most social workers view social problems as social is not to be taken too lightly, although it is self-evident to social workers themselves. We do live in a society, after all, that holds the ideal of individualism in very high esteem, as well as in one beset by profound doubts about the collective responsibility for the poor, for children, for minorities. Individual achievement is as important to social workers as to other Americans, and a mature view of communalism is largely absent in American society to this very day. Torn by dissent, philosophically and politically, it should hardly be surprising to read that even in the "people" professions there is little understanding of the relation of person and community, that is, the meaning of *social* (Falck, 1969, 1971, 1973, 1976).[1] Of particular importance in this connection, and particularly to psychiatric and medical social workers, is the strong inclination to think and talk of patients as having "the social environment" as if it were something outside of them, as an additional consideration regarding a personally held illness. That may be true in the medical tradition. I submit that it has no place in a social work view. From a social work standpoint illness is not a medical event; it is a social event. The members of the patient's social context are as affected by the person's illness as they are by all else he/she does. They are affected, they are responsible, their lives are influenced by it, they in turn influence the course and often the nature of illness: the situation is social, the event is social, the intervention is social. All of this defines and spells out our social work values, which deny American individualism, in its isolating forms; and they acclaim the interdependence of man, not only as ideal but as scientifically demonstrable fact. My reading of the social work ethic says that social work believes in the sacredness of *the person in the social context*, rather than in individualism apart from it, or at most marginally related to it. That is how and why illness is a social event, perhaps not even really illness as social work would see it, but social dysfunction along with or in addition to illness. It is also the place where our values and our knowledge merge, yet are clearly identifiable. From a social work standpoint, I submit, the needful unit is always a group (the meaning of social), although it is also true that the medical and psychiatric worker may talk with one person at a time. But what they talk about, what they focus on, what is of the essential concern is the person as part of others. That is a social view as I see it, and I recommend it in this context in order to delineate what social—irreducibly—ought to be about. The term "irreducibly," to emphasize my point further, means that man as part of the social context is not a part that one puts in and takes out, as it were, but that he is to be seen as individuated within the social situation, not separated from it and individualized.

[1]The author's main points have to do with viewing individuation as a result of and a contributor to groupness, referred to as the individuality-groupness (I-G) effect, rather than continuing to distinguish between individual and group.

It would be beyond the scope of a single paper to elucidate at length the linkages between social man and psychological man, or the relation of sociological and psychodynamic thought. Various attempts have been made in that effort (Falck, 1976; Parsons, 1958; Pollak, 1956). I shall confine myself here to a brief consideration of psychodynamically oriented work in a social framework.

Every helping (or therapeutic) interaction is social, simply because it presupposes two or more people, active in some relationship to each other. What makes it *social* or *psychological* (it is always both anyway) is the problem conceptualization which emphasizes the one more than the other. When the emphasis is primarily psychological the work is conceptualized as reflecting how by use of the client's personality he/she experiences himself/herself, and presumably, how modification in personality dimensions would lead to different and presumably more satisfying behavior. Social work is problem solution, both in the conceptualization of it as social and, therefore, in its method. It emphasizes not what the personality produces, but the options (choices) clients have that are realistically available in order to cope (behave) more effectively. *The test in both personality- and behavior-oriented work is more desirable behaving.* It is not in whether one or the other is better or deeper. It lies in what is needed by the patient and what works. Deeper is not always better, and coping more efficiently may engage so much energy and spell so many difficulties for the client that it would often be far better to try a more psychiatrically centered approach. There need be no conflict, therefore, between social workers, psychologists, and psychiatrists when the issue is viewed from the standpoint of resource availability. The problems arise primarily over power, domination, and envy. They are pushed under the rug when role blurring takes the place of making multiple methods and resources available.

The discussion, then, leads back to a logical extension of the concept *social* as here given. That in turn suggests that the medical concept *patient* (in distinction to Parsons' sick role formulation) ought to be revised to client. Client has the advantage of being consistent with the rest of social work, resolves the confusion over whether nonmedical people "treat" patients, clarifies that social workers help clients cope socially by invoking the client's family and/or other social structures, and thereby *dampen the individualistic bias that underlies everything from medicine to education, social work, religion, and business.*

Medical and psychiatric social work should come to terms with the fact, as I see it, that the central logic of its work is social, that is, group-related. This does not suggest that "one-to-one" work is not as legitimate as it ever was, but that the point of view workers bring to it is determined by the individuality-groupness dimension which irreducibly describes man to social workers.

I think that the educational implications of this intellectual attitude need to be spelled out, but not in this piece. May it be sufficient to point out that they lie primarily in the area of how man is viewed psychologically and sociologically, and by derivation how this affects the formulation of intervention theory.

Conclusions

The concept *social* has its own logic in both problem conceptualization and in intervention management. It is the central intellectual building block for social work practice. It does not need to stand in conflict with other approaches, either in problem conceptualization or in methodology of helping. Social work and social workers are defined as persons committed intellectually, attitudinally, and methodologically to the understanding and practice of social intervention.

If the tone of this article is "editorial," this is my intention. There are issues where the facts should lead one to suggest, also, how they ought to be changed.

References

Falck, H. S. Thinking styles and individualism. *Bulletin of the Menninger Clinic*, 1969, *33*(3).

Falck, H. S. Individualism and the psychiatric hospital system. *Bulletin of the Menninger Clinic*, 1971, *35*(1).

Falck, H. S. Magic in the perception of the self-made man. *Menninger Perspective*, 1973, *4*(6).

Falck, H. S. Individualism and communalism: Two or one? *Social Thought*, Summer 1976.

Falck, H. S. Interdisciplinary education and its implications for social work practice. *Journal of Education for Social Work*, 1977, *13*(2).

Parsons, T. Social structure and the development of personality: Freud's contribution to the integration of psychology and sociology. *Psychiatry*, 1958, *21*(4).

Pollak, O. *Integrating sociological and psychoanalytic concepts*. New York: Russell Sage Foundation, 1956.

Schwartz, W. The social worker in the group. *Social Welfare Forum 1961*. New York: Columbia University Press, 1961.

Schwartz, W. Between client and system: The mediating function. In R. W. Roberts & H. Northen (Eds.), *Theories of social work with groups*. New York: Columbia University Press, 1976.

9 Aspects of Clinical Social Work Practice

The three articles in this group of exemplars deal with various aspects of clinical social work process in health settings. The importance of a sound knowledge base to that process was outlined in Chapter 2; Judith Poole considers breast cancer and mastectomy within a format that follows the approach explicated in that chapter. Her article, "Mastectomy: Its Effects on Interpersonal Relationship" (C), reflects professional concern with social functioning in relation to a medical event. In addition, her discussion of the patient/client's reaction suggests the concepts of object introjection and symbolization.

Membership factors are apparent in Poole's exploration of the responses of the patient/client and her significant others to the events. She notes that the diagnosis of breast cancer and the mastectomy constitute crises, not only for the woman who experiences them, but for her family and friends as well. Perceptions of breast cancer and mastectomy may cause the victim to become secretive, thereby arousing the suspicions of others. Family members and friends attempting to help the woman cope with depression over the diagnosis and surgery may develop a sense of guilt and depression of their own if they perceive themselves as unable to help. Death fantasies and problems in the relationships of siblings may occur. Fear, anxiety, and perceptions of inadequacy may lead to psychosomatic reactions in the woman's male partner. These, in turn, may contribute to a deterioration of their relationship. Poole's discussion of these and other possibilities underscores the fact that adverse health conditions are social events which impact and disrupt the lives and abilities of people to manage their social memberships.

Poole concludes her article with a discussion of the implications of the findings from her study for clinical social work practice. Thus, she demonstrates how the study framework outlined in Chapter 2 can be used to organize knowledge and develop understanding with reference to a particular health condition, its treatment, and impact on the patient/client and her significant others. The organization of such knowledge is the precondition for effective clinical practice in health settings.

Despite frequent reference to the concept of process in the generic practice literature of social work, it has received little attention in the literature of health social work. In part, this lack of attention may reflect a common tendency among social workers to use the terms *method* and *process* interchangeably, for the notion of process is implied in most formulations of social work methods.

The close association of process with the concept of function may also be a factor. Both concepts were central to the initial formulation of functional social work theory (Taft, 1962) which, when it first appeared in 1937, represented a sharp departure from the mainstream of social work theory development. Most health social work writers of that period were within the mainstream, which emphasized the derivation of social work theory from Freudian psychoanalytic concepts. In contrast, with few exceptions (Gilbert, 1937; Cressman, 1944; Rappaport, 1964), emphasis in the development of functional theory was given to fields of social work other than health (Taft, 1943, 1944, 1946), and it was not until more recent years that the contributions of functional theory were recognized and incorporated into the mainstream of social work theory development.

"The Beginning Process in Medical Social Work" (D), by Jeanette Hertzman and Rachel Wyman, is, therefore, somewhat unique in its attempt to apply the concept of process to clinical social work in the health field. Because it was written in an earlier period, the close association of the concepts of process and function is apparent. As reprinted here, the more dated medical content in the article has been edited out so that the relevance of its basic thrust to present-day practice is more apparent. In the final analysis, the principles with which Hertzman and Wyman work are at peace with time and represent a useful starting point for the exploration of current clinical social work process in health settings.

Considering the importance of the concept of relationship in the practice of clinical social work, both historically and presently, the lack of specific attention to this concept in health social work literature is even more surprising than the neglect of process. Although present in some form in most formulations of health social work practice, Conway (1979–80) is one of the few health social workers to select out the concept of relationship for the specific exploration of health social work practice at various levels, that is, administration, supervision, clinical, education.

In "Mental Retardation: A Family Crisis—The Role and Function of the Social Worker" (E), Hans S. Falck does, however, address many of the dimensions of relationship in clinical social work in health settings. In his description of the role and function of social work in this particular health specialty, he identifies relationship qualities that are shared by families confronted by mental retardation and by clients and social workers in their mutual efforts to deal with the impact of mental retardation on client abilities to function effectively in community with others. Throughout this selection, Falck's discussion of relationship connections and qualities echoes the concept of membership, which he later developed.

References

Conway, Joan Bonner. The why and how of relationship for the social worker in a health care setting, *Journal of The Otto Rank Association*, Winter 1979-80, 14:2, 40-49.

Cressman, Edith M., ed. *Functional case work in a medical setting*. Philadelphia: The Pennsylvania School of Social Work, 1944.

Gilbert, Dorothea. The dilemma of medical social work, *Journal of Social Work Process*, 1937, 1:1, 127-147.

Rappaport, Mazie F. The introduction of a new service into an on-going program— A professional adventure in process, *Journal of Social Work Process*, 1964, Vol. XIV, 99-116.

Taft, Jessie. The relation of function to process in social case work. In Virginia P. Robinson (Ed.), *Jessie Taft, Therapist and social work educator: A professional biography*. Philadelphia: University of Pennsylvania Press, 1962, pp. 206-226. (Originally published, *Journal of Social Work Process* 1:1 (1937), 1-18.)

Taft, Jessie, ed. *Day nursery care as a social service*. Philadelphia: Pennsylvania School of Social Work, 1943.

Taft, Jessie, ed. *A functional approach to family case work*. Philadelphia: University of Pennsylvania Press, 1944.

Taft, Jessie, ed. *Counseling and protective service as family case work: A functional approach*. Philadelphia: University of Pennsylvania Press, 1946.

C Mastectomy: Its Effects on Interpersonal Relationships

Judith Poole

Introduction

The subject of this article is the female breast cancer victim who has had a mastectomy. The lives of a great number of women are touched by breast cancer. Nearly 25 percent of the total population of American women will eventually contract one of its forms (Schain, 1977). Abnormalities of the breast are the greatest cancer death threat to American women over the age of 35 (Schoenberg and Carr, 1971). Just as important, mastectomy affects the woman's social relationships and the quality of her life.

It is assumed that there are fears and problems related to the mastectomy that are not medical in nature. Some women may feel a loss of femininity and self-esteem. The woman's partner may also develop psychosocial problems that can lead to a breakdown of the relationship. Thus, while interpersonal relationships with significant others are of importance, primary focus here is given to the female/male relationship following surgery. Even though only one partner has undergone surgery, it is assumed that the psychosocial concerns of both are important and a healthy adjustment is dependent upon the attitudes of both.

A review of the literature published between 1970 and 1980 was undertaken to determine whether there is support for these assumptions. Material published by the American Cancer Society (1979) was consulted for biomedical information and other sources were consulted to supplement this material. Based on this review, implications for social work practice were drawn.

The Nature of the Disease

Cancer is a group of diseases caused by the uncontrolled growth and spread of abnormal cells. Under normal circumstances, body cells reproduce themselves in a way that insures growth. When cells grow into a mass of tissue, a tumor is formed. Tumors may be benign or malignant.

Benign tumors do not spread to surrounding tissue and are not life-threatening though they may require surgical removal. Malignant tumors

Published with the permission of the author.

destroy normal surrounding tissue and may result in death unless their growth is stopped.

A tumor can be located anywhere in the breast but is usually found in the upper outer portion. From there it can spread to the lymph nodes in the armpit, neck, chest, and can be carried through the bloodstream to other parts of the body.

Incidence

Breast cancer is considered the greatest cancer threat to the American woman. In 1980, about 109,000 new cases were predicted, 36,000 of which would be fatal (Bard and Sutherland, 1979). Women over 35 years of age are considered high risk, but it is not uncommon to find breast cancer among teenage girls.

Signs and Symptoms

The American Cancer Society (1979) has been conducting cancer research since 1959 hoping to find a cure, but also providing data for prevention. Any noticeable change in the breast should be enough to alert a woman to the possibility of breast cancer. The discovery of a lump, nipple discharge, swelling, redness, and skin irritations are indications of a possible abnormality. When any one or a combination of these signs are present, a physician should be seen immediately.

Diagnosis

The disease can be diagnosed by a physician in several ways. Mammography can detect tumors too small to be found by self-examination. Mammography uses low-dose X-rays to evaluate breast tissue. Xeroradiography is another type of X-ray used to detect breast cancer. Thermography, which shows heat patterns on the skin, can indicate the presence of cancer, but it is not reliable in certain stages. Biopsy is the excision of a piece of tissue from a living body for diagnostic study to determine if a malignancy is present.

Treatment

Surgery is considered the most effective treatment method, although radiation therapy and chemotherapy can be combined with surgery for good results. When a tumor is operable, a biopsy is necessary to determine if a malignancy is present. Depending on the results, on type and stage of the cancer, additional surgery may be necessary.

In all three types of mastectomies, the breast is removed. In a modified radical, the lymph nodes are also removed. A radical mastectomy includes removal of the breast, lymph nodes, and underlying muscles.

High Risk Factors

Of the 46 countries studied by Strax (1975), the United States ranks twelfth in breast cancer death rates. The highest numbers are found in Northern Europe, Israel, and Canada. There are fewer deaths in South America and Africa, while the risk in Oriental and Asian countries is one-sixth that in the United States.

Among ethnic groups, Strax found that black women and Puerto Rican women are less likely to have breast cancer than white women. The highest incidence is found among Jewish women, especially those in the upper economic brackets.

Strax cites data gathered by the American Cancer Research which suggest certain factors that affect the frequency of breast cancer. Age is important. The older a woman gets, the more likely she is to have breast cancer. Women whose mothers, sisters, or aunts have had the disease are also at a higher risk. There is a higher frequency of the disease among women who have never given birth. Recent findings suggest that a full-term birth prior to the mother's twentieth birthday increases her protection against breast cancer.

Psychosocial Reactions

It is not denied that mastectomy is life-saving. A woman's gratitude, however, may be tainted by the price she must pay to save her life—loss of the breast and disfigurement.

At present in American culture, a woman's breasts are critical to her identity and self-concept. Americans have been socialized to believe that there is great value in feminine beauty, of which the breasts are symbolic (Schain, 1977). Because of this view, a mastectomy carries a significant psychosocial threat.

There is concurrence in the literature that in America, female identification is symbolized by the size and shape of the breast (Schoenberg and Carr, 1971). It has been said that a woman's sexual attractiveness to a man is dependent upon her breasts (Bard and Sutherland, 1979).

Generally, mastectomy leaves a woman with a sense of mutilation and raises her fears. There is a natural anxiety that is associated with any surgery and the ever-present fear of death. With breast surgery, there are fears about the loss of the breast, concern over one's sex appeal, and concern about sexual relations and marriage.

The amputation of a breast leaves a woman with one remaining breast, a constant reminder of her loss. Body symmetry is disrupted. Asken (1975) found that this can produce ambivalence. Great psychological importance may be attached to the remaining breast—the sign of motherhood, femininity, and sexuality. It is, however, not thought of as stimulating when next to a mastectomy scar and few doctors permit it to be used for breast feeding. Ultimately, there is the fear of recurrent cancer.

For some women, the loss is similar to the loss of a loved one through death (Schoenberg and Carr, 1971). The stages of denial, depression, anger, acceptance, and resolution can be seen in the mastectomy patient as well as in the dying person (Wabrek, et al., 1979). These are normal reactions and part of the struggle in regaining self-worth.

Loss of Femininity and Self-Esteem

A woman's psychological adjustment is closely aligned with her individual self-concept. Some writers (Joiner and Fisher, 1979; Bard and Sutherland, 1979) suggest that the value of the lost breast will depend on the basis of the woman's self-esteem. To what extent is her self-acceptability based on her appearance? If her primary means of relating to others has been through physical attractiveness, then the removal of a breast may seriously impair one of her basic ways of relating to others. As perceived by the woman herself, her body has been marred, leaving her unacceptable to herself and to others. Self-worth and self-acceptance for such women is predicated on body image. To lose a most prized physical possession damages feminine pride and shakes the foundation of feminine identification. The primary emotional response to breast cancer is not so much the fear of death as it is the shock of the threat to the female role (Polivy, 1977).

Mastectomy changes a woman's value system, looks, self-image, and life style. This hypothesis has been investigated and the literature clearly indicates a decline in body image and total self-esteem following mastectomy (Gadpaille, 1975; Polivy, 1977; Ray, 1977). Pfefferbaum (1977/78) even found that some women experience such a profound loss of femininity that suicide is seriously considered. It is not uncommon for mastectomy victims to increase their intake of tranquilizers and alcohol following breast removal.

The fears the married woman experiences are multiplied in the un-attached woman. These women are said to feel doomed, all chances of marriage are seen as forfeited because of their appearance (Witkin, 1979).

Impact on Significant Others

It almost goes without saying that the problems a woman might have in accepting the loss of a breast stem from her fears of how others will respond to her after surgery. A woman must know how to cope, not only with herself, but with the reactions of others to her surgery. It is known that family members experience as much of a crisis as the patient herself (Joiner and Fisher, 1979). Bard and Sutherland (1979) found that some women were reluctant to engage in any activity that required close contact with others, such as shopping or traveling, because of feeling socially unacceptable.

Woods (1975) reflected on the fact that some women become secretive about their surgery and try to hide it from the community. This, in turn, gives the community reason to view her with suspicion, and the cycle continues and worsens.

It is the family who carries the greatest share of the psychosocial burden during the recovery period. In the postoperative period, depression is common and family members must cope with the depression while attempting to be supportive to the woman. Often, family members feel guilty or become depressed themselves over their inability to cheer up the woman (Nuehring and Barr, 1980).

Younger children may be plagued by fantasies of death stemming from their understanding of the mastectomy itself. They may not understand their mother's emotional state and may develop problems of their own, for example, in school (Asken, 1975).

Studies of psychodynamic factors (Schain, 1977) indicate difficulties in mother-daughter relationships following surgery. Teenage and adult daughters who fear for themselves find relating to their mothers during this time to be a strain.

Much attention has been given to the spouse's reaction to the scar itself, but other family members need to be desensitized to it as well. If revulsion is what other family members experience, feelings of guilty conflict may well follow (Nuehring and Barr, 1980).

Certain roles may change as the children and/or husband assume the role of caretaker and these changes, in turn, may reinforce the woman's role as invalid. There are also practical realities which the family must face. There may be sizable medical expenses to be met during a time when there may also be a loss of income. If the woman is the family's main breadwinner, this can result in further family dysfunction. The woman's life style may be temporarily, if not permanently, altered, leaving younger children in particular with the feeling of having been deserted (Nuehring and Barr, 1980).

The Male Partner

There is ample information in the literature (Asken, 1975; Joiner and Fisher, 1979; Pfefferbaum, 1977-78; Schain, 1977; Wellisch, et al., 1978; Witkin, 1979) to support the hypothesis that male partners develop psychological concerns following the mastectomy which can lead to marital or sexual dysfunction. Witkin, for example, found three major intrapsychic issues for the man: (1) his ability to accept the loss of his partner's breast; (2) his overinvolvement when he experiences her pain or trauma as his own; and (3) his feeling of helplessness and the fear that he will not be able to meet the woman's emotional needs.

Other issues emerge from these fears. Hall (1980) discovered that, in spite of all the information to the contrary, some men fear they will contract cancer themselves or that it could be spread to another part of the woman's body.

Most men suffer some psychosomatic reaction following the woman's surgery. Pfefferbaum (1977-78) includes insomnia, loss of appetite, weight gain, and a feeling of general malaise as typical reactions to the mate's surgery. Difficulties in work are also common, including trouble with concentration and preoccupation.

Men who do not, or cannot, express their negative feelings to the woman may experience some guilt. It can be expected in some cases that the man will experience some difficulty in attaining an erection. This, in turn, confirms the woman's suspicion that he finds her repulsive. Some of the man's ability to adjust to his partner's mastectomy depends on his own self-image (Hall, 1980; Schoenberg and Carr, 1971). If he already has a stable image of himself, he is less likely to be shocked and repelled by the surgery. There will be less chance of his assuming responsibility for the cancer (Wabrek, Wabrek and Burchell, 1979).

Asken (1975) and Witkin (1979) both discuss the mastectomy bind. Because the man may be unsure of how to respond to the woman following surgery, he may withdraw from her. This kind of bind results in the couple moving apart. Each one needs physical and emotional caring from the other, but finds it too risky to express those needs. The woman reacts normally with depression and crying spells. The man is convinced that she is indeed fragile and vulnerable. In a short time, the woman despairs because she believes the man cannot bear to look at her. The man, in turn, is guilt-ridden because he believes he has failed to help her.

The Role of the Male Partner

The support systems available to the patient are an important source of help. Male supports are especially crucial to the patient because the most important single factor in determining her response to the surgery is the reaction of significant males (Fortune, 1979). It has been found that acceptance of the mastectomy by the male partner is the woman's main concern. This fact crosses all age, social, and cultural lines. Clearly, the support of the male partner is of inestimable value in the psychosocial recovery of the woman.

Most men agree that the most stressful time for them was viewing their partner naked for the first time after the mastectomy. Confronting the missing breast is a critical moment in the male-female relationship and it can determine whether or not the couple will distance from one another or progress toward closeness. This confrontation can best be made if the man is present at the woman's bedside when the bandages are removed and the chest is exposed for the first time. This clinical setting helps the man to emotionally detach himself and to confront the wound in a less personal way.

The message that needs to be communicated to the woman from her male partner is that he still finds her desirable. This can be done by hand holding, by kissing, or by verbally expressing his love for her. Only the man in her life can mollify the woman's fears that she is only half a woman. He is the one from whom she needs compliments and support. He is the one with whom she needs to communicate on a deeply emotional level.

The data indicate that the man makes a better adjustment himself and can be more effective in the woman's recovery if he has been included in decision making from diagnosis to prognosis (Schoenberg and Carr, 1971). Hospital visiting by the man is seen as being strongly supportive in the postsurgical period. Visiting patterns have been found to correlate with subsequent psychosocial recovery and functioning (Wellisch et al., 1978). Those men who do not visit regularly are often at risk for emotional difficulty and are certainly not in a position to offer support and encouragement to the woman. Visitation is seen by the patient as the indicator of the man's commitment. From her point of view, he is, quite literally, either with her or he is not.

The Sexual Relationship

The couple is no different after surgery than it was before with regard to sexual wants and needs. Sexual foreplay and intercourse meet some of the most basic emotional needs. To forego or to lose that experience could result in emotional emptiness.

It has been shown that the postoperative sexual relationship, even the marriage itself, is usually contingent upon the status of that relationship prior to the surgery (Wellisch et al., 1978; Joiner and Fisher, 1979). Marriages that were stable, in which healthy sexual relations existed before the mastectomy, tend to have fewer postoperative problems of sexual adjustment.

It is not advisable to wait too long to resume an active sex life following the mastectomy. Early intercourse indicates to the woman that her partner still finds her desirable. It also helps her to accept herself and her sexuality. Unless hospital accommodations present too many obstacles, intercourse is recommended on the woman's last night there (Witkin, 1979). Any position is acceptable as long as the chest area is protected and the woman's physical weakness is taken into account.

In the period immediately following surgery, the male superior position is recommended, with the man supporting himself on his hands and knees. When the initial period is over, many couples prefer the front lateral position, rear lateral, or sitting frontal positions. Most women prefer not to use the female superior position because it is more strenuous and because it puts the chest in a more prominent position.

Implications for Social Work Practice

Social work intervention will likely cover a wide range of social functioning concerns, that is, psychological, sexual, and social. It is known that mastectomy brings about behavioral changes in women and that other family members may develop problems as well. The literature suggests that while it is the woman who has undergone surgery, the family unit is treated as the client.

The findings from this review have implications in four areas: (1) prevention; (2) the woman's fears; (3) the male partner's response and role; and (4) family dysfunction.

Prevention of Interpersonal Dysfunction

In order to be effective, the social worker needs to have an understanding of breast cancer in general and of mastectomy in particular. The worker needs to be well-informed about the psychosocial ramifications of amputations and the grief process. This knowledge provides the framework for determining whether behavior is within normal limits.

From the studies done on mastectomy patients and their families, some intervention is called for between diagnosis and the surgery itself. Usually, there is little time for such intervention, however, and the family is under stress when major decisions must be made. It would be well for the woman and her husband to make these decisions together. In this way, the woman is not isolated and she can experience her husband's involvement and support even before surgery is performed. The husband is not shut out, but feels part of the process and this may alleviate some of the helplessness men report they frequently experience. Fortune (1979) describes this short period as a crisis period and recommends that a crisis intervention approach be used by the clinical practitioner.

Crisis theory is a useful framework within which to view the stress caused by the diagnosis of breast cancer and the pending surgery. Coping mechanisms previously used by the client may not be effective in controlling associated anxiety and the clients may have to develop new coping skills. The client and her male partner can be helped to use their perception of mastectomy and to draw support from similar prior events in order to progress through the present crisis.

The Woman's Fears

Implications can be drawn from findings about the fears of mastectomy patients. Many women report fear of rejection and fear of death. Because some women name these and other fears does not mean they have all been identified. The depth and variety of fear begs a closer look.

Fear is individualistic. Whereas one woman may fear her tennis game will never be the same again, another may be afraid to wear her favorite dress because of the way she thinks she appears in it. The social worker who recognizes these differential fears as normal behavior is in a better position to help the woman dispel as much of this fear as she can.

Fear produces certain kinds of behavior following surgery. There may be an increase in suicide threats during the immediate period following surgery and a subsequent increase in drug or alcohol intake. The implication here is that if the social worker is knowledgeable, she may be able to anticipate such client behavior. Because she is sensitive to the potential problem, the social worker may also be able to help the woman find a more appropriate means of coping with her fears. The social worker should not overreact, however, to the possibility of drug or alcohol abuse. Clearly, pathology should not be sought when there is no reason to suspect it exists.

The Male Partner

There is sufficient documentation of the need for a supportive male to underscore the importance of his attitude as a primary variable in the woman's emotional recovery. This dynamic must not be overlooked, but must be clarified and encouraged. Implications are that this relationship can either be a healing agent or a source of more pain for the patient. Attempts must be made, therefore, to promote a positive attitude.

Before the male is able to offer emotional support, it may be necessary to attend to his own psychosocial needs. The partner of a mastectomy patient is a good group candidate if such a group is available. If not, it is time for the social worker to start one. The male has his own fears, anxieties, and depression to face and needs to be listened to, empathized with, and accepted. A properly planned group experience can provide all of this.

Research has identified certain predictors that suggest the man can expect some physical reactions to the woman's surgery. The social worker can educate the man so that physical symptoms will be taken at face value and not lead to questions about the state of his own health. Based on the documented experience of others, probable emotions and behavior can be identified and healthy means for expressing them can be identified.

The resumption of sexual relations is a critical point for the couple. It is problematic at best and traumatic at worst. Desensitization to the missing breast could be standard procedure in the hospital so that negative reactions can be dealt with in a safer environment than the intimacy of the couple's bedroom provides. If the social worker is aware that intercourse is recommended prior to hospital discharge (Witkin, 1979), this can be discussed with the couple and facilitated if hospital accommodations and policy permit and the couple desires such arrangements. Accommodations could be arranged by the social worker in a discreet, professional manner.

Social workers should not make the hasty assumption that a particular couple needs sex therapy just because they express concern about their sexual relationship. Mastectomy does not change the couple's basic need for sex, nor does it necessarily change the marital relationship. The post-surgery relationship is predicated, at least to some extent, on the pre-surgery relationship and counseling, if advised, should be directed to the former relationship.

Family Dysfunction

Certain role changes can be expected and have been identified above. If the family understands the new structure, there may be less friction and resistance to accepting different roles for a temporary period. A family therapy model can be successful for families of mastectomy patients and can be introduced as soon as the family, or the prospective patient, is made known to the social worker (Pfefferbaum, 1977–78).

Since it is known that young children and teenage or adult daughters may have difficulty relating to their mothers because of the mastectomy, the social worker should be alerted to the possibility and should be prepared to offer appropriate service or to make an appropriate referral, for example, to a group experience or a Reach for Recovery volunteer.

Conclusion

Each mastectomy patient and her family deserves sensitive attention to the psychosocial problems that mastectomy precipitates or exacerbates. The operation is traumatic and is made more so by cultural bias. Cultural emphasis on the breast is pervasive and the internalization of breast pride can lead to devastating consequences when a breast is lost.

Because of the mastectomy, the realities of male-female relationships are undermined by feelings of worthlessness on the part of the woman. This low self-esteem can be mitigated by the openly expressed love of a caring partner.

This review has discussed how mastectomy impacts the patient in all of her social relationships as well as the general problem of recovery, unless there is evidence of acceptance and support from significant others. Although there is research that documents relationship problems following mastectomy, more is needed in this specific area as is study of the concomitant fears. Social workers should reject the stereotyped concept of the mastectomy client as intrinsically unappealing and they should combat the attitudes of society from which such myths and fears arise.

References

American Cancer Society. *Cancer facts and figures, 1980.* American Cancer Society, 1979.

Asken, M. Psychoemotional aspects of mastectomy: A review of recent literature. *American Journal of Psychiatry*, 1975, *132.*

Bard, M., & Sutherland, A. M. Adaptation to radical mastectomy. In *The psychological impact of cancer.* An American Cancer Society Professional Education Publication, 1979.

Fortune, E. A nursing approach to body image and sexuality adaptation in the mastectomy patient, *Sexuality and Disability*, 1979, *2.*

Gadpaille, W. J. The middle and later years: New dimensions in sex. In Lucy Freeman (Ed.), *The cycles of sex*, New York: Charles Scribner's Sons, 1975.

Hall, R. C. Impact of medical illness on sexual-marital relationships. *Medical Aspects of Human Sexuality*, (February 1980) 14:2, 125-132.

Joiner, J. G., & Fisher, J. Z. Post-mastectomy counseling. *Journal of Applied Rehabilitation Counseling*, 1979, *8.*

Nuehring, E. N., & Barr, W. E. Mastectomy: Impact on patients and families. *Health and Social Work*, 1980, 5.

Pfefferbaum, B. A comprehensive program of psychosocial care for mastectomy patients. *International Journal of Psychiatry in Medicine*, 1977–78, 8.

Polivy, J. Psychological effects of mastectomy on a woman's feminine self-concept. *Journal of Nervous and Mental Disease*, 1977, *164*.

Ray, C. Psychological implications of mastectomy. *British Journal of Social Clinical Psychology*, 1977, *16*.

Schain, W. S. Psychosocial issues in counseling mastectomy patients. *The Counseling Psychologist*, 1977, *6*.

Schoenberg, B., & Carr, A. L. Loss of external organs: Limb amputation, mastectomy, and disfiguration. In D. Peretz and A. H. Kutscher (eds.), *Loss and grief: Psychological management in medical practice*, New York: Columbia University Press, 1971.

Strax, P. Factors affecting frequency. In *Breast cancer is curable*. New York: The Benjamin Company, a Benco Health and Welfare Publication, 1975.

Wabrek, A. J., Wabrek, C. J., & Burchell, R. C. Marital and sexual counseling after mastectomy. In R. Green (Ed.), *Human sexuality: A health practitioner's text*, Baltimore: Williams and Witkins Co., 1979.

Wellisch, D., et al. Psychosocial aspects of mastectomy: The man's perspective. *American Journal of Psychiatry*, 1978, *135*.

Witkin, M. Psychological concerns in sexual rehabilitation and mastectomy. *Sexuality and Disability*, 1979, 2.

Woods, N. F. Alteration of body image and sexual adaptation: Enterostomy, mastectomy, and hysterectomy. In N. F. Woods (Ed.), *Human sexuality in health and illness*. St. Louis: C. V. Mosby, 1975.

D The Beginning Process in Medical Social Case Work

Jeanette Hertzman and Rachel Wyman

In the field of medical social work, although there has been increasing clarification of function, very little published material has appeared related to the factors that are significant at the point in medical care when social work service is offered. Is the nature of the intake process essentially different in this setting where the primary function is not that of social work? Are there similar factors present in this setting to which

Edited and reprinted from *The Family*, March 1945, with the permission of the Family Service Association of America.

individuals bring problems defined principally in terms of physical disability and the need for medical care?

The thesis presented here is that more help is given the client if service is defined principally in terms of the function of the agency itself. Function is understood to be an intrinsic part of the social work process through which the client is enabled to utilize the agency services constructively. The actual experience of coming to the agency for help is viewed as a dynamic factor in the client's ability to mobilize his strengths.

In the medical setting the social worker frequently goes to the patient, who may not have requested her help directly, to explore with him whether or not he needs and wants service. This help may be offered at the recommendation of the physician; on the other hand, it may be part of the policy of the hospital to extend social work help to selected groups of patients because it is recognized that there are potential social problems involved in the experience of illness and medical treatment. It is true, in a sense, that the patient coming for medical help is asking for all the services a medical agency offers, including social work. However, because the patient does not request this special service directly and may be quite unaware that there is a social component in his situation, the process of enabling him to recognize his need for help is particularly important.

In those instances where the social worker goes to see the patient for the first time, without his having asked for her help, an exploratory process is initiated. The purpose is to determine with the patient what his problems around his illness are, whether he wishes help from the worker with these problems, and whether he can use this help to change his situation. This exploratory process, as already indicated, is initiated because of the conviction that illness is a life-experience that precipitates problems for many individuals. It is the medical social worker's responsibility to recognize whether a particular patient is able to handle these problems alone or needs the special help she is equipped to offer. She recognizes, too, that often—even though the patient has problems as a result of an illness—he may not be able to recognize these or use help because he is too threatened by the offer of this service at a particular point in his illness when he is unable to face the realities of his situation.

Very often patients have a generalized fear of hospitals, operations, medical procedures, and possible unfavorable end results of the illness, such as incapacity or even death. These fears are often not expressed directly but are projected upon other aspects of the situation. For this reason it is important that the social worker's approach to each patient be a very sensitive one, in order to recognize his fears and anxieties, even though he may be unable to express them directly. She must be aware of his need for help in expressing these fears, which are often diffuse and not focused upon a particular problem. If she is dependent only upon a verbalized expression of need by the patient, her real helpfulness may not be made available to him.

In medical agencies, the client or patient may offer his own diagnosis of what is wrong and indicate the kind of help that will be acceptable. [Patients often try] "to make the helping source a kind of extension of themselves by attributing to it qualities of their own making" (Gomberg, 1942, p. 8). Patients coming to see a doctor will often state their complaints, what they think is wrong, and then go on to offer suggestions for treatment. For example, one hears a patient complaining of "stomach trouble" and asking for an X-ray, or stating he has "heart trouble" because of pain in the region of his heart. Those who attempt to help him frequently question why the patient attends the clinic if he thinks he has the same skill and knowledge as the doctor.

> Actually the patient or client is not coming because he knows the same things as the doctor or case worker. He is coming for something he himself lacks, something he does not have, although frequently it is desperately hard to admit or to face this. Actually he is coming for the difference between them. Thus the help that may ultimately be the source for changing the untenable situation, will grow from the difference between the patient and the doctor—the client and the agency. (Gomberg, 1942, p. 9)

The medical social worker's recognition of these factors enables her to perceive the nature of the patient's difficulty in using the help offered by the doctor to interpret to the doctor some of the reasons for the patient's seeming need to prescribe for himself. Such a patient is obviously anxious about what is wrong with him and what is going to happen to him. He seeks reassurance and safety by prescribing treatment for himself in terms familiar to him. Very often he cannot accept the procedures recommended by the doctor until he feels secure in the situation. The medical social worker can play an important part in increasing the patient's feeling of safety and also in helping the doctor understand some of the reasons for the patient's behavior. The doctor regards the patient's presence in the clinic or hospital as an indication that he is requesting his professional opinion and help. The doctor's capacity to accept the patient's behavior as a manifestation of fear, rather than as a denial of the doctor's ability to help, will inevitably be an important factor in his relationship with his patient and will contribute to the security the patient may derive from this relationship.

In order to give help that is really meaningful to the patient, the medical social worker must be aware of the motivating factors that may be involved in an individual's request for clinic or hospital care. In the first place, of course, medical treatment is undertaken in order to get relief from pain and anxiety, but it is important to recognize that medical care may also mean fulfillment of other needs. Some patients may be seeking relief from difficult social situations by placing themselves under the protection of a hospital. Others who are not receiving satisfaction in their personal lives find special values in medical care because it may supply an unmet need for love and affection. Still others seek medical care in order to meet eligibility requirements of social agencies, particularly with regard to employment or rehabilitation. If we understand some of the basic needs that operate in the patient's desire for medical care, we are better able to help the patient use the appropriate services of the medical agency, which are focused primarily upon his medical problem and the use of reliable scientific methods of treatment. The actual nature of the care the patient receives may be enriched through broadening the understanding of him as a person by those who are responsible for his care.

Although the client may have decided what kind of help he wants, in many instances this must be clarified with him.

Although he [the client] wants help he also resists it. There is a part of him which prefers to get along without help and struggles against it. However, if this part of him is not out of proportion to the part which wants help, he does present himself and makes a request of some sort. This is the beginning of the case work situation, considered psychologically. (Aptekar, 1941, p. 126)

We see this concept as having real significance in the medical social situation. With many patients their desire to get well is in conflict with an unconscious wish to remain ill. Although we have assumed that the sick person usually wants to get well or receive relief from pain, very often he unconsciously needs to remain ill. However, if that part of him which wants to get well is greater than the part that does not, it is our feeling that such a patient meets one of the essential criteria for the effective use of social work help directed toward resolving enough of his ambivalence to enable him to use medical care realistically.

Many patients are overwhelmed by the necessity for facing and accepting the total implication of medical care. These patients often respond readily to help directed toward partializing the total problem and becoming active in thinking about a part of it. For example, a patient who had to undergo an operation for removal of the uterus expressed a great deal of fear about hypodermic injections and blood transfusions. She did not indicate any fears about the actual operation. [T]he social worker's help was focused upon her expressed fears about transfusion, which enabled her to move forward to fears about the operation itself. The service of helping patients to partialize their fears and to work through them may lead to an acceptance of the total medical plan.

The following case illustrates how a bedridden patient was blocked in her desire to participate actively in medical care because of factors influencing her relationship with the hospital. The social worker's help was focused upon enabling her to express feeling that she was afraid to display in the presence of the doctor and the nurse upon whom she was dependent for care. The worker also evidenced her own capacity to accept hostility from the patient and the rejection of her services if the patient did not wish them.

The patient, a 29-year-old single woman with chronic rheumatoid arthritis, was referred to Social Service by the doctor who had been treating her for over a year as a private case. She had been readmitted to the hospital as [an inpatient], and her symptoms were more acute than they had been during the former three hospitalizations. The doctor [thought] that since patient might be bedridden for a long time, the interest of the Social Service Department would be helpful, particularly with plans for convalescent care. Before interviewing the patient, worker had learned that the patient and her sister were estranged from the father and a stepmother. For seven years they both had maintained an apartment above their financial means. The sisters had always been very close to each other. The patient's present acute exacerbation occurred around the time that her sister became interested in a man of some social status. They were married during the patient's hospitalization.

When the worker first interviewed the patient following her admission, the patient questioned her directly as to the reasons for her interest. The worker replied that the doctor had thought she might be having some problems in relation to her illness. Patient thought that her problems were no different now than they had been before and asked why doctor had not suggested that worker visit her previously. As the interview progressed, patient brought out a great deal of feeling about not having visitors. At the same time she expressed some relief that no one had seen her in her present condition. Patient had thought herself attractive, but now described herself as "toothless" with hands like "claws." She immediately showed the worker a photograph taken when she was well which the worker thought was quite appealing. In spite of her dejection about her appearance, she indicated that she had hopes of looking better again. Since she repeated that it was better that none of her friends came to see her while she looked so badly, the worker wondered how she felt about her visiting. Patient responded that it was good to talk with someone besides the nurses and doctor; and since worker "belongs to the hospital," she knew about patient's illness and was not "shocked by my appearance."

After this statement, patient talked for some time about her younger sister and about the "nice" man she married. Sister had moved patient's clothing and furniture to her new apartment and patient had thought that when she left the hospital she would go to her home. Worker sensed that patient might have some feeling about sister's marriage, particularly since sister was several years younger, appeared more adequate, and was physically more attractive. Worker sensed that patient seemed to be making a controlled effort to cover up her true feelings and had made a great deal of effort to repress her hostility. This was indicated overtly in her rigidity and tenseness, which seemed to be a factor in her illness. Patient seemed to be able to relate positively to the worker and further indicated that she would like to talk with the worker whom she could accept as part of the hospital.

Patient looked even less comfortable physically when the worker saw her again. Her fingers seemed stiff and sore, and her fingernails were coming off. Patient told worker that her sister had visited her the previous week and had brought her some fruit. She emphasized the fact that she realized how busy the sister and her husband were, so that they could not visit often. She then went on to talk about getting well and said that she understood that recovery was slow in certain illnesses. Although she had been in the hospital for two months, she hoped she could leave at the end of another two months. Suddenly patient burst into tears, after which she seemed embarrassed and began to apologize. She said she had never allowed herself to show her feelings before anyone, although she did cry at night. She also mentioned that she hoped her doctor would not be told that she lost control. He has done so much for her and he might think her ungrateful. She really felt she could not tolerate being ill this way all her life. She brought out her fear of dying, which she thought might result from infectious process reaching her heart just as it had affected her fingernails.

At this point the worker was able to accept patient's fears and the fact that it was not easy for her to be ill. It was her thinking, too, that patient might be helped through a case work relationship to release some tension and thus lessen her rigidity. In talking with the doctor about this, he expressed discouragement that patient was not showing any progress. The infection seemed to be difficult to check. He felt, too, that patient's emotional state was a large factor in her illness and that, unless she were helped to resolve some of her feelings, the medical treatment would be ineffective.

Another case is illustrative of a beginning interview undertaken at the request of the attending surgeon, who was anxious that discharge plans be initiated promptly. It is interesting to note that, in spite of the external pressure created by the time element, the worker, cognizant of the reality situation, does not allow this sense of urgency to affect her service to the patient. This patient had been in the hospital for several months, during which time radical surgery had been performed because of malignancy. Patient had a functioning colostomy which was to be closed up within a two-month period. It was worker's thinking at the time of referral that this situation should have been referred earlier, since patient might have been able to use help in accepting the diagnostic and surgical procedures.

Worker introduced herself to patient and explained that the doctor had told her that patient was ready to go home soon and might have some problems about care at home. Worker commented that she was interested in helping her with this. Patient is an obese, middle-aged, gray-haired woman with a very pale skin. She has large dark eyes and appeared somewhat depressed. Patient sighed and replied that she was going home, but not to her own home. She was going to her sister-in-law, since she felt that she would need someone to take care of her. At this point, with a good deal of suppressed feeling, patient started sobbing and said she was afraid to go home but she did not want to remain in the hospital. After a short pause worker replied that it must be difficult for her because of the nature of her operation. Patient continued to tell worker that the operation really involved a radical change. She was terribly ashamed and upset about it. She did not want people to take care of her and she hated taking care of herself. Worker said that she knew about this. Patient with some feeling stated that the odor nauseated her and she was afraid that people around her would not want to stay near. She did not like anyone else to take care of her and she felt she must learn to manage.

Worker wondered whether she had discussed with the doctor the possibility of caring for herself. She replied that he had assured her that the colostomy opening would be closed up in two months. In addition, he had prescribed a diet so that she would be able to control the colostomy during this interval period. Worker commented that she knew of other patients with similar conditions who had learned to care for themselves. Patient replied that she never knew that anyone had this kind of operation. It was something entirely new to her. She really felt disgusted with herself and was fearful about reactions of people coming in contact with her. Worker commented that it was not easy to accustom one's self to something like this, but that perhaps it was her feeling about herself that was the important thing. Worker then suggested that perhaps patient would like to talk about this further. Was it that she might feel others were disgusted because she herself felt that way? With much less feeling, patient nodded and thought that might be the reason. Worker wondered if patient had been told about the nature of the operation. Patient replied that if that had been made known to her, she would rather have died first. Worker commented that not having known about it must have made it more difficult to accept. Had the doctors explained why it had been necessary? Patient replied that they had. She went on to say that they had promised to close it up, so that it was this present period that concerned her. With a sigh, she added she supposed she would just have to manage for two months. Worker wondered how she felt about the arrangements at her sister-in-law's home. She explained that she felt she was rather weak and did need to be with someone. She would have her own room and did not anticipate any difficulties in staying with the family. It was simply her own feelings about herself. Patient went on to tell worker about her family relationships and her feelings regarding being a free patient. This was the first time she had had to accept care without paying for it. She felt that she had received excellent care but was upset about her inability to reimburse the hospital.

After some discussion of the physical arrangements at her sister-in-law's house, patient and worker agreed that at present she would need a public health nurse to help her with her dressings and bed care. Worker arranged to send a nurse. Patient said she could make her own arrangements about leaving the hospital and returning to clinic.

In summary, the writers have attempted to analyze the use of function of the social worker in a medical agency as a dynamic factor in the intake process. Because of the complexities and limitations in the setting, the medical social worker often has to assume more responsibility for initiating the helping process. This occurs because the help offered by the social service department is only one of the many services in the total program of medical care of the institution. The patient's immediate concern in coming to a hospital is to obtain relief from physical symptoms, so that in the beginning he may not understand the social worker's services in relation to his medical care. It is often necessary, therefore, for the medical social worker to offer her services before the patient may be aware of the need for her help and to assume responsibility for enabling him to understand how she fits in with the rest of his medical care. In the initial interviews, both the worker and the patient actively engage in an exploratory process in order to discover together the degree to which factors within his environment and within himself are influencing his illness and his feeling about medical care. The patient's participation in the joint process has been increased through a recent emphasis upon the importance of enabling him to be an active contributor to it. This is in contrast with former procedures of obtaining social information *about* a patient rather than *with* him.

The [two] cases presented illustrate the worker's use of criteria to determine the patient's ability to use her services helpfully. [Both] patients presented a problem relating to medical care. Services were focused upon enabling these patients to participate more fully in medical treatment. An important factor in the social worker's offering of service was a recognition that anxiety, if unrelieved, utilizes energy needed for physical restoration. Because a certain amount of anxiety is present in any illness situation, the worker needs to gauge sensitively the amount of anxiety a patient can handle by himself and at what point he needs help from the social worker. In [both] cases, too, the patient's ability to relate to the worker and to the services of the agency was the basis of continuation of her activity.

Thus one sees in the beginning of the . . . relationship with the patient an attempt on the part of the worker to evaluate the patient's ability to relate to the medical agency and to use the services offered by the social worker. The extent and direction to which the patient can continue to use help is indicated by "the way he faces, works with, and relates to the agency services, requirements, limitations, and choices as a resource for changing the situation that brought him" (Gomberg, 1942, p. 37). Translated into the language of the medical setting, this means simply that the capacity of the patient to use medical help is measured by the degree to which he is able to take hold of what medical science has to offer and to use this help for achieving greater physical adequacy or comfort. For the social worker functioning within the medical setting, this implies flexibility and sensitive awareness of the problems created for the patient by the nature and demands of medical care, capacity to recognize evidence of the patient's own strength, and ability to perceive areas in which fear and anxiety may paralyze his power to assume responsibility. Her specific professional function becomes one of recognizing the essential nature of the patient's problem and of helping the patient to cope with it. Awareness of her special professional function becomes truly significant when she is able to integrate this professional awareness with a knowledge of the meaning of illness, understanding of the person who is ill, and skill in the process of offering help at the initial point when this special service is made available to the patient.

References

Aptekar, Herbert H. *Basic Concepts in Social Case Work*. Chapel Hill: University of North Carolina Press, 1941.

Gomberg, M. Robert. "Some Aspects of Diagnosis in Family Case Work," in *Studies in the Practice of Family Case Work*. Brooklyn, New York: Jewish Family Welfare Society, 1942.

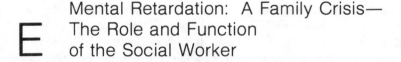

Mental Retardation: A Family Crisis—
The Role and Function
of the Social Worker

Hans S. Falck

It is my task today to speak here about the involvement of the social worker in the treatment of the mental retardate and his family. Since it is both necessary and desirable to limit the scope of my discussion, I shall try to stick to the social work role.

Let me say, first of all, that the functions of various professionals tend to overlap at certain points. This is true as between psychologists and chaplains, between chaplains and social workers. And, yet, there must still be some core functions that are somewhat uniquely the province of each.

Originally published in *The McCormick Quarterly* (1966), Supplement, pp. 26-39. Reprint permission granted by McCormick Theological Seminary.

Retardation is a pretty big word and includes a great many conditions. One must quite evidently know something about them, whether the diagnostic terminology came from medicine, education, social work, or somewhere else. And yet, for the social worker it is less important whether he knows all the ins and outs of the various forms of retardation than it is for him to see what happens in a family or other social unit when one or more than one of its members has a severe disability. This is particularly the case when the member is highly dependent in his disabled state, and so disabled that a) he cannot learn beyond certain more or less sharply defined limits; b) cannot exercise the kinds of intellectual judgments that would ordinarily make it possible for a person to make significant decisions; and c) may have severe difficulties in "reading" his cultural context in a way in which his expression of feelings and actions are within the outer limits of what is acceptable behavior.

From a social worker's point of view there are certain commonalities regardless of the specific differences. The most obvious of these, and the one on which I shall spend most of my time, is the fact that most of the retarded children we see have parents and siblings. If this were the only significant observation, we could see the job of working with the families of disabled children as easy. One might take family members one by one and give them the word: Tell them what to do, be sympathetic, encourage them to cheer up, in other words live in one way or another with the thought that one of the family is more or less severely retarded.

Unhappily and perhaps happily, things are more complex than that. What is actually the most relevant for the social worker to understand is that families are not collections of individuals but units—psychological and social units, and that the functioning of each members touches all. And so, one might well point to a person and label him retarded, but one must also understand that to the degree that one person functions in a particular way, the rest of the unit, of which he is a part, must adjust its functioning to him. And this is a very complex story and of exceedingly great difficulty in practice.

Before I go on, however, I must say a word in defense of a very concrete approach in helping families with retarded children. It is very frequently the case that in our eagerness to understand the complications of relationships in the people we serve, we undervalue the concrete parts of helping. Getting adequate medical care for a retarded child, getting him to a clinic, arranging transportation to get him a training program, making financial arrangements, obtaining help for mother in the home— particularly if she should have several retarded children—and a host of other services that are needed are all activities worthy of the most sophisticated of us. When we think that such work is not "treatment" and thereby imply that such activities are unworthy or only clerk's jobs, then it is usually because we fail to see the real opportunity to give of ourselves which may be as meaningful as the complex, relationship-focused activity that so many workers find so very satisfying.

Having said all this, one must nevertheless recognize that a family with a retarded child must have other kinds of help, also. Let me then make some observations about the way at least this social worker looks at the problem of retardation.

The first impulse is to lump all under a single heading called "re-tardates." This sounds both neat and totally inaccurate. Now you expect me to say that each retardate varies from all the others, but that is both quite untrue and too simple. What sounds just as simple, but is much more complex, is the observation that they are all *people*. I myself often have trouble with that so obvious idea. I think I have it because basically I think we have a certain tendency to shrink away from severely damaged persons and find it quite convenient to symbolize this by lumping them into categories. When challenged, we intellectualize the situation by re-marking that after all, the categories are convenient diagnostic devices. Which is true. But limited. The fact is that the attitudes that are implicit in speaking of retardates, rather than people with certain difficulties, tend to be rejective ones that say: "I will look at you in general, but don't come close." There is a deep current and a long tradition in categorizing and depersonalizing the outsider, i.e. the person whose condition or behavior deviates from social norms that make us feel comfortable, especially when we do well by them. And there is no sense merely in telling workers to change their attitudes, be they openly rejective, covertly rejective by patronizing, or, superficially accepting by doing too much "for" and too little "with." There are tough attitudinal choices social workers have to make in working with retardates and their family units, and they are highly complex besides. It is for this reason that I cannot find it in my heart to be too critical of my colleagues who struggle with their feelings and attitudes. But be it said that whatever one feels and expresses in subtle ways, there is a lot of confusion on the inside. So please, I would say, less preaching about what other people ought to feel and more understanding perhaps about what persons who try to help do feel, without excessive self-congratulation or know-it-all criticism.

I put the attitudinal part first because I think that it is the most important of all. How I handle myself with the families is much more revealing than how I handle the family, as we sometimes tend to say. Then I can talk with you about other people: the retarded person, his family, the relationships of a married couple who have produced a less than satisfying product, and so on.

On to the family. Let's take the easier things first. I already pointed out that there are quite often facilitative services that are rendered by social workers. This is where the work ought to get underway once the family has some first and surface understanding of the fact that the child is retarded. Facilitative services deal with housing, finances, transportation, recreation, babysitting. Relationship-focused services deal with danger to other children, what the neighbors might say, how to tell grandma and grandpa, whether to send out birth announcements, and so on, can all be of immense concern and carry a great deal of worry and often do.

Yet all this and more complicated problems of which I shall speak later need one essential element without which all come to naught. This is the importance of relationship.

Relationships are not established, as people so often say. Relationships are processes, are changing interactions, which include most particularly the sharing of feelings. And so a worker should ask himself what it feels like for the client, if he can detect this, to be with him. Of course, relationships can also be built by the exchange of information and very frequently by "just talking." The subject can be anything and it is deplorable to conclude that the client is "resisting" when he doesn't right away indicate that he's just been waiting for us to barge into his life. Of course he resists. Which I see as a sign of health within certain limits.

I said before that relationships are not established. The word here ought to be "establishing" because they must be worked on in a thousand ways all the time that you are trying to help. This becomes important in another sense also.

We have in our culture a tendency to have to deal with the publicness of our misfortunes. I am constantly aware in my work at the Washington University Medical Center about how public the drama of illness really is. And so one might say, that we have the greatest privacy available when we are healthy and well. We shut the door, turn the lock, draw the blinds, and go to bed. But when we are ill—especially seriously ill—we are more in the open public and the social worker or any other "helper" are part of the larger public. To move into another's life especially when he is in great need is an invasion of his privacy. It is necessary and unavoidable; it is welcomed or resisted: yet, it is an invasion nevertheless. This, you see, gets tied up with the relationship notion. I think that Martin Buber—may his memory be a blessing—would perhaps agree that one must make oneself a welcomed part of another and another a welcomed part of oneself if help, and especially long-term help dealing with intimate matters is to be truly helpful. This, I think, presupposes the understanding of what I suggest here: no relationship, no help.

I have already said enough, perhaps, to indicate in what direction my mind runs. I believe in the efficacy of a personal approach in social work practice. This includes work with the retarded. I do know indeed, that much good work is being done of a high governmental level by the various agencies concerned; I know that many difficulties need to be met in regard to better research, in regard to larger programs that deal with problems of mental retardation. But I also know that here in this place and before this audience—if anywhere at all—it is proper to realize that all the money in the world and all the professional books are but means to what will ultimately go on when the office door closes or the mother has admitted you to the home and the social worker is face to face with his client. That will still be true when we have 400 million rather than 200 million people in this land of ours. Who is he then and what kind of bond will begin there? Do you hear the overtones of where social work came from and where your tradition originated as well? Do you sense the affinity?

Now then, we can talk about concepts, science, diagnostics, treatment approaches.

What do I see or attempt to see when I work with the family of a retarded person? I see a unit here, a family unit in which all members are intersticed, interpenetrated, interwoven with each other. This is also the reason why, I would suggest, the family must be seen in the sense that it is afflicted, that a part of it is not in too good shape. The family is a system; touch a part, you touch the whole system. I do not really believe that there is an *individual*; only individualization which is a group phenomenon, a result of and a part of the ongoing group processes of which all people are a part.

The result of such a view as here outlined is the tendency for workers who accept it to be less concerned with the reactions of individual members of the family group but rather with *inter*actions within the family. Consequently, questions should deal with the relationships of family members to each other.

One often makes the mistake of assuming that the child has a deficit without recognizing that the child is also a powerful force within that family unit. Being retarded is not just what one is not, it is most importantly also what one *is*. One is, for example, the person who gets more attention than anyone else. One is the person whose needs tend to be met prior to everyone else's. One is the person who is talked about often. One is the person about whom many family members feel the anger of the deprived without the ability to say so aloud. One is the person about whom mother may feel guilt. One is the person whose father silently accuses mother of having given birth to. One is the person whose medical bills are high. One is the person whose future is very much in doubt. One is the person whom siblings regard as the burden they may need to bear after father and mother are gone. One is the person about whose condition people often whisper. One is the person who has dashed the fondest hope of a father who wanted a successor son; of the mother who dreamed of some far distant wedding day in white. One is the person whose disability parents wish away and about which they press social workers and attempt to induce them to tell them that the child really is not retarded. One is the person about whose institutionalization there is much doubt and guilt and shame. One is the person who is unreasonably suspected of being uncontrolled sexually (especially if one is of teen age). One is the occasion and target of old wives' tales by nosey neighbors. One is the object of dire prediction—often justified, most often not. One is the person whose life span is supposed to be short. One is the person about whose diagnosis more mistakes are made than about almost any other disability. One is the person about whom we try to find nice neutral words so that our own discomfort and rejection doesn't show through quite so much.

But one is also a human being who feels. One is also the person who can sense rejection and love. One is also the person who wants to be protected, loved, patted, talked to, taught, thought well of. One is the person who indeed can feel lonely. One is the person who often to a limited degree learns to do things for oneself if only people were not so rejectingly sympathetic and made reasonable demands to perform tasks. One is a person who feels the cold and the warmth, the comfort and the joy, the warm hand and the cold words.

All these things one is and is not, are those that deal with the relationships the patient has with other people. And it is for this reason that social work attention must be given to the relationship patterns in and out of the family group. The most frequent and often the most destructive element in the life of the retardate *and* his family are isolation from effective contacts with others, plus guilt and shame, plus unexpressed anger; plus the feelings of worthlessness for having produced a defective person. One may add other pluses.

In other words, retardation is not only a condition; it is also a social role. It is a *social* role because it not only involves the self but other people: sozius, i.e., citizen or person. It is thus an interactive role and as is true of all roles, deviant or not, it is a learned role. It is learned because although many children—though not all—already come into the world with a deficit of endowment, the ways of responding to the deficit and the society in which the person lives are learned. They are learned because they are taught. And if one may say one thing that is true about the retarded person, it is that he acts as a retardate not only because he is disabled, but also because he learns to respond to the way he is treated. Treat him as a retardate, and even if he is not, he will act like one. This is a not inconsequential situation that prevails all too often.

Yet, there is another dimension. This is the dimension of denial. I have seen workers and have been one of them who were subjected to the most intense of pressures to say to parents that really the child is quite without problems or is "growing out of them." These are very sad experiences.

They are so sad because one feels that one wished one could agree with the anxious parents, say it is not so bad, imply that Johnny will be o.k. But one can also make some bad mistakes when one assumes that this is really what parents wish to hear all the time. I often think that parents, knowing what the diagnosis is and what the future might be like, really need to test out the professional person and really do wish a confirmation of the condition rather than a sugary denial in the form of a conspiracy of workers with parents, all involved knowing all along that it is a sham. It results in lack of trust by parents of whoever the gullible or weak-kneed professional might be: whether social worker or physician, whether chapplain or nurse.

All of this deals, of course, with the problems of interpretation so many workers must deal with. Some workers, aware of the pitfalls I have cited, decided that they must be brutally frank. But I have a friend who once said to me that to be brutally frank is often much more brutal than frank. So let's rule that out. But this still doesn't mean that one has a right to mislead. One can be frank without being brutal. But way beyond this kind of information approach lies the much greater need to help people take a look at what they already know anyway. The complaints and questions of parents are rarely as much the symptom of the lack of information as the inability to know what to do with it.

As I have attempted to suggest here, having a retarded youngster is a feeling that—I am sure—those of us whose children are not retarded cannot really imagine. I don't know how close we can come. But we can listen and encourage people to talk out what they feel. We can help them feel that it is normal in any close human relationship to love and hate, to treasure and to reject. Only when such feelings can be truly accepted by a worker who is not merely a technician but a feeling philosopher, a man who both knows and speculates about meanings, that is to say a professional in the best sense of the word, can real help be given.

Retardation is a tragedy for all involved. But being a tragedy it is also not a Greek drama of irrevocable fate. The retardation may always be there and yet parents can be helped to make decisions and be seen and treated as persons with strength, rather than just deficits. Do not deny the retardation. Do not deny the future. But also do not deny the energy and the strength that people possess potentially and actually. The retardation may not be reversible. But education can take place in many cases. But beyond this, retardation is a mental health problem for the family that can be managed well or poorly. In most cases, there is nothing given or inevitable about that. Mental health can and must be dealt with. And one way to do that is to encourage persons to understand the meaning of what has happened to them and to make responsible decisions as to what to do about that. That is why one must not stop with the exploration of feelings. That is why I said in the beginning that the environmental needs, such as housing, transportation, schooling, finances, and so on, are important social work activities. For, if skillfully handled, father and mother, brother and sister can be helped to feel as being on top of the situation, not mere dependent reactors to a family tragedy that all resent because of its own tragedy but also because of the tendency to react passively, that is to say, as the innocent victims of a hostile universe. It may be hostile and the illness may be tragic. But there is no excuse in the vast majority of cases for just simply giving up.

The balances one must draw are complex and, therefore, also difficult ones. One must be feeling without being mushy. One is asked to give information and be sure it is understood without assuming that just saying words results in reassurance and joy. One must be frank without being brutal. One must be realistic without being overly discouraging. One must have hope and express it without denying the reality of the present and future. One must help the person understand that it is not his fault that he or she is the parent of a retarded child without denying that the child is a product of the union. One must know as much as possible about the condition without merely intellectualizing about it. One must be supportive without encouraging too much dependency. One must have intimacy, objectivity, and empathy. One must be Solomon. One must most of all be all those things that mortals cannot ever hope to be.

Now, I would like to say a few words about parent organizations and about the institutions for the mentally retarded. The reason that I list both in one sentence is that there are important connections between the two.

Undoubtedly one of the most remarkable developments of the last twenty years in the voluntary social welfare field has been the emergence of the National Association for Retarded Children (NARC). I have had repeated experience with local units, served on the board of directors of one of them, and chaired committees made up of parents of retarded and non-retarded children.

Until recently, NARC has had a difficult time. It is no more than five years that even remotely the attention has been given to retardation that it deserves. I don't need to go into the reasons for this slow development. Let me just say that had it not been for determined parents no NARC would exist even now. NARC's concern has been with research, legislation, public relations, and education about retardation, and quite importantly, in many places NARC has begun to raise very serious questions about the institutions for the retarded and the quality of care given there.

It is not always easy to work with parents whose children are retarded and who sometimes have a tendency to reinforce each other's problems in

NARC meetings. But this can be worked with provided that skilled staff is available. In many units this is not the case. Much more needs to be done about the quality of institutions. I am currently consultant to two of them.

And so the parents of NARC should be encouraged, especially in their efforts to persuade legislatures to spend more and more money for the institutionalized retarded child and the parents.

But the story does not end there, for parents have a very special relationship to the institution that harbors their child. I have already spoken of the guilt and the anxieties that go into the recognition that one's child is retarded. In addition to that, it is important to call attention to the fact that in a child-centered culture such as ours, where supposedly every child is to have parents and a fine home, good food, and education, it becomes a somewhat suspect matter when one places one's child. For placing a child is an admission that, for whatever reasons, one is unable to give the child what he needs and deserves. And that admission is the admission of inadequacy. Inadequacy is a very short step indeed from failure.

This precisely is where parent groups come in. This is also why there is such a special relationship between such groups and the institution. It is the institution that does what the parents cannot do. Thus it is admired because of its skill, its facilities, its ability to cope; it is deeply and bitterly resented precisely for the same reasons: it can do and does what the parent cannot do. "My child," says the parents in effect "is not my child" because I cannot take care of it. Add this to the not infrequent feelings of anger and subtle hostilities towards and about the child and you have a potentially explosive situation. The result is what we call ambivalence. "The child is mine and I want to love it and take care of it," says the parent. "I am no good, my child is no good and I wish it had never happened," says the same parent. "I want my child at home, rear him, raise him!", says the parent. "I cannot take care of him, the institution does it so well and he is so much better off there," says the same parent. One might perhaps be excused if one finds it occasionally a bit difficult to work with whole groups of parents who express these ambivalences towards their children, the staffs, the institutions.

And yet, the work must be done. I would strongly suggest that there be fewer tours of hospitals, fewer lectures, and more meetings where with a trained worker (social worker, physician, nurse, psychologist) there'd be some real opportunity to talk and work out some of these seemingly contradictory feelings. This not an easy job, but it can, at least to a degree, be done. It seems ideal for a properly trained chaplain. Thus also, workers might learn not to see parents as bothersome appendages who are tolerated by giving talks, tours, and refreshment. Work with parents must never be a public relations gimmick. It should and must be a matter of treatment.

And so, what then is the role of the social worker? Obviously, he has many roles, all of them difficult and complex. He must give advice, he helps persons understand what the facts and feelings are with which they inevitably deal. The worker must pull in community resources, especially around some of the concrete, environmental possibilities that can be made use of. The worker must be able to reassure and also set limits. He must have clear convictions and very specific knowledge. And let me say that this must include more than information about the various forms of retardation. He must know as much as possible about small group process, especially as this relates to family life. He must have accurate perceptions and knowledge about the psychological make-up of persons. And above all he must know himself, or perhaps better, sense himself in the helping situation. That he must have respect for the other members of the treatment team is elementary but harder to achieve than to suggest.

And finally he must have the ability to come close, not because he may believe in Buber's personalism or Tillich's existentialism or Kierkegaard's suffering but because he wishes it and is willing to make the sacrifices necessary to learn it.

"Open your heart," says Professor Allen O. Miller at Eden Theological Seminary, "and let me come in."

10 Examples from Practice

In this group of exemplars, four articles were selected that suggest the variety of clinical social work practice in health settings. In "The Social Work Home Visit in a Health Care Setting" (F), Sarah N. Cohen and Bernadette Egen discuss the use in current practice of a modality that dates back to the beginnings of medical social work. Indeed, they describe the home visit as "the modality of choice for the home care social worker." Although focus is on the home visit, the practice Cohen and Egen describe makes use of the one-client method in a multidisciplinary context.

Cohen and Egen use case vignettes to illustrate their points. In all, five cases are described. Each case consists of one client who lives alone, is elderly, and is receiving multidisciplinary health care services in his or her home. This person is the medical patient and the social work client. No other clients are involved directly, yet significant others "cause" problems in the giving and receiving of health care services in each case.

What is so striking about these cases is the power of membership in the life of each client. In all five cases, these memberships are "unseen." Depending on the case, those with whom the client shares membership are dead, living elsewhere, or part of a period in the client's life that is long past. Nevertheless, the influence of these unseen members on the client's behavior and health situation is dramatic. In these cases, problems manifest themselves in the interactions of the clients with other health care professionals who then request a social work home visit to get to the root of the problem. It is the social worker in each case who perceives the symbolic clues that lead to the resolution of what is essentially a problem in the management of unseen memberships that influence the client's ability to deal with the medical situation in a positive way.

Barbara Leff, in "A Club Approach to Social Work Treatment within a Home Dialysis Program" (G), illustrates the use of the nonkinship group method in the chronic care sector of the health field. Leff notes that people with similar problems are often able to accept help from one another. This observation implies the utility of the nonkinship group method. She makes another observation, however, which is important for clinical social workers in the health field. In discussing previous efforts to form a dialysis group, Leff points out that they failed because the clients associated the notion of "the group" with psychotherapy. Already dependent on machines for their physical survival, they feared the additional burden of being regarded as emotionally ill. As a consequence, they rejected the idea that they needed psychiatric treatment. This reaction is not uncommon among health social work clients and Leff's use of the nonkinship group method demonstrates its utility in clinical practice.

Throughout the article, the reality of membership is apparent. Indeed, the sense of social isolation, the various forms of acute psychosocial stress, and the chronic nature of the condition and its treatment underscore the importance of membership. As the group moves through various stages, its membership and activities are defined and redefined in ways that suggest the effectiveness of the nonkinship group method in recreating for clients a sense of "normalcy" and a series of activities that approximate the social relationships of everyday life in community with others. In this particular case, "business, educational, and social activities" were mixed with helping clients to cope effectively with "problems, fears, and anxieties." Basic amenities, such as food and drink, pleasant surroundings, and attractive furnishings, are highlighted as important factors in group formation and activities.

Finally, Leff notes the range of clinical roles inherent in the social worker's interaction in the group as its expert member. These range from enabler, to clinical specialist, to liaison to other members of the medical team.

The next two exemplars are illustrations of practice in collaboration with other health professionals. "Social Work and Nursing: Collaboration as a Method of Meeting Family Needs" (H), by Margaret A. Kaufmann and Edith Shapiro, is a rare exemplar of dynamics that effect the collaborative enterprise. In this article, the authors recount an example of successful collaboration, but begin their discussion with a reflection on the purpose, knowledge base, and educational preparation of each profession. Although the more dated aspects of this reflection have been edited out of the article as it is reprinted here, the basic principles that Kaufmann and Shapiro identify remain constants, and they go further in delineating the way each profession's purpose shapes the way knowledge is used than do most authors of similar articles. They also denote more clearly than most the similarities and differences between the professions and how they complement each other.

The final exemplar in this group, "Pediatrician and Social Worker as a Counseling Team" (I), by Randy Lee Comfort and Michael S. Kappy, is unusual in that it focuses on a type of, and setting for, collaboration not generally found in health social work literature—the private physician's office. Attention in this article is directed to the kinds of problems, both medical and social, encountered in the physician's office, and to the ways the physician and social worker collaborate to provide medical and social care.

Although exemplars H and I are somewhat unusual examples of collaborative practice, they are particularly effective in covering a range of concepts and variables discussed in Chapter 6. The attitudes identified in the chapter as prerequisites for effective collaboration are easily discerned in these readings. The notions of commitment to one's profession, belief in the holistic approach, the interdependency of practice, and respect for the expertise of colleagues are touched on in different ways in both selections.

The Social Work Home Visit in a Health Care Setting

Sarah N. Cohen and Bernadette Egen

ABSTRACT: Along with many other professions, current social work interest is focused on exploring the relationship between people and their environment. When this environment is a health care delivery system, the relationship can give rise to many problems. The authors demonstrate how a social work home visit can ameliorate some of these problems in a home care setting and suggest its applicability in other health care delivery systems.

Social workers traditionally have been interpreters and negotiators between individuals and the situations, systems, or environments in which human beings find themselves. At different times in our professional history, we have emphasized different aspects of this role, sometimes concentrating our efforts on altering the system/environment, as in the early days of social and industrial reform, while, at other times, we have focused more sharply on supporting the adaptive and coping abilities of

Social Work in Health Care. Vol. 6(4) Summer 1981. © 1981 by The Haworth Press, Inc. All rights reserved.

individuals. At present, we are attempting to better understand the relationship between people and their environment so that we may achieve an "ecological perspective," as Germain puts it (1977). We try to use newly discovered information regarding the impact of various environments upon the behavior and well-being of individuals by aiding these environments to become more responsive to the needs of individuals while, at the same time, we continue to aid individuals to understand and cope with the problems which these environments may engender.

This perspective is particularly useful in dealing with the stresses and complexities of the acute care hospital and for developing strategies to deal with them. Social workers in these institutions are keenly aware of the loss of privacy and personal dignity which hospitalized patients often experience and of the sense of depersonalization which they may feel. Though not deliberately foisted upon patients, these experiences and feelings appear to be the not easily controlled by-products of the highly specialized nature and ever accelerating pace of modern medical care. Ironically, this kind of stress saps the very physical and emotional stamina required to assist in the task of restoring health. This, in turn, puts further strain on a health care delivery system already beset by a multitude of problems. Such phenomena are not confined to acute care hospitals alone, however. As social workers in the home care department of a large urban hospital, we have noted its occurrence even when health care services are delivered in the patient's own home.

Home Care

Most home health care agencies are charged with the care of the recently discharged patient who requires skilled ancillary medical services to insure continued recovery. The patient is usually less ill than when in the hospital. There is, therefore, a reduction in the sense of medical urgency, and an opportunity for members of the home care team to take a more holistic approach. The primary mission of a home care agency, however, continues to be the delivery of concrete medical services. This requires an organized approach which, at times, can be impersonal or even arbitrary. The result, once more, is that the patient's life space is invaded, his/her time, movement, and decision-making powers are infringed upon. Strangers appear (visiting nurse, physical therapist, home health aide, etc.), usually needing to meet the demands of their own busy schedules. They issue medical directives which the patient must follow. Awkward pieces of clinical equipment may make their appearance (hospital beds, grab bars, etc.) and displace the patient's own furnishings. All of this, in addition to remaining symptoms, may cause a patient to continue to feel depressed, angry, and uncooperative with home care personnel, who in turn feel frustrated and are stymied in their attempts to render adequate medical care.

The problems which occur at the interface between the patient and the home health care system are, therefore, similar to those which occur in acute hospital settings. The role of the home care social worker also remains the same: to help the patient cope with the system and to help the system respond to the individual needs of the patient. In fulfilling this familiar role, however, the home care social worker has available an extremely effective tool, not nearly so available to the in-patient worker, and this is the home visit.

Home Visit

While an in-patient worker may make an occasional home visit, it is the modality of choice for the home care social worker. Home care patients are, by definition, homebound, and home is the arena in which the interaction between the patient and the health care system takes place. Presumably in recognition of this fact, and as noted by Axelrod (1978), many medical insurances reimburse for social work home visits. This also would seem to indicate some recognition that a social work home visit is a cost-effective modality due to the opportunity it provides for rapid and highly effective assessment and intervention when problems do occur. It is, in fact, our conviction, based on our experience and the available literature (Axelrod, 1978; Paterson and St. Cyr, 1960) that the social work home visit can allow us access to problems not evident or available during a patient's hospitalization, can yield information not obtainable from most other sources, and can provide us with opportunities for intervention less likely to occur in other settings.

When problems arise during a patient's hospital stay, engendered either by the illness or by the stress of the hospitalization as noted above, the professional hospital social worker is most often able to intervene in a meaningful way. However, not all such problems make themselves evident during hospitalization. The patient who is intimidated by the hospital is not likely to bring forth his or her concerns. On occasion, a patient is simply too ill to participate in discussion, and there may be no family members or friends to contact. The patient may deny or minimize observed or anticipated problems.

Once home, however, it is difficult to continue this minimization or denial. No matter how intrusive hospital staff and medical procedures may have been, they also were supportive and reassuring in the face of pain and anxiety. At home, the patient is alone for most of the day, except, perhaps, for the presence of another family member and the critical but brief visits of home care personnel. Patients who underestimated their need for help at home become quickly aware of their mistake. Others who idealized family relationships find that a few days of tension may put a dent in the best intentions of spouses and children. Patients who readily accepted home care services may discover themselves beset with the same feelings of invasion and of being controlled which they assumed they had left behind in the hospital.

There are also positive reasons for greater accessibility to discussion of difficulties once patients have been discharged. An obvious and major reason is that patients are likely to be less defensive and more open in their own homes than they were in the hospital. As Richmond (1917) observed, "In the office hospital, the clients are on the defensive and justify their visits by their replies. In the home, the social worker is on the defensive, the host and hostess at their ease." While an occasional patient may sense the worker's visits as another kind of invasion, most appear to welcome an opportunity to play host. There seems to be an increased sense of comfort from familiar surroundings, a feeling of control, a reenhancement of self-image, and, at the same time, a sense of relief that the social worker has come to offer help.

A home visit also affords us unique opportunities for extrapolating information about the patient through what we are able to observe about his neighborhood, home, interrelationships with family and friends, and the artifacts of his/her environment. As Richmond further observes there is "an avoidance of the need to ask so many questions, some of which are answered, unasked, by the communicative hostess and her surroundings. To the quiet observer, the photographs on the wall, the framed certificates of membership in fraternal orders, the pensioner's war relics, and Sunday school books, the household arrangements are all eloquent." The artifacts may have altered from Richmond's days to ours, but their significance remains constant.

Other members of the home care team may also be more accessible to the social worker than were their professional colleagues in the hospital. Generally speaking, those attracted to a home care setting are likely to be well oriented to a public health, educational, and team effort approach to delivering health care. The visiting nurse, physical therapist, and home attendant who are part of a home care effort are trained to work in close conjunction with the home care social worker. Schedules allow for regular communication, and there usually is a marked willingness to participate in social work planned or initiated intervention.

Nevertheless, difficulties do occur. Following are five illustrations of cases in which marked difficulties arose between the patient and the home care system. In the first case, a perceived invasion of privacy caused a patient to be surly and uncooperative with health care providers. In the second case, a patient's strong attachment to certain personal possessions, which represented a cherished self-image, blocked her from accepting appropriate medical care. An inadvertent disregard for the patient's sociocultural values caused a crisis in the third case. In the fourth case illustrated, a sudden acute depression occurred due to the patient's misperception of certain medical information. In the last case, a strong phobia inhibited the patient's acceptance of a necessary hospitalization. Since the causes of these difficulties were not immediately evident, the home care social worker was asked to make an assessment. In each case, a social work home visit, or series of them, was instrumental in ferreting out the source of the problem and in mounting an appropriate and successful intervention.

Case Examples

Invasion of Life Space

Mr. T., a single, 74-year-old, German-born, retired porter, was referred for home care following a partial amputation of his left leg. Due to his age, marginal income, poor physical health, deficient housing, and lack of social supports, Mr. T. was seen, and in the hospital saw himself, as needing maximal services on discharge. The home care plan called for twice-weekly visits from the visiting nurse, daily visits of a home health aide, and twice-weekly visits from the physical therapist. In addition, homebound meals were ordered, and referral for a friendly visitor was made to a community agency.

Despite the extent of the services Mr. T. was receiving and which he had agreed to in the hospital, he soon became surly and uncooperative with service providers. He refused appointments and would not follow medical directives. Those trying to help Mr. T. became frustrated and angry with him, which, in turn, caused Mr. T. to be even less cooperative. On his visits to the hospital clinic, Mr. T. was not responsive to inquiries by the social worker aimed at evaluating the cause of his behavior. It was thus decided that a home visit by the home care social worker should be attempted.

Only one social work home visit was required to make an assessment and to initiate interventions which proved to be effective. The rapidity with which this was accomplished was largely due to the abundance of evidence in Mr. T.'s apartment which gave the worker insight into the personality and value system of this elderly, essentially nonverbal man. This evidence underlined the value which Mr. T. placed on cleanliness, efficiency, self-determination, and privacy. His household effects and furniture, though sparse and threadbare, were neat and clean, and had been placed with a great deal of ingenuity so that everything was within reach from his wheelchair. When the worker made this observation verbally, the patient responded with obvious pleasure and pride. When the worker commented on how difficult it must have been for him even before his surgery to climb the four flights of stairs to his apartment, Mr. T. retorted that it also kept busybodies away from him. The multiple locks, which the worker also noted, were explained in a similar way—not to discourage criminals so much as to keep nosey neighbors out of his room.

Mr. T.'s dilemma was now fairly simple to understand. On the one hand, he recognized his need for many of the services he was receiving. On the other hand, he greatly resented the frequency with which his life was being invaded and the restrictions which this placed on his privacy and self-determination. When the worker stated that his dilemma might be partially resolved by assessing which services were obviously essential and which might be diminished or terminated, the patient appeared greatly relieved, participating fully in the ensuing discussion with the social worker. Mr. T. realized that his doctor, visiting nurse, and others on the health care team also would have to be consulted, but asked that the social worker explain his feelings to them. As a result of this interchange and the ensuing discussions held by the social worker with other service providers, the home health aide's visits were cut down to three per week, the visiting nurse's to one, and the friendly visitor was dispensed with. The meals-on-wheels continued to come, however, and the physical therapist increased her visits to three times a week to support Mr. T.'s striving for rapid independence. Within a week, Mr. T.'s mood changed to one of cooperation, the service providers worked without frustration, and Mr. T.'s advancement toward independence and cessation of home health care services was expedited.

Artifacts as Clues

Miss J., a 71-year-old single, diabetic woman, was admitted to the hospital for amputation of her right foot due to gangrene. Once in the hospital, however, she refused surgery and also refused to discuss her seemingly irrational behavior with the floor social worker. After a psychiatric evaluation which revealed Miss J. to be mentally competent, there was no choice but to discharge her home. The home care department accepted Miss J. for service with some trepidation. A visiting nurse and home health aide began visiting. Though not an optimal medical plan, it was hoped that if the infected foot could be kept clean and dry, it might detach spontaneously from the leg, with no spread of gangrene. Attempts to pursue this plan were greatly hampered, however, by the conditions in Miss J.'s home. Her basement apartment, dark and damp, was extremely dirty and vermin-infected. An untrained pet cat urinated and defecated freely, so that Miss J.'s foot came into frequent contact with cat hair and waste. Furthermore, Miss J. seemed either unable or unwilling to follow nursing directives regarding bathing her foot and keeping it covered. Attempts by the nurse to convince Miss J. to get rid of the cat, allow the apartment to be thoroughly cleaned, be readmitted to the hospital for amputation, or enter a nursing home so that her foot could be properly cared for were all met with stony refusal. At this point, a request was made for the home care social worker to make a home visit.

It took four visits for the worker to discover the causes of Miss J.'s seemingly irrational behavior and to mount an intervention. The reasons for Miss J.'s behavior became more apparent when the contents of her apartment could be observed more closely. Though the apartment was extremely dirty, noxious, and an obvious threat to Miss J.'s health, it also held many mementos of an earlier time in her life when she had been an aspiring actress, dancer, and singer. Though she had not received recognition as a performer and had ended her working days as a secretary, her closets were filled with worn evening gowns, traveling suits, and dancing shoes. She had many scrapbooks filled with clippings and photographs of herself as an attractive young woman, often on the arm of a male companion.

At the beginning of the initial interview, Miss J. was unwilling to have her mementos touched and warned that the cat was vicious. As the worker continued to show an interest in the patient's past life, however, Miss J. began discussing with pride her early career and her social and emotional decline in the recent years caused by aging, illness, and the deaths of many contemporaries. She was finally able to admit that it was her attachment to the contents of her home and to the past image of herself which made it impossible for her to consider altering in any way either her belongings or herself. She imagined dying after surgery in the hospital and having strangers discard or destroy her life's treasures. She imagined her "poor puss" without a home.

It took several more visits before the worker was able to help Miss J. work through some of these feelings. During this time, the social worker maintained close and frequent contact with the visiting nurse and home health aide so that information could be shared and mutual goals decided upon. Finally, after a new home was found for the cat with neighbors, after her clothing was dispersed to her few remaining friends or given to a deserving charity, and after Miss J. was assured that she could take all of her scrapbooks with her, she agreed to move to a nursing home. Shortly after arriving there, her foot did detach spontaneously, there was no further spread of the gangrene, and Miss J. remained at the nursing home until her death several years later.

Sociocultural Factors

Mrs. D. was an 85-year-old, Italian-born widow of a prominent Latin scholar. She was being seen twice weekly by the visiting nurse and a home care physical therapist following hospitalization for an acute phase of her osteoarthritis and a chronic heart condition. In addition, a Medicaid-paid home attendant, arranged by the hospital social worker, came daily to Mrs. D.'s home. Mrs. D. had been enthusiastic about these arrangements before her discharge. Once home, however, she began a series of daily phone calls to the home care department to complain that both the therapist and the home attendant were fresh and lazy, though she was unable to describe what they did that so offended her. A subsequent home visit by the home care social worker did much to clarify the situation.

Mrs. D. lived in a large, rent-controlled apartment which was filled with ornate Italian furniture which she and her husband had brought with them from Rome in the 1920s, as well as various books and art objects that had belonged to her husband Dr. D. Though he had died 10 years ago, Dr. D. was still a palpable presence in the apartment. When the worker made a comment to this effect, Mrs. D. proudly acknowledged the fact. Though she herself had come from a prominent family and appeared to be a strong-willed and articulate person, she seemed to have gained her greatest pleasure from being the wife of a prominent academician. Their childlessness seemed to have drawn them even closer, and she described her life as being one devoted to caring for her husband and helping him to advance his career. Among her contemporaries, and those aware of her husband's status, she was referred to still as "Signora, Dr. D." Upon revealing this, Mrs. D. broke into tears and described the anger and humiliation she felt when the physical therapist had addressed her by her fist name and encouraged her to walk by beckoning with a finger and "talking to me in a funny high voice as if she were speaking to a child. I am not a child. I am a respected woman!"

When made aware of her error, the physical therapist was most willing to try and alter her behavior, but Mrs. D. would not accept this, and a new, more "respectful" therapist was installed, with whom Mrs. D. was most cooperative and happy. She was more willing to accept compromise in the case of the home attendant whose laziness, it appeared, consisted of her refusal to dust Mrs. D.'s books, pictures, and other memorabilia on a daily basis as Mrs. D. had requested. When the social worker explained the emotional value these objects had for Mrs. D., however, the home attendant agreed to dust them three times a week. This gesture appeared to satisfy Mrs. D. From that point on, there were no more telephone calls to the home care department, and Mrs. D. was fully cooperative in her future dealings with service providers.

Misperceived Information

Mr. H., a 77-year-old widower, had recently undergone colon surgery to remove a malignant tumor and had been left with a permanent colostomy. Mr. H. had been informed of his diagnosis, had been told by his surgeon that there was a very good chance that the malignancy would not recur, had learned colostomy care quickly in the hospital, and remained in good spirits for several weeks following discharge. Suddenly, however, and with no apparent precipitating experience, Mr. H. became markedly depressed, stayed in his night clothes and in bed for most of the day, and complained to the visiting nurse of a heaviness and lack of energy. Though an apt pupil in the hospital, Mr. H. became less adept and motivated in carrying out his colostomy care. Given assurance by his surgeon that his current symptoms were not physically caused, Mr. H. then discussed awareness of his depression with the visiting nurse. He could not fathom its cause, however. At this point, the visiting nurse asked the home care social worker to make a visit.

Two home visits were required to evaluate Mr. H.'s problem and to assist him in beginning to resolve it. Even before discussion began, however, it was possible for the worker to gain visual awareness of Mr. H.'s usual personality and life style. A picture of his long-dead wife was on the mantelpiece, but a picture of his current woman friend sat on his night table. His closet door, half ajar, revealed many youthful sports clothes. Though old, the furnishings of his apartment were solid and ample, purchased during his career as a successful clothing salesman. Based on these observations, it was an easy matter for the social worker to begin her conversation with Mr. H., and Mr. H. readily revealed that before his surgery, he had enjoyed playing cards with his cronies, eating out in fancy restaurants, and taking trips abroad with his woman friend. Now, he had lost enthusiasm for all of these things.

With the worker's help, Mr. H. retraced his experiences in the hospital and since, trying to pinpoint the event or thought which had triggered his depression. Finally, after considerable discussion, Mr. H. thought that his feelings had to do with what the doctor had said about chances of recurrence of his malignancy. "A very good chance" that the malignancy would not recur seemed to Mr. H. to be about 60-40 odds against recurrence. He wondered, however, if he might increase his odds by settling down to a more sedate life style, giving up late night card games, foreign travel, and rich foods. He wanted to resume a sexual relationship with his woman friend, but worried that this too might cause stress that would lessen his chances for survival. He found it difficult to articulate these concerns, even to his doctor. Recently, when Mr. H. had obliquely joked with his doctor about "being able to satisfy my girlfriend again," the doctor had joked back and said that Mr. H. was "too old for sex anyhow." This had discouraged further discussion.

It was equally difficult for Mr. H. to discuss these kinds of concerns with a female worker. The worker had a marked advantage, however, in being able to see the patient at home. Evidence regarding Mr. H.'s prior life style was abundant. This precluded the necessity of the patient having to carry the bulk of the conversation himself. The worker was able to guess and fill in when the patient found it difficult to speak. Gradually, the patient took the initiative, deciding, finally, that he would like to try once more and discuss these worries with his doctor. This he did, apparently receiving information which was helpful to him. Following several frank discussions with his physician, Mr. H.'s depression lifted, he resumed self-care, he continued in his medical recovery, and was able to return to most of the activities which had given him pleasure in the past.

Phobia

Miss C., a 64-year-old librarian, had fractured a hip and was receiving physical therapy at home following hospitalization. During one of her sessions with the physical therapist, she revealed that she had been experiencing heavy vaginal bleeding for some time, but was terrified to see a doctor about it, presumably because she feared a malignancy. She had no internist and refused to discuss this situation with her orthopedist. She also refused, though she was able to ambulate, to come to the hospital and discuss her immobilizing anxiety with a social worker. She did agree, however, to have the home care social worker pay her a visit.

Miss C. lived in an attractively furnished studio apartment. She seemed happy to see the worker and was relaxed and voluble in sharing information about herself. She readily admitted to understandable anxiety regarding a possible diagnosis of cancer, but offered that she did not think this was the real reason for her anxiety. She seemed unable to state what this real reason was. As the interview stretched on, it appeared that it might end without its having revealed the cause for Miss C.'s reluctance to see a doctor about her bleeding. Suddenly, however, Miss C. excused herself to use the bathroom. Since Miss C. had appeared physically uncomfortable for some time, the worker had wondered why Miss C. had not excused herself earlier and was even more puzzled when, with great embarrassment, Miss C. asked if the worker would please stand out in the hallway until she had finished using the bathroom. When the worker returned, Miss C. then explained, with a great deal of discomfort, that she had suffered from a lifelong "urination phobia," something she had been unable to shed even with psychotherapy. This phobia required that she be alone in her apartment with both apartment and bathroom doors locked before she was able to urinate. This, then, was the reason for her reluctance to see a doctor. Miss C. knew that a hospitalization would be required, and in the hospital, she would not be able to urinate. On her previous hospitalization, she could not void for several days, and a catheter finally had to be installed, much to the irritation of the medical and nursing staffs who had been convinced that the patient could have voided "if she had wanted to." The patient had felt humiliated and frightened by the obvious anger expressed, but had been unable to share her feelings with the floor social worker. Miss C. now dreaded a repetition of this experience.

Armed with this information, the home care social worker was able to make appropriate arrangements so that Miss C. could receive necessary medical care. With the patient's permission, her orthopedist was alerted to her problem and referred her to a sympathetic surgeon. The appropriate hospital social worker was involved and was able to help the floor medical and nursing staffs gain a broader understanding of Miss C.'s inability to void. The patient was catheterized immediately upon admission, underwent a routine hysterectomy for nonmalignant fibroid tumors, and was discharged without further incident.

Implications

The foregoing sought to illustrate the effectiveness of the social work home visit in a particular health care setting when difficulties arose between patients and the home health care system. Emphasis was on the kinds of information obtainable and the kinds of interventions available via the social work home visit. It is also important to note that there is an enhancement of certain psychodynamics which, though present or potentially present in all therapeutic relationships, become especially prominent when the arena for interaction is the patient's own home. These may include a rapidly accelerated pace of relationship development between patient and worker occasioned by the sense of relaxation and openness which the home engenders, a tendency for the occurrence of strong transference and countertransference in a setting suggestive of prior life experience, and a desire by the patient to "deprofessionalize" the worker-patient relationship. This last tendency is understandable in that, as mentioned, the patient at home may feel like a host and expect the social worker to behave as a friend or social visitor. Well-refined skills are thus required to avoid the obvious problems which can result from the foregoing. At the same time, one must take heed of the positive value which may be achieved from the sharing of a meal or of not rejecting outright a small gift which the patient may have selected from his or her personal possessions.

Finally, home visits offer us an opportunity to reassert historical social work values, such as the right to self-determination, privacy, and control over one's life (Axelrod, 1978). While these are basic social work values and must be kept in mind in all settings, they take on an especially strong meaning when visiting in a patient's home. The need to make appointments well in advance of our appearances and, if at all possible, to the patient's convenience is critical. It is also helpful to dress conservatively, comport ourselves in ways which add to the patient's comfort, and to abide by the simple rules of etiquette. Attention to such details make it all the more likely that the patient will be open and at ease with us, responsive to our questions, suggestions, and interventions.

When one considers the benefits which accrue from home visiting, one might assume that it is a more commonly used modality than is the case. As long ago as 1961, Fawcett noted that "the home visit was a usual procedure in all social work undertakings and during the formative years of our profession," but "fell into disfavor a few decades ago." Pumphrey and Pumphrey (1961) and Behrens and Ackerman (1956) make similar observations, and it would appear that this trend toward disuse has continued in the years since these observations were made. We base this conclusion on the lack of reference to this modality in most current social work literature and on our discussions and correspondence with colleagues and schools of social work. Surely, there are many understandable reasons for this to have occurred in health care as well as other social work settings. Hospital social work services often have to be delivered with such rapidity that there may be no time to make a home visit, even if it is clear that such a visit might be of significant help. Urban sprawl and constantly rising crime rates discourage travel. Home visiting is, on occasion, both uncomfortable and harrowing. However, old biases would also seem to be at work. Mary Richmond's affection for home visiting was, no doubt, due to considerable personal experience with this modality when our profession was in its infancy. It may now seem to be a relic of our distant, "nonprofessional" past. More recently, home visits have been associated with welfare investigations and the invasion of privacy.

We think that such judgments and associations, however, unnecessarily discourage more frequent use of the home visit in health care settings where it could serve a variety of roles. In the case of the patient with frequent readmissions to the hospital, a social work home visit might do much to tell us about the conditions which contributed to this situation—often more than the patient's verbal recounting alone. Following discharge, such visits might be extremely helpful to patients in maintaining social, emotional, and economic conditions which are health-supportive and further reduce the need for hospitalization. For the elderly outpatient in particular, there often is great difficulty in understanding and negotiating the intricacies of the clinic setting. Though some of these patients become affiliated with and are seen at home by community-based social work agencies, these agencies themselves may experience problems in comprehending the structure and complicated procedures of the hospital and its clinics. As a result, many older patients are lost to follow-up medical care. One can only conjecture upon the benefits which might be derived from the planned, intermittent visit of a hospital or clinic-based social worker, sensitive both to the problems of the patient and to the workings of the health care system. There is no doubt that the social work home visit could be used in many health care settings to the advantage of both the patient and the health care delivery system.

References

Axelrod, T. Innovative roles for social workers in home care programs. *Health And Social Work*, 1978, *3*, 49–66.

Behrens, M., & Ackerman, N. The home visits as an aid in a family diagnosis and therapy. *Social Casework*, 1956, *37*, 1, 11–19.

Fawcett, E. A re-evaluation of the home visit in casework practice. *Social Casework*, 1961, *42*, 9, 439–445.

Germain, C. An ecological perspective on social work practice in health care. *Social Work In Health Care*, 1977, *3*, 1, 67–77.

Paterson, J., & St. Cyr, F. The use of the home visit in present day social work. *Social Casework*, 1960, *41*, 4, 184–191.

Pumphrey, R., & Pumphrey, M. (Eds.). in *The heritage of American social work*. New York: Columbia University Press, 1961.

Richmond, M. *Social diagnosis*. Philadelphia: The Russell Sage Foundation, 1917.

G
A Club Approach to Social Work Treatment within a Home Dialysis Program

Barbara Leff

ABSTRACT: *This article discusses one approach to helping patients and their families cope with the stresses of a program where dialysis treatments are performed at home. The "Home Dialysis Club" includes many facets and levels of group work treatment. The need for support is unending for families with this difficult life style. The club approach offers ongoing services with flexibility to change as needs change.*

Within the past 15 years a new patient population has emerged: a group of people totally dependent on a machine for survival. These are people with end-stage renal disease, who except for advances in medical technology would have died. Now, however, they are functioning members of society, their "lifeline" being the artificial kidney machine.

This is a group with many stresses imposed upon them daily as a result of the treatment process and the life style they must now adopt in order to survive. "The stresses of kidney disease and hemodialysis contribute to a continued series of crises which involve all phases of the patient's existence."[1]

A new medical technology created this patient group. "Hospital Social Work now must concentrate on combining service to patients and their families with study of the new problems in living associated with new technologies. The aim is always not merely to extend life but to allow a better quality of life."[2]

This article describes one approach to helping those patients and their families with the stresses involved in a program where they perform dialysis treatments in their own homes. The club approach is one example of a new social work treatment method created to serve this new patient population. It has been used successfully for two years with a group of home dialysis patients at an urban Veterans Administration hospital.

Characteristic Stresses on the Home Dialysis Patient and His Family

At no time can the dialysis patient isolate his illness from the rest of his life. The machine in his home is a constant reminder of his dependence. It

Social Work in Health Care, Vol. 1(1), Fall 1975. © 1975 by The Haworth Press, Inc. All rights reserved.

also represents the responsibility he and his family have assumed for his health and safety. Medical care prescribed by a distant hospital staff must be maintained by the patient and his family. He needs to be on dialysis an average of three days a week, six hours a day, and when not being dialyzed he must adhere to very stringent dietary restrictions.

The dialysis patient experiences constant loss and change.[3] A critical body function has been lost. Since other vital organs are often affected by the lack of kidney function, the threat that they will be damaged is ever present. Social and business functions revolve around the dialysis regimen. Such constraints affect work, finances, status, and life styles. Even short vacations and business trips are contingent on proximity to a hospital or clinic where treatment can be scheduled.

Patients cannot know when they will feel sick or need medical attention. Many are fearful of injury each time they are "tied" to the machine and watch their blood leave their bodies to be cleaned by an artificial kidney. They experience changes in body image. Weight loss necessitated by strict diet control results in changed physical appearance. Stringent dietary restrictions are frustrating. Often sexual desire and potency change radically. Family equilibrium may be affected as role assignments are changed or reversed. The wife may become the major income earner. These changes are traumatic and render the family crises prone.

These changes, losses, and stresses result in pressure that may be intolerable to the most stable and well adjusted.[4] Long-term counseling and support are essential for successful mastery of this life situation because the pressures experienced are beyond the scope of normal coping mechanisms. "What dialysis patients do manifest are various emotional-behavioral reactions, of varying intensity, to a condition and treatment that present them with an incredible barrage of acute and long range stresses."[1]

The Group Approach

Since people are often able to accept help from others with similar problems, the group approach seemed an obvious modality to employ.[5,6] However, twice in the past this approach had failed. This was puzzling, but the answer soon emerged from discussions with patients. The group approach had been flawed for them by previous experiences where the word "group" had come to mean psychotherapy group.[5] Patients had resisted the idea that they in any way needed psychiatric treatment, and had greatly feared being seen as emotionally sick. It was burdensome enough to cope with being physically sick.

Because of this they were closing doors that might give them access to help in coping with their problems and their reactions to them. "Dialysis patients' intense emotional reactions are rooted in reality and do not necessarily merit a psychiatric or psychopathological label."[1] Yet at the same time they need to share experiences with other patients. Those we spoke to felt that the home dialysis program was growing so large they were losing the closeness and support they once received from the hospital staff. Since a home care program carries the expectation of independent functioning, the patient's sense of isolation from traditional hospital support provoked anxiety.[4] Also apparent were the needs of wives of home dialysis patients. They needed an opportunity to get together and share their feelings about common problems growing out of their having become dialysis "attendants."

Out of this need assessment came the concept of the "Home Dialysis Club." The club includes many facets and levels of group work treatment. In format, it is a mixture of business, educational, and social activities and, most importantly, is perceived by the members as a place where they are able to share and receive help with problems, fears, and anxieties. It is a norm of the home dialysis program that all patients and their families participate in the club's activities.

Development and Early Themes
of the Home Dialysis Club

The Home Dialysis Club was established in August 1972. It began as a wives' club, a place where they could gain support and understanding for what they were experiencing in their daily lives. It was also a place where they could receive warranted recognition from each other as well as from the staff for what they were doing on behalf of their spouses.

Clearly the wife's attitudes and feelings significantly affected the patient's adjustment to his illness and the quality of life for both. Cummings[1] feels that "the family is the primary adjustment support system in the dialysis patient's life."

In order to encourage the wives to attend, it was important to make the initial contact as attractive as possible. Invitations were sent out to all dialysis wives announcing the formation of the club. Refreshments were served at the first meeting in a room designed to create the ambiance of an afternoon club meeting. Their conversation, however, was not that of an "afternoon tea." They felt that neither family nor friends could understand the problems they were experiencing. They recognized that they had no outlet for their feelings and no resource for advice and support on how to cope with their unique responsibilities. The wives had hesitated to "bother" the doctors with their "minor" concerns. Here there was some exchange of ideas about dialysis routines which diminished their sense of loneliness and isolation.[7]

The worker thought all home dialysis wives should know what went on at the meeting even if they had not attended. A newsletter was sent to all "members" announcing when the next meeting would be held and briefly describing what had transpired at the last. Other wives expressed interest and did not want to be left out. By the second meeting, it became clear that husbands were also feeling very "left out" and wanted to know what they were missing. Some anxiety developed among the patients that such an experience by their wives, without them, could create a division in their relationship. The wives felt that a place where they, patients and wives together, could meet and discuss common concerns would be helpful. Some wives also felt they could more easily express their feelings to their own husbands with the support of others in the same situation.

Meetings were held once a month, on a Saturday. The available three hours had to encompass all aspects of the club's activities. Patients had to travel too far and were too tied to the dialysis routine to meet more frequently. The group handled business and organizational aspects of the meetings. There was also the need to have a place and opportunity to share more personal problems. Common themes were problems in coping and adjusting. The group was large, with an average attendance of 22 members. Much of the work went on in small subgroups. Having coffee and cake served during the last part of the meeting facilitated the members forming into small cluster groups around the room. Many important issues were discussed here, often issues that members felt were too intimate to be brought out in the large meeting. This clustering around refreshments served three vital purposes: First, it gave members the option of talking to someone they knew shared a similar concern. There was a correlation between what was brought up in the larger group but not fully discussed and what discussion continued in the small group. Secondly, the member was able to move to another group if the topic became too anxiety-provoking for him to handle at that time. In such an event, the member could get up for a refill of coffee and settle down elsewhere where a less threatening topic was being discussed. It would appear to others that his interest was simply diverted, thereby offering him a comfortable and needed defense. Thirdly, it gave the worker an opportunity to move easily from group to group facilitating discussion and noting which members needed more individualized attention with particular problems.

By the fourth meeting the members began to take increasing responsibility for the group. Elections were held, and members took on the various roles that the worker had once assumed.[6] Dialysis couples often feel they have lost control over their own lives because of their absolute dependence on the kidney machine. The club gave them a small vehicle for control and planning. On the basis of membership decision dues were collected to be spent on social events during the year. Since dialysis couples have had to alter their membership in many outside social activities because of their medical restrictions, the club's provision of opportunity for them to enjoy themselves without feeling so different from everyone else was important.

At this point, the club was well established as an ongoing experience with many different facets. Members who lived too far away to attend were kept informed by the monthly newsletter, and they too began sending in dues so they would not be left out. Being excluded had become the fear, rather than being labeled as "sick" for being included. The club had achieved one of its original purposes in that group membership was perceived as a positive, ongoing experience.

Highlights of the Home Dialysis Club

The group has served many different purposes. When a crisis occurred in the Home Dialysis Unit, the group became the place where feelings could be expressed. When patients needed information on a topic of great concern to them, such as the long-range effects of dialysis or the risks involved in a kidney transplant, the group became the place to get the information by inviting a speaker to the meeting. The worker encouraged the group to invite their own medical staff to speak as often as possible. In this way not only would they get the information they needed, but also communication between members and staff could become more open. Dialysis couples feel so dependent on staff that any gap in communication can create great anxiety. Patients often express the fear that staff have the power to take away their life-sustaining treatment at any time. As a result of this open communication there are fewer misunderstandings between patients and staff. Staff members are helped to see the patients as people, and their understanding of how they can best serve patients' needs is enhanced. Medical team workers have been enabled to put more emphasis on overall good adjustment to dialysis since they have discovered the complexity of these families' social needs.

Communication among members is also vital. Many members realized for the first time that they were not alone with their problems and that other members were able to cope with the same problem that they felt could never be resolved. Often members express conflicts that cannot easily be resolved. It is in this respect that the worker's role as therapist becomes extremely important. The worker must be able to assume the role of specialist, not only as enabler, and must use expertise as the treating person. Members look to the worker for guidance when attempting to deal with their feelings and fantasies surrounding their very difficult lives. As in individual treatment, the members must be able to derive from the worker the sense that no subject is taboo and that whatever is of concern to them may be discussed. Just because the group is not a traditional therapy group does not presuppose that very intimate problems are not discussed. As the members have become closer to each other, they have been able to discuss many issues in depth that at one time they would have avoided. The group's structure and flexibility allowed this to develop naturally over several years.

The need to feel normal has been a theme since the club's inception. Members expressed the desire to once again live as other people and share the good things in life. Vacation planning and social activities took on great significance. When seen in connection with the couples' struggle to cope with all the restrictions put on their lives, the social activities take on new meaning. It is the goal in any social work intervention to help patients be as "normal" as possible and to help them utilize the options they do have in their lives. One attempt by the group to have a good time without feeling so isolated from everyone else around them was their inquiry about going on a cruise and dialyzing each other while on board ship. With group support they felt they could follow their restrictions with less difficulty than when going on vacation as individuals. They received an encouraging response from the president of a steamship company. Dates for a Bermuda cruise were offered with one free stateroom to be used as a dialysis room. Although the members were not able to go this time for a variety of reasons, the important thing is that the group attempted to cope with life as it is and tried to make it more fulfilling.

Sometimes activities may seem purely "social" when they are not, and the worker must be aware of the dynamics operating within the group. From the beginning the members have expressed an interest in being informed, by the worker, when someone is hospitalized or when someone dies. The expressed reason was that an appropriate card could be sent. Although feeling there was more significance to this request, the worker offered no interpretation and allowed the members to disguise what they were feeling until they were ready to reveal its meaning. Eventually the members were able to talk about their feeling that their lives are so tenuous and that they were acutely aware that when someone was ill, it could easily have been themselves. They wanted to know that others would show concern if they were to become ill. Knowing about others was their way of mastering their own anxiety about being alone when in crisis. Since their life situations are so threatened, it is very important to help this patient population cope with issues at a pace that is manageable for them. This necessitates the workers' constant evaluation of the underlying dynamics and the skilled timing of intervention.

Taking care of each other was expressed also in their willingness to be "sponsors" for new people entering the home dialysis training program. During initial psychosocial evaluations, the worker found that many new couples needed different support than the professional team could offer them. They needed to talk to someone who had actually lived through the training and was doing home dialysis. When the group was approached with the idea of helping the new people by being "sponsors," every member volunteered. New members were thus assigned to a more experienced member who lived in their area. This has served two purposes: The new trainees have another couple to turn to for support in addition to that provided by staff, and the club is presented to new people as the norm for home dialysis couples.

As the group progressed, another phase developed. Children were invited to attend some of the meetings. As members learned that open communication with each other was safe, they began to share some of their feelings with their children more openly.[8] Since children are involved, it is appropriate for them to be included in some discussions. The whole family is affected by home dialysis, and they too need a place to talk about how they feel.

Over the two years, many members have requested individual interviews to follow up on something that has happened in the group or to pursue an issue they feel is too personal for group discussion. Members who may never have sought help before have found the group a means of getting involved in individual treatment. Since they have already tested out the worker they are less fearful of involving themselves in treatment. Some of that great anxiety around needing psychiatric help has been dissipated through the nonthreatening group experience.

Conclusion

Dialysis never ends except through transplant or through death. Likewise, the need for a sustaining, supportive environment is unending for families destined to this difficult way of life. While the resistance of patients and families to joining a group was an immediate spur to using the "club" approach, the format has demonstrated serendipitous features. For people whose need is forever, the club is a natural ongoing experience with flexibility to change as individual members express their changing needs. Thus firm connection to a helping source is an imperative component. Families new to the program can take in help at their own pace, while those who have partially integrated the hazards of a life-threatening situation are strengthened by the offering of aid under conditions protective to the helpers and those being helped.

The essential limitation of the structure is that a quasisocial situation complicates the handling of resistance. For a group whose defined needs are forever, there is, however, more time to allow for the breaking down of such barriers to help. The club approach has been demonstrated as an unconventional but effective means of offering services to home dialysis patients and their families in a manner consonant with their needs for dignity, self-respect, and more control of the structure than is needed by some clients.

References

1. Cummings, Jonathan. "Hemodialysis: Feelings, Facts, Fantasies." *American Journal of Nursing* 70 (1970):70-76.
2. Morse, Joan. "Family Involvement in Pediatric Dialysis and Transplantation." *Social Casework* 55 (1974):223.
3. Wright, Robert; Sand, Patricia; and Livingston, Goodhue. "Psychological Stress during Hemodialysis for Chronic Renal Failure." *Annals of Internal Medicine* 64 (1966):611-21.
4. Joel, Sheila, and Wieder, Susanne. "Factors Involved in Adaptation to the Stress of Hemodialysis." *Smith College Studies in Social Work* 43 (1972-73): 202, 205.
5. Tropp, Emmanuel. "The Group: In Life and in Social Work." *Social Casework* 49 (1968):267-74.
6. Hartford, Margaret. *Groups in Social Work—Application of Small Group Theory and Research in Social Work Practice.* New York: Columbia University Press, 1972.
7. Smith; McDonald; Curtis; and DeWardener. "Hemodialysis in the Home, Problems and Frustrations." *Lancet* (1969):616.
8. MacNamara, Margaret. "The Family in Stress: Social Work before and after Renal Hemotransplantation." *Social Work* 14 (1969):93.

H Social Work and Nursing: Collaboration as a Method of Meeting Family Needs

Margaret A. Kaufmann and Edith Shapiro

The myth that we can achieve collaboration simply by the act of conferring about a specific patient from time to time needs to be dispelled. Collaboration is an intricate process which involves the selective use of knowledge and the effective interplay of action between two or more professionals who share a common goal: comprehensive patient care.

Collaboration is a process by which two or more differing professional persons or groups work toward a common objective by the use and interaction, both individually and jointly, of their unique professional knowledge. It also involves a philosophy that underwrites the value of interdependence among professions, and the importance of coordinate use of resources within a given period of time, to the end that greater effectiveness is achieved.

In their coordinative efforts, social work and nursing often tend to see their respective roles as those of conferring and consulting rather than collaborating. Consultation involves the deliberation of two or more persons upon some matter; the seeking of opinion, advice, information, or instruction. It may be one-directional, or it may be a mutual giving and receiving. Collaboration, though it consistently involves conferring, formal or informal, presupposes a more active relationship involving conjoint participation toward a goal that has both mutual and individual facets. This common goal is one widely supported by the health professions. It involves the improvement at all levels of services to patients and families so that comprehensive patient care may be realized with minimal destructive effects on family equilibrium and functioning.

The effects of collaboration and noncollaboration are many and have implications for community as well as for individual planning. A result of noncollaboration may well be the placement of responsibility for synthesis of service as a burden upon the patient and family, rather than as an anticipated outcome of professional function.

Fundamental to the achievement of successful collaboration is a comprehension of the nature and roles of the potential collaborators. Too often the expectations that professions have of each other are limited by incomplete or inaccurate knowledge, and perhaps also by a degree of timidity in approaching another discipline.

Edited and reprinted, with permission, from *The Journal of Social Work Process*, Volume XIII, pp. 33–50 (1962). Published by the University of Pennsylvania School of Social Work.

Currently social work and nursing educators and practitioners are tending to be less concerned with uniqueness and overlapping of function per se than with definition of discrete role and focus in collaborative efforts. For this reason it is important to outline knowledge areas in training and practice that are more specific to the individual professions.

Similarities and Differences

Certain similarities exist in the educational backgrounds of nurses and social workers. A wide variety of educational preparation exists for each practitioner group. The largest proportion of the workers in both professions have not had graduate education. In social work, the majority of the practitioners have completed a baccalaureate program but the emphasis on social science background has been variable.

By contrast, in nursing, the largest group in staff level positions do not hold a baccalaureate. There is, however, an increasing number of practitioners who hold an Associate in Arts degree (the two-year Junior College program) or the baccalaureate, but these still remain in the minority. Social science content in nursing is highly variable. It increases in depth and breadth in the baccalaureate and higher degree programs, but does not completely approximate the scope found in the graduate programs in social welfare.

Both the medical social worker and the nurse have areas of discrete role and focus. They also have areas in which there is purposeful blending of both role and focus that lead toward their joint goal: comprehensive patient care. The role and focus of the nurse is twofold. She shares the ultimate goal held by all health workers: the promotion and maintenance of optimum health of individuals and groups. In addition she holds a specific goal that involves individuals or groups under the stress of a health-illness nature. This goal has as its primary purpose the relief of tension and discomfort to the end of restoring or maintaining internal and interpersonal equilibrium. (Johnson, 1959, p. 292)

It is with these backgrounds, having both similarities and differences in their natures, that nurse and social worker approach the collaborative effort.

Collaboration in Patient Care

Perhaps one of the best ways to demonstrate the principles of collaborative patient care is through an analysis of a successful practical experience in comprehensive care for a particular patient.

Such a case is that of Mr. Charles Dolan, age 61.

Charles Dolan

Mr. Dolan looked like a man who should have had a twinkle in his eye, but he didn't; and his skin didn't fit him too well. Until the time of his retirement, Mr. Dolan had been with the Chicago police force. He was a bachelor and lived with and cared for his mother until the time of her death. Following her death, his life socially became rather isolated. He moved to Los Angeles, where he lived by himself in a hotel room not too far from his nephew and his nephew's family. It was to his nephew that Mr. Dolan turned at the point of crisis—the beginning of his acute symptoms. Mr. Dolan was first confined to bed in the nephew's home. From there he was admitted to the hospital where his nephew regularly visited him.

Mr. Dolan's medical problem was one of urinary retention, which resulted in severe kidney damage and infection of the right kidney. The condition was complicated by an abscess formation, which necessitated a right nephrectomy. Because of concurrent abscess involvement of the intestinal tract, a temporary transverse colostomy (the creation of an artificial anus on the abdominal wall) became necessary. Surgical closure of the colostomy in approximately three months was anticipated if no complications arose.

Mr. Dolan's appearance was that of a seriously ill individual. His color was poor and he was almost totally lacking in physical energy. He ate little, and scarcely responded either to his physical surroundings or to the nurse. During the periods when the nurse cared for his colostomy he retreated even further. Something beyond his physical situation was obviously affecting Mr. Dolan. The primary blocking appeared to be related to the colostomy. It is well understood that a colostomy has many psychological and social overtones. In Mr. Dolan's case these were not clearly defined. The matter was discussed with the physician, and upon his concurrence, a referral was made to social service.

The nurse discussed the situation with the social worker, indicating that although, from the physiological standpoint, Mr. Dolan was making some progress, he was not moving toward any degree of acceptance of his colostomy, a first step in achieving self-care. Plans were made for the social worker to see Mr. Dolan to ascertain more clearly the nature of his behavior and attitude in regard to his adaptation to his illness.

When the social worker first went into the room to see Mr. Dolan, he was lying on the bed and staring at the ceiling. He looked as someone looks when the present is unbearable and the future hopeless. The social worker hoped to convey to this man that life was still worth living. His medical reality was such that following the projected surgery (closure of colostomy) he would, in fact, feel better than the year before he became ill. She mentioned his name softly as she crossed the room and he turned his head in a tired way. She introduced herself and asked if the nurse had mentioned that she would be stopping by. He turned and looked at her, challengingly. His whole manner said, "What can you do to help me?" words he was too polite to utter. She answered anyhow, saying "I know that people in your position are generally worried about what is going to happen later when they leave the hospital." She had hit the right chord with

Mr. Dolan and he opened up. In the course of several interviews he conveyed in numerous ways his fears, fantasies, and concerns about the surgery, treatment, and future. The social worker clarified where she could. His loaded question, "Do women have this too?" was answered factually and carefully by stating that the colon and kidneys were common to both men and women, and that both men and women suffered illnesses which necessitated colostomies.

She learned he was blaming himself for the delay in coming to medical care and for causing the really horrifying experience in his nephew's home in which there was a "mess" when he lost urinary and bowel control. He told of the relationship between himself and his nephew and his nephew's wife. Later, of that between him and his mother. It all helped to clarify that this lonely, frightened man was torn by his fear of being abandoned, and by his concern that the only way to avoid it was a situation he saw as intolerable: being cared for by his nephew's wife. She had apparently gone to pieces during the ordeal preceding hospitalization. He expressed grave concern about the smallness of the nephew's house and exposing the children to his problems.

When the social worker was certain that Mr. Dolan was sufficiently informed to know he didn't have cancer (an underlying fear of many surgical patients) and that he understood the nature of the past and future surgery, she used the fact of the temporary colostomy as a lever to stimulate Mr. Dolan to think about his role in his own recovery and to enable him to use the nursing guidance available to help him achieve self-care and return to independent living again. At the end of the first series of contacts, Mr. Dolan and the social worker were aligned to find out from his nephew his thoughts and concerns about the situation—Mr. Dolan to find out in his way and the social worker in hers. Thus he prepared his nephew to see the social worker as a person who could help plan for convalescent care.

Most people know the pain of the relative who wants to help but is afraid that his way of helping will be refused, belittled, or altered. It was not difficult with the intelligent, thoughtful, and anxious young nephew to see that he felt responsible for his "mother's favorite brother," that his wife was terrified and repelled by the colostomy (they had one bathroom, two children). When both agreed that a nursing home would not be *second* best, but *first* best for everyone, including Mr. Dolan who had expressed a preference to use professional nursing help and needed it, the nephew selected a nursing home close to where he lived so he could visit frequently. His nephew made the financial arrangements necessary, using savings of Mr. Dolan and giving some supplementary help. In a few phone conversations with Mrs. Nephew, she was reassured about Mr. Dolan's need for a nursing home and was informed that nursing is a highly technical kind of skill that many untrained people could not provide.

From this point on, the social worker's role was secondary to the nursing role. Mr. Dolan began to assume responsibility for his colostomy, slowly but steadily. He also began to act his usual self and to enjoy the concern and interest of the nurses who were teaching him self-care. Because Mr. Dolan knew that he was no longer alone with the problem and would have help in adjusting to his life in the community, he was better able to participate in his life in the hospital.

During the next ten days Mr. Dolan began to take an interest in what was going on around him. He changed physically through increased appetite and energy, and emotionally by a willingness to discuss his post-hospital plans and to involve himself in learning to care for his colostomy. He was involved slowly, gently, and firmly, paced and balanced by the progress he was making in coming to terms with his reality. Nurse and social worker alerted each other to the progress he was demonstrating with each facet of his care. The nurse noted he first began helping with his bath, while the social worker noted he was talking about the changes he was faced with in social living.

A week after the referral to Social Service he looked at his stoma (the intestinal opening on the abdominal wall) and about that time he began talking with the social worker about his colostomy. Nursing began to do the colostomy care with the head of the bed up so he could observe if he wished. He began to assist the nurses by holding the top dressing, later by washing around the area, and finally by assisting with the irrigation (a procedure similar to an enema, which patients ultimately do by themselves). Although proud of his achievement, he never more than tolerated the fact of the colostomy. He worked toward the day when he would be rid of it.

As he progressed it became apparent that transfer to a nursing home was feasible. Social work handled this by describing the nursing home and involving him in the selection and arrangements for payment. He involved his nephew in carrying out the plans. The nurse then secured the same equipment he would have in the nursing home and helped him learn to use it. Thus he was prepared for two changes: one in equipment, the other in location. He saw himself as an ambulatory person in the nursing home taking care of his own colostomy.

The date of discharge arrived. It has been said that Mr. Dolan's colostomy was temporary and that it was this which served as a stimulus to fairly rapid and not too stormy functional adjustment to it, and to self-care. What if the colostomy had been permanent? The situation would have changed markedly. Mr. Dolan would undoubtedly have gone through a much longer period of mourning, and a more stormy transition as he was faced with a radical revision of his own concept of himself as a man. He might have required an extension of his period of hospitalization and far more intensive support from both nursing and social service. He might have needed considerable postponement of the initiation of even the introductory phases of self-care until he could achieve some degree of acceptance of the reality situation, even though he would never like it.

With the transfer of Mr. Dolan to the nursing home, the nurse had an opportunity not always available. The nurse was able to go to the nursing home and to discuss with the nurse there Mr. Dolan's progress to date, to guide her in understanding the procedure Mr. Dolan had adopted in his self-care, and to be there to support and guide him in his first irrigation in this new and different setting. Whereas in most cases the staff nurse may not be able to go to the patient's home or sanitarium post discharge, she should not be hampered from communicating with those who will be participating in the patient's future care to the end that they are apprised of the situation and better able to formulate their own roles and purposes.

Implication of Collaborative Care

Mr. Dolan serves as an example of the collaborative effort toward total patient care. In summary, we might for a moment look at an overview of the joint and separate roles of the nurse and the social worker as they move toward a common objective.

The case of Mr. Dolan illustrates the discrete role and focus of both professions as well as the purposeful blending of these. The case-finding was done by the nurse who assumed responsibility for referral to social service for analysis of the social factors and the ensuant delineation of discrete areas of social work and nursing intervention at specific points in time. Following the initial evaluations made by each practitioner, the activities of both nurse and social worker were basically interdependent. The context of the collaboration between the two professions took into account where Mr. Dolan was in his patient role, and how that role was affected by individual, family, and community factors. It was carefully attuned to changes in Mr. Dolan's physical and psychological states, and was geared toward facilitating his movement toward positive acceptance of his medical-social situation.

In the blending of roles of nurse and social worker, it might be well to point out an actuality that may foster disintegration of an otherwise cohesive plan. The *nurse* is often referred to as a single entity whereas, in effect, *the nurse* is a group of individuals who contact the patient over 24-hour periods, seven days of the week. A single nurse may be with one patient one day, another the next. If this situation is not recognized and dealt with it can lead to discontinuity of observation, plan, and action. Adequate and continuous communication may never start, or may be interrupted. Communication is essential between nurses as well as between nurse and social worker.

In the Dolan case, the social worker utilized the casework method to study the situation, define the problem, and intervene effectively. The caseworker individualized her knowledge and understanding of the hospital, nursing, people, programs and helping process, to help Mr. Dolan become involved in participating in the definition of his problem in terms of his psychosocial situation, which included his physical condition, the hospital and professionals, his family, and his socioeconomic status. Once he perceived his situation in social terms, he was better able to muster his adaptive capacity to utilize effectively himself, his family, the social worker, the nurse, and the community. By being encouraged to take hold of one aspect of his situation and consider possible solutions, his sense of being overwhelmed lifted, his stress was reduced, and he regained control of his life situation.

The social work function included communicating to the nurse and doctor and others the facts about the social situation and the social diagnosis that influenced her use of medical and nursing services for predictive and planning purposes. She also shared knowledge of other agencies and resources.

Modes of communication between nurse and social worker include conferences, consultations, recording, interagency referral forms and, especially, keeping up to date with informal exchanges of ideas. Continual exchange is important because the situation changes both as a response to treatment and a cause for treatment. One of the things that seems to interfere with effective communication is the fact that the nurse and social worker may be speaking from two different frames of reference or levels of abstraction so that the shared interest in helping the patient is lost in the misunderstandings of reasons for actions.

Through shared communication and joint planning, nurse and social worker can achieve mutual awareness of the patient's needs at the same point in time. This communication process may be time-consuming in its initial phases but requires less time as concepts of timing and mutuality of goal are incorporated.

In the hospital, the nurse is frequently the person who recognizes that the patient's needs are beyond the scope of nursing to evaluate and manage and it is she who makes the decision to involve the social worker. In a sense, she is a case finder. Her effectiveness varies with her varying degrees of knowledge about social service and her varying degrees of commitment to the collaborative process. The reverse is also true when the social worker is a case finder. In the hierarchy of administration within the hospital, social work and nursing have different relationships and connections to the administrative structure. Their activities, both formal and informal, are influenced by the varied expectations stemming from the different administrative levels which, in turn, affect achievement and functioning in the collaborative process.

The nurse and social worker have different clinical skills in interviewing, knowledge of disease entities, knowledge of medical diagnostic and therapeutic programs, technological case skills, manipulative skills psychologically and environmentally. If the sharing of knowledge and skill is interactional rather than simply additive, the whole achieved thereby may be greater than the sum of its parts.

Toward Improved Communication

It is knowledge of the differential content and focus, the similarities and differences in training, the variable depth and breadth of understanding and action, the attitudes and expectations of role performance both achieved and ascribed, and the goal and values that make collaboration possible.

It is essential within the common goal of total patient care to recognize that there are lacks and gaps that cannot be filled by either social work or nursing *alone*. The strong cultural need of social worker, nurse, and patient to ascribe omniscient and omnipotent qualities to the physician's role has been a deterrent toward effective communication between nursing and social work. These needs are lessening as social work, nursing, and medical training and practice broaden their base of knowledge in social and cultural understandings.

The dangers inherent in lack of collaboration or ineffectual collaboration are many. These dangers include fragmentation of service, incomplete and costly duplication of service, and the inability to achieve the goal of comprehensive care. The anticipated outcomes of effective collaboration give greater promise of patient and family gains, professional worker gains, and reduced fragmentation and duplication occasioned by omission and commission.

Reference

Johnson, Dorothy E. "The Nature of a Science of Nursing," *Nursing Outlook*, Vol. 7, May, 1959.

Pediatrician and Social Worker as a Counseling Team

Randy Lee Comfort and Michael S. Kappy

Pediatricians are currently expected to assume more varied roles in child health care. They must now involve themselves not only with the diagnosis and treatment of diseases and the health supervision of a child, but with the developmental and behavioral growth of the patient, as well as his family environment. Recently, paramedical personnel have been used to facilitate the physician's ability to provide high-quality care. This article describes the work of a pediatrician and social worker who acted as a team to provide in-depth family counseling in addition to medical care.

The pediatrician, who is in solo practice in a large county adjacent to a major metropolitan area, works five half-days a week. His patients are from various social, economic, religious, and racial backgrounds. The social worker has a master's degree in social work, with experience in family counseling and child behavior. During her three half-days per week at work, she interviews, makes reports, contacts other agencies, and makes referrals. The patient is charged according to a preestablished sliding scale that is based on income and number of dependents, but adjustments may be made.

Patients are helped to understand that counseling will enable the pediatrician to handle a particular problem more effectively, or that counseling might be beneficial for a parent to help him cope with the presenting problem. Family counseling seems less threatening to many patients if they are helped to see it in the context of medical care.

The pediatrician can refer a family to the social worker if his initial evaluation of a child's problem does not seem adequate or if there are additional questions about the case. Schools and welfare departments are frequently helpful in identifying and referring children with behavioral problems or family difficulties or those in need of medical consultation and emotional support. Appearing in significant numbers are abused children and their parents as well as the offspring of "prebattering" or "inadequate" parents.

Depending on the needs of the family, an appointment with the social worker can be at the office or in the patient's home. Counseling sessions in the office are conducted during the pediatrician's absence, although all familes are assured of continuous contact with him.

Following the initial interview, the social worker determines what services the family needs and how best they can be provided. Short-term counseling, from three to ten sessions, is generally used as a tool for crisis intervention, for preventing cumulative disorders, and for teaching healthy, effective patterns of child-rearing. Patients from relatively intact families are more receptive to brief therapy than are those from antagonistic families, most of whom either require long-term counseling or reject it entirely. The social worker must not only assess the needs of the family, but its ability to accept counseling at a particular time. As pointed out by Barten and Barten:

> Small successes can provide models for problem-solving, and catalyze the individual's and/or family's independent experimentation and change without risking the dependency or passivity that longer therapy sometimes engenders.[1]

If long-term counseling is indicated, the family is usually referred to the mental health center or to private agencies or psychiatrists. The social worker arranges for this herself and tries to maintain contact with the family. If another agency is already involved, the family is urged to continue working with that facility to insure that there is no overlap of services.

Close contact between the social worker and the pediatrician is maintained to provide continuity of service and better understanding of the patient. All reports of counseling contacts are submitted to the pediatrician in writing, and are supplemented by frequent telephone conversations and weekly conferences. Attempts are also made to work closely with the schools and other community agencies. Family members are counseled individually, but group sessions may be instituted also.

Description of Cases

In nine months, fifty families—involving twenty-eight boys and twenty-two girls—were counseled. Twenty children were between the ages of two and five years and twelve were younger. Eighteen children were of school age. The kinds of problems they presented seemed to fall into five major categories: home behavior, school behavior, enuresis, inadequate parenting, and special problems, including medical, retardation, personal or social, and marital problems.

Home Behavior

Fourteen families indicated that this was their primary reason for seeking help. They included parents who had difficulty controlling their child or felt that he manifested a specific behavior that was intolerable, as well as families referred by the pediatrician who felt the home situation was not conducive to the well-being of the child. Children of school age also exhibited difficulties in class.

> Mrs. I is the divorced mother of five-year-old Ann, a child with slight hearing and speech handicaps. Mrs. I could not control Ann's behavior, which she described as extremely stubborn and insolent. In four interviews, two of which included Ann, Mrs. I was helped to control the child so she willingly dressed herself, went to bed at the appointed hour, and began to cooperate. Mrs. I was made to see how her inconsistent management and her unwillingness to make demands of Ann were working against her. Both parent and child were referred to a speech and hearing clinic at which Ann would receive therapy and Mrs. I would be given counseling to help her understand what realistic expectations she might make of her child.

In general, supportive counse'ing that focused on a better understanding of child behavior was found o be expedient with parents of preschool children who also needed direct counseling on parenting and behavior management.

School Behavior

School problems were frequently reflected by difficulties in the home as well, and constituted a separate category only if it was the school that first identified the problem. In nine cases it was judged to be the primary reason for counseling, and in each case the worker contacted school personnel in addition to meeting with the parents and child. In some cases it was the child's behavior that was of primary concern; in others the problem was manifested by poor academic achievement, apparently related to physical or emotional handicaps. School phobia was evident in two cases.

> A 14-year-old girl was a consistent truant from school and suffered from rashes and abdominal pains when she did attend. Her physical examination was normal. After a period of short-term counseling, her schedule was changed to a half-day program. Since then, her physical symptoms have subsided, she has attended school regularly, and is earning better grades. She continues to carry all academic subjects and does baby-sitting in the afternoons.

Enuresis

Parents of enuretic children over four years of age were all referred for counseling, although some did not follow through with the referral. In all seven cases, behavior modification and supportive counseling were used; in only one instance was medication indicated as well. All have shown considerable improvement, and five have stopped bed-wetting almost entirely.

Inadequate Parenting

Eight families fell into a group of inadequate or prebattering parents. Parents included in this group are those with children who have non-organic, failure-to-thrive syndromes, who suffer unexplained or repeated injuries, and have persistent eating, sleeping, or behavioral problems with no medical basis. The parents frequently express extreme concern over minor behavioral difficulties and are unsure of themselves or unaccepting of their children. All these families have been visited at home by the social worker and have been given supportive counseling over time.

As has been substantiated in studies by Evans et al., inadequate parents seem to have little support from their own families or friends.[2] Frequently they are divorced or remarried. They are lonely, evasive people with little companionship and almost no recreational or social outlets. Financial struggles are prevalent. Although they tend to be involved with a variety of community agencies, contact with these is irregular and inconsistent.

Despite persistent efforts, maintaining medical or social service contact with these families has been impossible. Many move from the area or decide to discontinue counseling "because everything is all right now." Clearly, these families require more intensive help than could be provided.

Mrs. L is a young mother of two children, aged two and three years. The two-year-old boy had been seen on numerous occasions for persistent diarrhea, poor eating and sleeping habits, and general ill health. He had been hospitalized for pneumonia and failure to thrive. His older sister was also small for her age and showed mild developmental delay. After many months the pediatrician was able to convince the mother to accept counseling.

Counseling took place in the home, for the mother's convenience. The home and children were not well kept. In counseling, Mrs. L expressed her loneliness and frustration with the children. Mr. L was home infrequently and did not have much tolerance for the children. Finances were of concern to the family. Mrs. L seemed able to accept suggestions of play activities and of general health procedures for her children, although she had previously been almost totally unaware of these things. Her expectations of her children were unrealistic, and her demands were impossible for a child to meet.

Since there was a possibility of child abuse and the time involved in home counseling became excessive, Mrs. L was referred to a public child welfare agency. Contact with the family was lost in the change from private to public health care. It was the fifth change of physicians the family had made in 1½ years.

Conclusions

Early intervention into family disruption is the purpose of social work counseling in this pediatric office. It is felt that the team approach has been valuable in dealing with the many pediatric problems presented by the child and his family. [See table that follows.]

Included in the category of "continuing contacts" are those families who are still actively involved with counseling, as well as those who are contacted only periodically for follow-up or "maintenance" service. Because many of the families no longer in counseling still receive medical care from the pediatrician, office contact with most patients is continued.

Outcome of Family Counseling

Follow-up Contact	Number of Families
Continuing contacts	15
Service completed	12
Did not keep follow-up appointment	7
Referred to another agency	6
Referred for residential placement	3
Referred for school follow-up	3
Referred for private counseling	2
Family moved	2
Total number of families	50

Although the program has shown a financial deficit in its first year, the benefit to those families using social service has far outweighed the slight financial imbalance. It is hoped that as the practice progresses, familiarity with the family counselor and with the idea of social service will convince more patients to make use of this aspect of medical care.

References

1. Harvey H. Barten and Sybil S. Barten, *Children and Their Parents in Brief Therapy* (New York: Behavioral Publications, 1973), p. 13.
2. Sue L. Evans, John B. Reinhart, and Ruth A. Succop, "Failure to Thrive," *Journal of American Academy of Child Psychiatry* (July 1972), pp. 440–457.

11 Clients, Colleagues, and the Future

Because the articles in this last group of exemplars direct attention to *the why* of clinical social work in health settings and to its future, it might be argued that they should have come at the beginning. In this sense, they provide a vivid rationale for all of the other exemplars. In a second sense, however, they are well-placed because they provide a dramatic affirmation of where health social workers have been for more than three-quarters of a century and where they must now go.

In "Notes of a Dying Professor" (J), Archie J. Hanlan writes in strong terms about the impact of severe illness with a terminal prognosis on himself and on others. That relationships with professional health care providers can be negative from the client's point of view is made dramatically clear in the writer's descriptions of his first clues that something serious was involved, how he felt when hospitalized, and his need for the social worker as the only person in the system with whom he felt he could relate as a human being. Embedded in these paragraphs is the justification for social work's clinical presence in the health field.

"Notes" poignantly chronicles the abrupt changes in life patterns brought about by the diagnosis of a terminal health condition. The impact on objective and subjective membership attributes is revealed by Hanlan in his description of his relationships with health professionals, his wife, his children, and his friends. The concluding paragraphs of the article suggest Hanlan's ultimate transcendence of his crisis in a way that underlines its tragedy and simultaneously inspires the reader.

The next exemplar, "Dear Medical Social Worker" (K), was written by a pediatrician, Louise F. Galvin. This article is the only one included in this book that is not authored or coauthored by a social worker. Moreover, Dr. Galvin's "letter" to medical social workers is published here for the first time. Dr. Galvin's "letter" was selected as an exemplar because it provides a rare, retrospective summary of health social workers as col-

laborators in health and medical service from the perspective of a representative of a major discipline in the field, medicine.

In this selection, Dr. Galvin notes that as a physician she was ill-
prepared for joint work with social workers and found her encounters
with them during a long career both mystifying and rewarding. In review-
ing her experience, she poses a question which structures her "letter":
"What have these creatures got that such a void is left when we lose one?"
In answering her question, she touches on a range of social work roles and
functions and how social workers contributed to her own enlarged understanding of patients as social beings. In Dr. Galvin's letter lies the affirmation of social work's contributions to enhancing the delivery of service by
other professionals in the health field.

The final exemplar is a paper presented by Rosalie A. Kane at the
Annual Meeting and Educational Conference of the Society for Hospital
Social Work Directors of the American Hospital Association in 1981. In
this paper, "Toward a Science of Hospital Social Work" (L), Kane ex-
plores a number of themes. The paper is divided into five major sections:
historical beginnings; current context; types of knowledge; measures,
outcomes, and values; and conditions for building our science. Kane's
paper affirms the past and present, but looks to the future.

In the paper's first section, Kane affirms the contention that social work
is both an art *and* a science. She notes the long tradition of scientific
inquiry that characterizes health social work—a theme traced in the last
chapter of this book—and stresses the importance of records as a basis for
study. In making this last point, Kane cites Cannon who clearly understood the importance of recording practice.

In the second section, Kane asserts that the social work profession *and*
the health care system are the two major reference points for health social
work and adds that health social workers are part of both. This theme was
sounded throughout this book in its stress on the importance of a synthesis
of knowledge pertinent to these two reference points as the basis for
effective health social work practice. Kane follows these points by identifying problems of access, quality, and costs as overriding concerns of
both the health care system and health social work and she emphasizes the
need to develop effective screening tools for social work services.

In the paper's third section, focus is on empirical knowledge and the
author highlights facts about the population served, about social work
services, about social work intervention, and the need for clearly defined
concepts as particularly important. All of these themes were highlighted
in the chapters of this book.

In the fourth section, Kane reiterates the need to conceptualize practice
in reproducible units and notes that measures used to study practice must
have clinical relevance. When they do, she asserts, they become thresholds

for action and provide opportunities for the demonstration of clinical social work effectiveness. In this section, Kane also notes the need for health social workers to make explicit the value dilemmas inherent in health care choices.

Kane closes her paper with the assertion that health social workers must be willing to ask questions about their work and its usefulness. She adds that they can do so with confidence since such questions lead to the improvement of practice and do not call into question the worth of the whole profession or its place in the health system. One might add that asking such questions is not only an important aspect of the health system, it is also a hallmark of health social work.

J   Notes of a Dying Professor

Archie J. Hanlan

When he was asked last fall at the University of Pennsylvania seminar which gave birth to this article what good recounting his own experiences would do, the author replied:

I have some knowledge and skill in understanding myself and in understanding other human beings, which is part of my professional bag of tricks. So I have something to bring. And my own life happened to turn quite suddenly, so that I was put in a position through my own intimate life experience of having to live through something that I in some ways taught or studied intellectually but did not experience emotionally.

In granting permission to use this incisive account, the author, a member of the faculty of the University, made only two requests: one, that we make it clear that the hospital mentioned is—and medical experiences recounted here occurred— outside the Commonwealth of Pennsylvania. And two, that the article be published anonymously; to that end, a few names and places have been changed.

The editors wish to publicly thank the author for the extraordinary contribution to our readers that follows.

There is a commercial on television (I've watched more television in recent months than I ever watched in my life), a stupid little commercial for Alka-Seltzer that shows this guy woefully sitting with people in a café or restaurant, and the waiter says, "Try it, you'll like it; try it, you'll like it." And the guy says: "I tried it—and I thought I'd die."

Originally published anonymously in *The Pennsylvania Gazette*, March, 1972. Reprinted with permission.

I listen to things like that differently now. It's a clever commercial: it's funny. But the punch line is: I thought I would die. That, to me, is kind of symbolic of what it means to die, in our society. The actor didn't describe how he felt when he tried it and didn't like it—he thought he would die. That conveys what? "He thought he would die" means it was terrible— how worse could you feel than wanting to die? As though dying is something inherently painful, undesirable, stigmatized in our society.

Several months ago I was told that I am dying. I want to recount to you the process I went through in finding that out. I was hospitalized and told on the day that I was discharged, a week later, that I had a terminal illness and would have six months to three years to live.

So how did I get to that point?

I had been examined by my physician, an internist with all the equipment in his own office who does very thorough examinations, and I was given a thorough bill of health. Some weeks later, I returned to him because I had this peculiar symptom: I found that I could not trim the fingernails on my left hand by operating the fingernail clipper in my right hand. I thought: "Gee, that's stupid! Why can't I push those silly little tweezers together? I can do it with my left hand and clip the nails on my right hand, but I can't do it with my right hand."

I mentioned it to my wife. I had been to my doctor earlier and he said I was in good health, and this was beginning to bother me; I didn't have any strength in my right hand. And she said what I wanted to hear at that point, I guess: "Don't put it off." So I went back to the doctor. And he thought it was some kind of arthritis or whatever, some mild problem, but he said it ought to be checked out by an orthopedist, that he himself couldn't check out what it was.

On a Thursday afternoon I saw an orthopedist. He looked at my hand, and he ran some simple tests of my arm and concluded—well, let me see if I can recapture what happened with him.

A very nice man. My internist is a rather cold, impassive kind of guy. The orthopedist is a warmer, friendlier, outgoing middle-aged man. After his cursory examination I began to realize that he was becoming increasingly noncommunicative. And that alarmed me. It frightened me a bit. *What* is he not telling me? And he became very grave and serious in his general demeanor. I asked him what he thought it was, but could get no reply.

He then let me know that this was something he could not diagnose and that I should see a neurologist immediately. Now, I was feeling fine, outside this stupid little complaint, so I thought whatever the worst was, it couldn't be all that complicated—until this nonverbal communication and the tightening up of the orthopedist, letting me know, in his own way, that it was serious and I should go to a neurologist. He arranged for me to see a neurologist that evening.

I remember going back out into the waiting room where my wife was, feeling very frightened and confused. She, of course, knowing me very well for 22 years, felt my own feelings coming through very quickly. We both figured out that something's up, that it's not just a simple matter of arthritis in my wrist. What it was, we didn't know. Some kind of neurological problem—but there are thousands of those. Whatever it was, it was serious.

So at seven o'clock that night I was at the neurologist's and he was more like my regular doctor: cold, aloof, highly efficient, a prominent researcher in the field of neurology. I tried to engage him in conversation but to no avail. He ran through the usual neurological examination, the whole routine, very standard procedure. It took maybe a half hour at the most. I tried to read his nonverbal responses, since I couldn't engage him in any verbal responses. And that was very difficult to do, because he's really a very masked kind of man, except that again there began to be a growing sense from him that this was something serious, that there was a gravity about what the examination was revealing.

I kept pressing him for a response, but there was absolutely no response at all. And the nonverbal response, the avoidance itself, generates considerable anxiety, fear, confusion, on the part of any patient in that kind of situation. While I may be hypersensitive to nonverbal clues because of my clinical training, I also think that most people, regardless of how sophisticated or unsophisticated they are psychologically, pick up these nonverbal cues, so that this effort on the part of the physician or the neurologist to contain himself and mask whatever he was finding or whatever he felt about his findings really served the function of making me increasingly anxious.

As he concluded the examination, he told me that I would have to be hospitalized the following morning.

I said I wanted to know why I was going to the hospital. He said: To run a series of diagnostic tests. I did not want to go to the particular hospital he mentioned. I knew that hospital very well and I had a preference for another one. But he did not practice in that hospital, so I did not pursue it. The point I want to make clear is that I began to respond to his directive to be hospitalized. I didn't know what in the world I was being hospitalized for. I was not unwilling to be hospitalized, but I certainly had a particular choice of hospitals.

But suddenly I felt this fear and panic and kind of being put in a position of passivity, as though decisions were being made for me, that I didn't take part in those any any more. What right did I have to make a big issue of what hospital I was being sent to?

Under ordinary circumstances, I would have made such a stink. What is significant is that I didn't. I did not feel able to fight even at that point. And this was only the first day of my discovery that something was radically wrong with me. I mentioned this because that process—feeling myself reduced in making decisions about my own fate—became increasingly reinforced and became very destructive psychologically.

The next day (Friday) I was supposed to go into the hospital, if a bed could be found. I had my bag packed and said goodbye to my wife and kids—and Saturday they finally found a bed. Saturday afternoon.

I had been in the hospital once before when I was 15 years old, for an appendectomy. So although I've seen the whole system of a hospital structure, both medical and psychiatric, I had never been very much on the patient end of it. I was greatly negatively impressed with how one gets processed as a patient. I went into the business office, the admissions room, and I was put in a wheelchair. And there wasn't a damn thing wrong with me. I could walk. The only limit to my physical activity had to do with my fingers, and other than that I had no physical impairment whatsoever. But I was put in a wheelchair.

Again, the sense was one of being passive, inactive; you immediately assume the role of the patient; this is the way you behave in a hospital. Also, I went through what seemed to me the incredible Alice-in-Wonderland business about my finances. I had to guarantee the hospital that I would pay the bill—and I didn't know what I was in the hospital for and how long I would be there—but I was supposed to sign a statement that I would pay whatever the cost was before I left the hospital.

That was just one more phase in that process of being identified as a patient. It struck me as: *This isn't for real!* But it was for real. And I refused to sign such a statement. It was ridiculous to commit myself to pay an amount I didn't know. I didn't know whether I had that much money. Anyway, they had to scurry around and ask the supervisor how they could go about admitting such a patient, who wouldn't sign this piece of paper.

But I got admitted as a patient. I got out of the admissions office and I was taken to a ward where postoperative neurosurgery patients were kept. I stress that because there were few patients like myself. The hospital was crowded; that's why I couldn't get in on Friday—and because there was no bed on the floor where my neurologist usually worked. I was put on the floor below that, where essentially the largest number of patients were failures of neurosurgery.

I had seen lobotomized patients in the back wards of psychiatric hospitals, but that doesn't sufficiently convey what I saw when I first came into that ward. Again, this was Saturday, I didn't know why I was in the hospital, I didn't know that I was in the wrong ward. My God, am I going to have some kind of brain surgery where I will wind up totally destroyed by some failure of the brain surgery, as these patients I saw being wheeled around the ward—totally speechless, grunting, staring, disheveled men?

That was my first sight when I was put in that ward, and I was pretty shaken, to say the least. The time sequence from that time on becomes more clear to me. The neurologist was not on duty again till Monday. Why in the world was I put there Saturday and Sunday, when nothing could be done, no instructions could be left even in terms of beginning routine procedures? So I sat there through Saturday and Sunday.

Monday, things began to move a little bit. The neurologist showed up and introduced me to three resident interns—no, they were in their latter years of medical school. They were students of the neurologist, and they administered several of the examinations that I was to have. He ran through the neurological examination of me in bed. And again I got a reinforcement of the sense of not only am I a patient who is supposed to behave in a certain way, but I'm almost an object to demonstrate to people that I'm not really a person any more, I'm something else. I'm a body that has some very interesting characteristics about it, which include twitching of the muscles, rather symptomatic of this particular disease.

And because it's a rare disease and not much is known about it, it was very instructive for these medical students to see these symptoms. But the point I want to make is that I felt treated as an object. Being a patient is one thing, but being an object is even less than being a patient. And I began to feel not only the fear of this unknown, dread thing that I have, that nobody knows anything about—and if they know, they're not going to tell me—but an anger and a resentment of "Goddamn it, I'm a human being and I want to be treated like one!"

I felt that if I expressed that anger, I could be retaliated against, because I was in a very vulnerable position. One, nobody is going to tell me what the hell is wrong with me, anyway. And two, if I do strike out, what's going to happen to me as a consequence? So there is a sense of anger, a sense of being terribly vulnerable—all of this setting in by Monday.

I might add that Sunday night was a bad night for me—this general malaise, this fear of being in the hospital. And I distinctly remember one of the few human beings I came in contact with during these first two nights was a black woman on duty during the night. It was nothing very dramatic that she did, but it stands out vividly in my mind that she was kind and gentle with me, concerned that I was fitful and disturbed. And she reassured me in a very spontaneous kind of way.

But she was one of the few people in that enormous institution who really dealt with me as a human being. That's why I recall it, because she treated me as a human being—and very few people did, the whole time I was there. So somehow I got through Sunday night and Monday night.

Monday started the routine. Take your temperature, check your blood pressure, urinalyses, etc.

Then we got down to the more basic stuff. On Tuesday, the two main examinations I had were both horribly painful—physically painful and psychologically devastating. I had no pain connected with the illness and still have virtually no pain connected with the illness, but I had excruciating pain in the examination.

It was on Tuesday that the team of young medical students were instructed to prepare me for a lumbar puncture, a spinal tap. I was frightened. Two of the medical students were a husband and wife. I found the wife more responsive, less uptight, I guess, than the two young men, and I got through to her that it was important to me to know what was going on: "I want to know about the lumbar puncture, everything about it, tell me what you're going to do, explain it to me very carefully, it's important to me to know what's going on."

And she did. So I had the lumbar puncture. Part of the diagnostic value of that is not only to take fluid from the spinal column, but to test the pressure of the spinal fluid. The spinal tap in itself is painful, but my recollection is that that was very minor compared to the other part of that examination, which was placing a collar around my neck and inflating it to exert pressure on the spinal column itself and take readings as the pressure is built up on the spinal column, to detect the extent of damage in the spinal column. This is an excruciatingly painful experience. It's the weirdest kind of pain, as though someone had inflated a balloon inside my spinal column and the pressure would almost explode inside my spine. It's a bizarre pain.

And this was administered in the ward where there were a few other patients. I screamed out and grunted with the pain. I remember thinking: This is nutty. The least they could have done is take me off into a room by myself. I asked for a towel to shove into my mouth, so I could grit my teeth and muffle my scream, so I wouldn't disturb the patients. I began to feel, even as I was having this horrible pain: My God, we're people; why should my going through this disturb the other patients: why should my screaming upset these other people?

Did anybody think about this? Somebody around this place ought to know that an examination this painful ought to be done in a place that at least provided privacy to the patient, and not put the burden on the patient like this.

The students did an efficient job. I was very exhausted and very frightened when it was over. They did not tell me anything at that time. I asked the physician the next day about any results and he was very evasive. In fact, there was very little I did know while I was in the hospital, until the last day.

The next exam was either on Wednesday or Thursday, but I want to tell a little about the time between the first and the second exam. I did a lot of reading. I read rapidly. My escape reading is fiction, which I do not ordinarily indulge in, so I had taken a couple of books, a very large novel of 800 pages, and I read about 400 pages the first 24 hours I was there. Then I declined in reading as an escape. I couldn't concentrate.

There was a little day room right off the ward, with windows, and it was sunny there, so I went in there on Wednesday, the day after the lumbar puncture. There was a man there in his early or midfifties, with grayish-black hair, a stubble, just growing back after his surgery. He was strapped into this wheelchair, so that he could not get out or harm himself. He sat in the wheelchair grunting. At one time he seemed to want something. I asked him if he wanted something and he growled.

He had a pile of stuff in his lap and I was very curious as to what it was. As I looked at it more carefully, I saw that it was pieces of old canvas. As I sat there a few minutes more, he began to fix himself upon this pile of canvas and he began to rip apart—with this intense, livid, violent expression on his face and his whole body—to shred this canvas. I had rarely seen a human being so violent, with such an intensity of focus—upon this canvas—and have it become the symbol of all his rage and fear. It seemed as though the surgery had excised everything but his soul. All he could do is give vent to his rage at this outrage that had occurred to him.

I felt pretty shaken after I watched that fellow and I had to get out of there. I wondered why I was so upset and finally had to accept that I was simply too vulnerable myself to deal with that kind of situation.

I guess there was some kind of learning in that. I throw that in because it was a point of looking at myself and maybe accepting that there were some things I couldn't deal with any longer. But along the way I had some excellent help from a social worker. It was the only real help I had, besides the terribly essential support of my family. I did have critical help from the social worker and I've had some help from another social worker since then, and I disagree with Elisabeth Kübler-Ross—the author of *On Death and Dying* (1969)—in some of the comments about why social workers seem to deal better with dying people.

It was very critical in maintaining my own sanity in this situation. I needed a social worker after my experience with that man. I was beginning to confront myself with what this was all about.

But I want to get to the second examination. This was called an electromyogram—*myo* meaning muscle. (The symptoms of my disease are a continuing deterioration of the muscles, all the major muscles in my body.) The examination consists of long steel needles with an electric wire attached to them, so that an electric charge can be generated by the control of a technician through the needle into the muscle. A needle is stuck into every major and minor muscle in the body during a two-to-three hour examination.

The electric charge creates a response in the muscle, which is recorded on an oscilloscope and measures the response of the muscles. The oscillo-scope makes a permanent TV tape of the test. I mention this because the process relates to the way in which that examination was conducted. There was relatively little pain involved in the insertion of the needle, but the way in which that examination was conducted was more physically exhausting and more psychologically upsetting than anything else that had happened in the hospital to me thus far.

The person who administered the electromyogram was a young girl who had been out of high school three or four years, a bright girl who had special training.

She is an interesting person for me to attempt to describe to you, because in some ways she symbolizes, at least for me, treating the patient as an object, this dehumanizing of a person, particularly of a dying patient, more clearly than some of the professional staff in the hospital. Physicians, nurses, others have a variety of ways of defending themselves against the impact of procedures in the hospital. She had her own ways, but they were not subtle at all.

So what I could see, as I thought back on that exam, were some of the same psychological processes operating with her as well as with physicians and nurses, but not as subtly covered up. She was a little more direct and open about how she tried to handle her own feelings not only about the unpleasant examination, but—knowing that anybody who takes that exam is suspected of having a very serious neurological disease, if not terminal.

The way she dealt with this was to be very cheerful, bubbly, charming in some ways, purely superficial, using her charm and humor to maintain this mask of a cute little girl attending me, and so on. But it was very apparent to me, as we got into this interchange, that she was treating me as an object. It was my body, not me. Sticking needles into me and joking "Oh, I got the wrong muscle!" She did have a sense of humor, but I didn't appreciate it as such. She had this banter which on the one hand seemed like she was being very friendly, but really there was nothing friendly about it at all. I was being treated like an object.

The point I'm making in regard to that technician is that she was less sophisticated, her defenses were less well developed and complex, let's say, than the physician's, but essentially they were no different.

I remember at one point I was terribly anxious and sweating, and her nutty humor was finally getting to me, and the sense of being treated like a thing was making me angrier and angrier and I wondered how in the hell do I deal with her. I'm not just going to sit back and take this. Finally I decided to play her own game. I'll engage in this banter with her. She said something about the wrong muscle and I said: "If you make another mistake and I die, I'm going to sue the hospital." And she thought that was hilarious.

I figured I could communicate with her at that level, but it was purely premeditated and hostile: if she was going to keep her distance, I was going to keep mine, too.

Anyway, I got out of there thoroughly spent and psychologically exhausted, a mixture of physiological and psychological utter exhaustion which became insufferable. It was a kind of exhaustion which had no comparison in my previous life.

I met with the social worker briefly Wednesday, Thursday, and Friday morning, before I saw the neurologist. I'm not sure how well I can convey the importance of having someone there, aside from my own immediate family and my own personal friends, in whom I could confide my own fears and concern about the gravity of the illness. There was no one in the hospital (around the clock) with whom I could engage in any real contact about the fact that I was there for something that was terribly serious. The only human being on that hospital staff I could talk to was the social worker.

And it was pretty important to have somebody who could acknowledge that I may be facing death, that it is a likely prospect, that I could cry about it, I could convey some of my rage, some expression of my own feelings, which were such a critical part of where I was at that point in my life. I can't underestimate the importance of that fact.

If I hadn't had that person in the hospital, I really don't know what psychological condition I would have been in. I could talk with my wife when she came to visit me and I could discuss with one of my friends that visited me, but I needed somebody on the spot to be able to communicate with, somebody who represented that hospital in all its treatment of me as an object, somebody who could confirm my doubts about whether I was a human being anymore or just a thing.

By Friday the tests results were all in. I knew that the major examinations had been completed. The main conference confrontation with the physician was about an hour before I was discharged. I had been in the hospital seven days. I was tired, irritable, angry—angry at the doctor who was still being evasive. I had told him from the start that I wanted him to be open with me, that I wanted to know the full implications of whatever it was that I had. And up until the last hour I was there it seemed to me that he could not face me with what he had to say.

He did then do essentially what I asked him to do, that is, to level with me regarding the diagnosis. It was a very hard thing for him to do. If he could have found any way of avoiding telling me, he would have. It was a terribly painful thing for him to have to lay it on the line. But he did. The way in which he did it was a kind of staccato, impersonal, matter of fact. This is what the symptoms are, this is the progression of the symptoms. How long do I have to live? Six months to three years.

The only break in his facade was when I asked him to clarify. He had prepared a little speech. But any time I asked him for a little bit more information or a judgment on those facts, I could almost see his shell coming back.

Out of the hospital, there were other matters to consider. One was my dealings with my family. I don't think one ever deals with anything with finality, in any one point in time, either with living or with death. I recall a Sunday *New York Times* review of a book by Robert Penn Warren. There was one quote from it: "The dream is a lie, the dreaming is true." Perhaps death is a lie and dying is true. The difference is between the nouns and the verbs. It's the "dealing" that is the truth, not the "deal."

That's a poor analogy, but at any rate, I haven't "dealt with" my feelings about my family. I am constantly dealing with them, as I always have, but in a new and different context since my illness.

Although there are relatively few physically painful aspects of the illness at this stage, the psychologically painful aspect has certainly been my feelings about my family.

I have a son at college and a daughter in college and a 10-year-old boy at home. And while I would like to see all my children well into adulthood, I find it particularly poignant and difficult that I may not see my youngest child into adulthood. I feel a personal responsibility, and always have, for seeing that my children are on their own and psychologically and other-wise prepared to assume responsibility for themselves. And I certainly cannot expect a 10-year-old boy to be responsible for himself.

There are a variety of reasons why I feel very strongly in terms of my own family, which aren't terribly relevant here except that that was a strong part of my reaction, my depression, in the hospital. I never cry very much, but I certainly cried very profoundly, a depressive crying, in the hospital. And being self-analytical, I tried to ask myself what I was so depressed about.

At an intellectual level I could tell myself that I had some guilt feelings about my family, particularly about my children, and not deal with it very much beyond a kind of superficial recognition that it wasn't the illness or dying itself that was really bothering me, but something more related to my relationship with my family and my feelings of not really having been as good a father as I should have been.

I was able to discuss some of this with the social worker while in the hospital, but I did not really come to terms with it then. I might add that the social worker told me, the last day I was in the hospital, that she had never seen a patient with a terminal illness, who knew he was dying, to accept it so readily. I thought that was very interesting and complimentary, but I expect myself to be able to deal with whatever I have to deal with and I really didn't know what she meant until a colleague loaned me Kübler-Ross's book and I read about the "stage of acceptance."

I certainly have not come to terms with my conflicted feelings about my family—a sense of not having been as good a husband and father as I should have been, and which I never would be, anyway.

I guess there's one incident I want to relate to that. When I came out of the hospital, that Saturday and Sunday, my wife and I made a point of having a few selected friends know about my illness and wanting to talk with them. I wanted some close friends with whom I could discuss this, and I needed some practical advice, particularly financial. My life seemed a total disaster economically at that point, and that concerned me, especially regarding my children. I figured that my wife, who is a trained professional, could fend for herself financially but certainly could not carry on the financial burden of getting three children through school.

I called a business friend, who came out on Sunday. He and his wife were among our close friends. We had had some other friends the day before and I was not feeling depressed. My friends were cheerful and I guess maybe I was, but not excessively so. But when my businessman friend came over and I told him about my feelings of desperation about the financial situation, I found myself getting increasingly depressed and somehow out of control emotionally, with the depression setting in a little bit like it had been in the hospital, a kind of overwhelming sea of depression.

I wondered why in the world just talking with him about finances—I had never been that uptight about money—why in the world was it upsetting me?

What he did was to refuse to accept what I stated as a problem—the money. And while he certainly is a whiz at finances and insurance problems and so on, and could give me the practical advice I needed, he refused to deal with me only at that level, and kept saying "Why is it so urgent; what is really making you so upset?"

I kept getting more annoyed with him. Why the hell doesn't he give me the advice I want and get it over with? Then I took the other track and wondered what *is* bugging me so much. And it suddenly hit me. I just feel horribly guilty about the children. I can't provide for them. And it's not just that I can't provide for them financially, but that I'm terribly guilty about my role with the kids.

At that point I burst out sobbing and my poor friend was sitting there with tears streaming down his face. I guess the point I'm trying to get at is that it took some while, and particularly that friend, to get me to the point—and that was a critical point—of my feelings about my family, of really acknowledging to myself the guilt and inadequacy that I felt about my role as a father. If I hadn't arrived at that point then, I would have had to reach it sometime or else be overwhelmed by the guilt and the depression that comes from it.

And I've not been depressed since then. A couple of months after I was discharged from the hospital I had a couple of periods of suddenly crying and saying to my wife, "It's not fair to David" (our youngest son). I had to blurt that out and cry about it, but after that I didn't have to cry about it any more.

In terms of dealing directly with the children, when I got out of the hospital Friday, I think that very afternoon, we all gathered—my older boy was away at college at the time—I guess it was in my bedroom—and I told them the nature of my illness, the prognosis, and so on. And I remember crying as I told them that I wanted to be with them as long as possible, that I didn't have any fear of death or of dying, but I simply wasn't ready to die now, and I didn't want to leave them. And they cried.

I don't think we discussed at any great length the implications of my illness in terms of how long I had to live, although we have discussed as a whole family, when my son has been home from college, not only the implications for me of the illness, but for them in the plans for their future.

I suppose the most painful parts of the whole business—and it's still painful, but it's a reality and there isn't much I can do about that reality except to take what responsibility I can, particularly in terms of insuring their getting through college, however we can do that. I still don't know how we can do that, but we're trying.

I had a social worker for some two months after I got out of the hospital. (Not the same social worker I had in the hospital, but another one.) During that period of time I remember discussing with this social worker the guilt about my role as a father and what kind of father am I, becoming a cripple and so on, for a 10-year-old boy, and was it really better for me to think in terms of not being in the family, whatever that might mean. Perhaps I should make some other plans for myself, particularly in terms of this being a very hard time for my younger boy, and what can I really contribute to him by being in the home, what role as a father can I play.

Very quickly, with the social worker, I decided that that's a lot of baloney, and that I can play a role, an important role, for him and for me, regardless of what physical shape I'm in, and that it was important to him and important to me, as long as we can keep it that way, as long as I'm physically able to be around.

So I came to terms with that part of it. And that was very difficult, because I had some conflicting feelings about what this would mean psychologically for my young son. The other two children were old enough to psychologically take some greater responsibility for themselves.

I didn't feel that a 10-year-old boy should have this kind of burden, but on the other hand there is nobody who's going to take the burden from him, either, so I may as well take some responsibility as his father. And we do have a very nice relationship.

My wife and I deal very honestly with one another. We did when I was in the hospital and we certainly have since. That was less of a direct conflict for me. My wife is a most unusual human being. The comment of the social worker at the hospital about coming to the acceptance of my illness was directed as much at her as it was at me.

It's not easy on a 10-year-old boy. He varies from week to week or day to day in how he deals with it. There was something that came up recently and I said, "I don't think this is something we should discuss with David." (The point is that there are very few things we think we shouldn't discuss with David.) I think it had something to do with planning or attempting to plan the terminal stages of my illness—to anticipate it—and we agreed that was not something he should be involved with. But short of that, he has been a part of everything. He has his own life. He has to help me in and out of the bathtub, whether he likes it or not. He's very gentle and kind about doing it. Sometimes he'll gripe—like he would any time, like any preadolescent. My illness has not inhibited that.

An interesting question sometimes put to those in my predicament is whether personal values have changed as a result of knowing about such an illness. I myself wondered whether I would just want to go off on a wild binge or something. (All the hidden fantasies that I've never committed—now's the chance to do it, if ever.) But I've done my thing for a long, long while. I have very few regrets, if any, about what I've done.

In some ways I've lived a more liberated life than most people have. My wife and I, when we were first married, finishing up college, took off without any money and spent a year in Guatemala. There weren't many people of our generation who just took off into the wilds of Guatemala. But we did, and we had a fabulous year working with the United Nations, a UNESCO project.

And even before I was married, I had a variety of friends. I lived with a black family for a while in Watts, California, long before Watts became a terribly imprisoned ghetto. I've had a rich life with a variety of people. I have a great appreciation of black culture, of black music in particular. I don't ordinarily tell people this, but the point is that my life has been good enough for me, rich enough and varied enough, and it's been a great life. It's a cliche but both my wife and I have always done our own thing.

So knowing that I'm dying, knowing that I've only got a limited number of years to live, there is no sudden surge of "My God, I've got to start living!" I want to continue to live and enjoy the things I've enjoyed as long as I can, but there hasn't been any radical change. I get frustrated because there's some things I can't do. I wanted to hear a Ray Charles concert recently and I couldn't make it, or I was afraid to. I had a real fear of falling. That's a real fear, because I have fallen down, and I have to be very careful. So my world is getting restricted.

A lady once told me that death is a part of life, which is a very pragmatic statement. This was after someone we knew committed suicide, maybe 20 years ago. It made sense to me, simple as it is. And I have had for some time a kind of existential approach to life, not with the full-blown philosophical and psychological paraphernalia of existentialism, but in a more pragmatic way. What is that little phrase we sometimes see printed up: "Today is the first day of the rest of your life." Which is an existential kind of statement.

I find that very nice. That's the way I live and have lived—in that sense, existentially, my wife and I—ever since we were married.

Immortality is rare, and I never thought of being immortal.

K   Dear Medical Social Worker

Louise F. Galvin

For quite some time I have been mulling over in my mind this mystery of the medical social worker. As our work load becomes heavier and our problems more involved and the scarcity of medical social workers more acute, I ask myself in frustration and annoyance, "What have these creatures got that such a void is left when we lose one?" My mind runs back over the years to my first introduction to medical social work, and because to some degree my impressions and experiences must parallel those of other physicians and also because I wanted to crystallize them for myself, I have begun this rambling introspective and retrospective letter. There will be nothing in it of professional knowledge but rather a journey into the past to review these impressions and experiences and to gather them together into some kind of meaningful whole.

I remember the day in 1935 when I was working in the pediatric clinic at the Medical College of Virginia which was then being held with all the other clinics in the old Virginia Hospital building. A clerk registered the patient, a nurse undressed him, student and resident staff examined him,

Published with the permission of the author.

visiting pediatrician checked the examination, and he left the clinic with his mother perhaps clutching a prescription for vitamins or a formula for his milk. From the unknown he had come, into the unknown he returned. Could his mother read? Did she have a cent in her pocket to buy the vitamins? That was in the lap of the gods. I don't believe it occurred to us that we carried any responsibility for the patient beyond the threshold of the examining room which, as I remember it, was curtained with white sailcloth hung on picture wire. All of a sudden there appeared a new creation—tall and stunning with beautifully manicured nails and tasteful jewelry. She seemed to be here and there in a nonspecific way and yet things seemed to begin to happen. As if a catalyst were at work, a broader realization of the problems of patients and their environment seemed to come to us. I cannot honestly say that I remember much being accomplished in those very early days about removing these problems but the consciousness of them was there. As time went on and the department expanded, we became more and more conscious of the worker assigned to us. Although we did not comprehend her possibilities, we knew we could call on her for anything there was no one else to do. I can remember her serving as messenger and clerical worker (or so it seemed to me, at that time). I remember her warm and chatty conferences about patients and their problems. We found her friendly and intelligent and were glad to spread our lofty medical knowledge for her admiration. I do not believe we comprehended at all that she was "orienting and coordinating" us into her team approach to the patient's problem but we knew she was there and we used her after our fashion. Looking back on it, I believe she realized the necessity of establishing her presence and making herself useful and welcome in any way she could as the *first* step in teaching us to use the medical social worker in the proper way. She knew that we had absolutely no background or preparation in the utilization of this professional worker.

After a period, it became obvious that the medical social service department had decided the time had come when *concentrated* efforts must be made to interpret their role to other personnel, particularly the doctors, and that they were attempting a gradual withdrawal from duties not properly theirs. We resented this, not only because of the withdrawal but because we were not interested in definitions of other people's jobs. We were interested only in being waited upon and in having our orders carried out—for the good of the patient, of course. All operations are painful but many are necessary and this phase was, in a way, such an operation—and gradually there did emerge the idea that the *medical social worker was concerned with social needs and problems as they relate to illness.* But how far was she concerned? Where did she come in and where exit? A confused picture persisted here because of the inadequate number of workers, a persistent lack of understanding of their work by certain other departments in the hospital, and lack of agreement as to their role relative to economic screening and financial need of the patients. Now and then the glimmer would glow steadily for a brief while, crystallized by actual accomplishment with a knotty problem in some particular case, only to flicker again as red tape, protocol, lack of true understanding, and lack of personnel clouded the picture. On the whole, however, steady growth continued.

I do not believe that the idea of *direct service versus partial casework service versus consultative service* was ever understood by us. We, therefore, were never able to understand why some of our requests brought results and some completely bogged down. Also, many requests which should have been made by us were not made because of our lack of comprehension. We had probably been told but it was seed on barren ground. The soil simply had not been prepared in our student days.

When I began to dabble in public health, although still on an individual patient basis, a new world began to open up. I became more aware of the home setting away from, yet inextricably linked with, the hospital and clinic, the larger community setting, the interplay between the various community individuals and organizations, and the way this affected the patient and his illness problem—the zealous, poorly informed local minister, the narrow-minded, inadequately trained welfare superintendent, the bumptious, penurious superintendent of schools, the rural isolation of the family, superstitions of the neighbor, the influence of grandparents, and many, many others.

It seemed there were so many problems brought to light in this small public health program; yet somehow, things seemed to get done. There was a feeling that we with the patient and his family bought the groceries, cooked the meal, served and ate it. What was the alchemy that brought about this sense of satisfaction and the feeling that a job was being carried through? I began to realize the medical social worker's role as a coordinator, a liaison person, as well as a member of a professional team and an individual case worker.

Still later, through actual demonstration of function with the program, I began to understand the concept of partial case work service woven in with a consultant service. It became apparent to me that this consultant service was skillfully given, often when it was not asked for, by clever maneuvering of whatever entering wedge presented itself. The scope and variety of consultative service began to emerge for me and frequently did not take the pattern I would have expected. I still retained much of the old doctrine that "the doctor knows best what is good for the patient." I had not learned we must go along with the patients (or the team partner as the case might be) and not sail out ahead of him. More and more it became apparent that this consultative service required a knowledge of all available resources, of the strong points and the limitations of persons involved, of an understanding of and empathy with the patient and his family, and the ability to suggest—never force—the right thing at the right time, as well as the ability to take whatever fact or request presented itself and transform it into whatever tool was necessary to get on with the task.

I began to see more and more why it was necessary in any partial case work service (which must include some consultant duties if any undertaking is to be consummated) as well as in any straight consultant job to have those workers who were competent and secure in those areas in which they gave consultation and who were also pretty well aware of the basic knowledge and competence of the persons and agencies with whom they consulted.

Now, having become intrigued with the public health aspects of medicine particularly as they related to medical care programs, I moved over into the administration field. I saw other administrators with various kinds of assistants—business managers, accountants, public relations persons, general office managers, efficiency experts, nurses, part-time doctors. Each was fine in his place but his place was limited and his actions more or less rigid. Not one could carry the thread of continuity through a program for chronically handicapped children for medically indigent families. Not one could understand enough of the other's work to tie them all together in a meaningful way at the same time never losing sight of the reason for it all—not as a patient or a chart or a hospital bill, but as a personality whose physical, emotional, and social needs and environment are inextricably intertwined. And the worker who must possess all these traits must also have the initiative, security, and ability to step into almost any role from director to supervisor to staff worker, as the occasion demands. For some reason which I did not clearly understand, the medical social worker seemed the person to do this. I came gradually to know that this administrative function was not truly her function but it did not alter the fact that for some reason she seemed peculiarly fitted for it. I began to realize better why I felt this way after reading a paper on the administrative process in social work by Arlien Johnson. She defined administration as a "process and method by which objectives of a program are transformed into reality through a structure and mode of operation bringing about the coordinated and unified work of people in a movement toward the defined objectives." I was relieved when I found other people felt the same way I did and that the medical social consultant of the children's bureau felt this was a logical development and that the same person could properly carry two functions if the agency was clear as to what was involved in each function and that time for carrying on each was allowed.

I now truly feel that in ours and in similar public health programs, the chief medical social worker fits in as an assistant (and often as a mentor) to the director, and as a consultant on the handicapped child to all staff members, to other state agencies, and to local agencies, hospitals and clinics. If the program is fortunate enough to have other medical social workers giving direct service, she should give supervision to these workers. If there are no other workers, she should give partial case work service on screened cases, carrying through with strong consultative emphasis. She is also the best equipped person to guide and coordinate volunteer groups who take as their projects some part of the program. As routine work is carried on in the program, she is the person who seems to discover the types of problems not being met and the gaps in existing setups, and who, as these needs are discovered, unearths ways to develop services for them whether it be boarding homes for club foot children, volunteer agency sponsoring of a toy fund, or planning staff conferences for case or program discussion. Her field seems to have few limits and these are mostly time and strength, not ideas or opportunities.

As I actually watched our medical social consultant function in all these ways, I frequently wondered why it was so difficult for me to answer the questions put to me as to why I felt she was indispensable. Why did it seem impossible to explain just what she was and what she did and what made her so? And then I got hold of a paper by Margaret Jacob, assistant professor, social casework at Western Reserve University, which answered some of these questions for me. Jacob said in part: "One reason our function is so difficult to define is that it is so variable. In its simplest term our job is to do what needs to be done under the circumstances and—in spite of the reputation we are sometimes given—not to do what does not need to be done." Again she says: "Uniting of efforts is in itself a skilled process. Often it is the Social Worker who carries the theme," and again, "The topic of team work is one of the variables." The larger the community, the greater the degree of specialization. In a city the patient and worker may be connected to a number of available services. In a small community there may be only three persons involved—the patient, the doctor, and the worker. This means the worker expands her role and this is one of the reasons her role is hard to define. The worker may become health educator and vocational counselor, she may actually get a job for the client, she should put him in touch with appropriate sources for financing, education, and recreation—in short, do what needs to be done when there is no one else to do it."

I believe Margaret Jacob has put her finger on the basic philosophy of the good medical social worker—her expandable quality, total evaluation, imagination, tact, and initiative, which along with sound professional training, comprise the unique set of tools which make her indispensable in any good public health program.

There are several things in this letter which may be subject to debate or contradiction and one real reason I had for writing it is the hope that you will discuss them and thus further my education.

L Toward a Science of Hospital Social Work

Rosalie A. Kane

Historical Beginnings

Were you aware that a few lines from *Alice in Wonderland* were used to symbolize the rationale for the first department of social work at Massachusetts General Hospital? I quote from Cabot's first annual report, "Social Work Permitted at Massachusetts General Hospital" (Cannon, 1952).

> "Have some wine," said the March Hare in an encouraging tone.
> Alice looked all around the table. "I don't see any wine," she remarked.
> "There isn't any," said the March Hare.

Why was this quotation included in Cabot's first report of the first hospital social work department submitted to the Massachusetts General Hospital's trustees in 1905? I would suggest it emphasized the discrepancy between the world of the medical practitioner and the realities—physical and emotional—that patients faced.

In a less ephemeral literature, Cabot (1915) wrote of the backgrounds and foregrounds of medical care as the purview of social work—both backgrounds and foregrounds were seen as blind spots for physicians bent on curing or diagnosing disease. Backgrounds were the social, psychological, economic, cultural, and environmental factors that contribute to the etiology of a disease and that influence the course of recovery. Foregrounds were the immediate observable needs or feelings of patients that might be overlooked by those bent on diagnosis and cure. (A thirsty person in a waiting room might be an example of the latter.) In his discussion of foregrounds, Cabot anticipated the recent recognition that existential fears, discomforts, anxieties, or alienation may negatively

Paper delivered at the Annual Meeting of the Society for Hospital Social Work Directors of the American Hospital Association, Philadelphia, Pennsylvania, April 3, 1981. Reprinted with permission of the author.

affect compliance and health and will certainly play havoc with the quality of life. Here was a great challenge to a budding science—the research agenda for social work in hospitals was (and still is) to articulate the foregrounds and backgrounds of health care delivery.

Social work is both a science and an art. Today we focus on the science. One hospital social work director in this tradition wrote:

> In many instances it is worthwhile to make a simple study of a clinical or ward service previous to starting social service in connection with it, for in several places, results of the study changed the plans for carrying on the work. (Cannon, 1913, p. 165)

The comment could have been made today, but, in fact, those words were written by Ida Cannon almost 70 years ago. Cannon also recommended surveys to test the values of a service, once established:

> For instance, at the Eye Clinic of the Boston Dispensary, a study was made of all the new patients who came to the clinic for three months in 1910 (263 patients), and again for three months in 1912 (301 patients). Social service was begun in 1911. In 1910, 66 2/3% of all glasses prescribed by the occulist were not called for. During a corresponding three months in 1912, only 8% of the glasses prescribed were not called for. (p. 106)

In the same book, Cannon spoke to still other modern themes. She deplored social workers who neglect records because, while they "find a patient's distress very appealing, the record of it seems dry, dull, and academic." This, she wrote, is "a superficial point of view and should never be tolerated by those responsible for standards in hospital social work."

I could continue with examples. From the beginning of hospital social work, Cannon was concerned about how social workers choose their clients and how they decide what to do. She recognized that social work coverage in a hospital may not be related to need. A particular physician's pet project, a wave of public sentiment about a particular disease, or the interest of a donor could bring social work coverage. Today's equivalent of the donor (or maybe I should say yesterday's) might be a government granting agency. Cannon looked forward to the development of "more comprehensive methods of measuring the need of social service in a given institution and organizing more effectively to meet those needs." She categorically asserted that physician referral was too haphazard a way to pick up cases and was looking for a better method of casefinding. She also noted that some test of truth and merit for the introduction of a new hospital-based service was needed: she suggested that test be whether any existing agency or group in the community could serve as well or better than the proposed service and whether that group could be persuaded to offer that service.

This was a promising start for the infant science of hospital social work. But, of course, the context of 1910 was different from today. The first social workers were not allowed on the wards. They were squarely located in the dispensaries and outpatient departments. They worked with the interface between the community and the hospital—helping the individual and the family make the decisions and the arrangements to come in for care. Now we work with the interface between the hospital and the community—helping patients make the decision to leave the hospital and, of course, we are disproportionately located on the wards.

Current Context

Hospital social work today refines its science with two reference points: the social work profession and the health care delivery system. We are part of both. Tasks facing hospital social workers that face our whole profession include the proper allocation of responsibility between MSWs and BSWs, the structure and quality of social work education, the tensions between psychotherapy and concrete service, between professionalism and social activism, between social reform and social control. The entire profession is concerned about the degree to which specialized education and credentialing should be encouraged—for social work in the health field, it sometimes looks like specialty interests are running amuck. These questions are internal (and eternal) to social work.

Other questions facing social workers in hospitals mirror those facing the health professions as a group. The three overriding issues in health care delivery are access, quality, and cost. Like colleagues in other health disciplines, social workers must continue to be concerned with distribution of our services, their quality, and their cost. The concern for access in social work translates into an emphasis on developing screening tools so that social services can be allocated to those most in need or most likely to benefit, or both. Our concern with quality has led us to try to define the processes associated with good social service protocols and even to examine the outcomes. Once we are sure that the outcomes can be achieved, we can think of costs. Bear in mind, no service is cost-effective unless it is also effective. But given an effective approach, we can determine whether the same outcomes can be achieved with smaller increments of service or with less expensive methods.

The knowledge—the science—of hospital social work must be developed in practice settings. In fact, of all social work practice settings, perhaps hospitals offer the best conditions for knowledge development, if we care to seize them. Hospitals may seem beleaguered to us, but, on the whole, they are resource-rich. Moreover, the medical tradition (which still dominates the hospital) values empiricism. If we ask a good question, we are likely to receive good support from our medical colleagues in our attempts to answer it. Claudia Coulton (1981) has mentioned that every profession has discovered the psyche. Her comments were couched in terms of threat to social work, and in some ways the psychosocial sophistication of other disciplines is a threat to social work's uniqueness. In other ways, it is an opportunity. I have said before that we must give up tilting at the windmill of the medical model (Kane, 1982). Our task on the team is no longer to convince medical colleagues that psychosocial factors are important. That message is too simplistic for the leadership we need to give to psychosocial care. We now need to bring our content to a new level of specificity. We would not be impressed with a physician who kept exhorting us that germs cause disease or of a physical therapist whose major message was that activity is important. Similarly, our challenge is to add much more detail to our slogans about the needs of the "whole person."

Types of Knowledge

My main theme revolves around three related facets in developing our practice science—outcomes, measures, and values. This attention will help us resolve basic questions about the proper distribution, quality, and cost of hospital social services. Coulton (1981) has addressed four kinds of knowledge—authoritative, intuitive, rational, and empirical. This paper focuses on empirical knowledge, which can be subdivided into various types.

Facts

The keystone of empiricism is straightforward, factual information. For example, it is true that I am delivering this talk here and that today is sunny and fair in Philadelphia. If we went to more trouble to marshal the facts, we could say that this room contains a certain number of people, some percentage of whom are from hospitals employing more than 10 social workers. All these are facts, subject to verification. There are three types of facts I would like to see hospital social workers collect.

1. *Facts about the population served by the hospital or the clinic.* We must be concerned with the incidence and prevalence of various diseases, the demographic makeup of the community, and the conditions that pertain in the social environment. Note that these facts are to be mar-

shaled not only about the population served by social service but about the population at risk. Only this way can we know whether the group we serve in a social work department or a single service is in some way atypical of the larger group.

2. *Facts about our service.* These are most familiar to this audience. They are the head counts of hospital social work—caseload size by worker, number of services offered by types of service, dropout rates from our social work groups, and so on. They are needed to link our services to the need and to examine our efficiency.

3. *Facts about the interventions we offer.* Some of you have heard me emphasize this point before (Kane, 1980). Social workers need to describe practice interventions in reproducible terms. This means that another worker should have all the information needed to repeat the intervention, confident that he or she has included all essentials. This does not take away from the artistry of practice—to take an analogy from music, all pianists do not share the artistry of a concert soloist, but when the notes are written down, it is at least possible for many people to know they are playing the same piece of music. Such factual information about our interventions—the individual techniques of bereavement counseling, anxiety reduction, and so on, and the plethora of proposed group work techniques—are essential so that our practice may steadily evolve in a building-block fashion, with new variations added to the old. The facts are also needed so that, as the effects of practice are studied, we will be able to know exactly what those interventions were that were proved effective or ineffective.

Concepts

Sometimes we make statements that cannot be treated as facts without considerable clarification. It is a fact that the hospital sees X number of mastectomy patients, and Y of them are referred to social service. It is also a fact that the average length of stay for mastectomy is Z days. But is it a fact that 60 percent of postmastectomy patients seen in your hospital are depressed? Or that elderly persons recently bereaved tend to be socially isolated? Or that support systems for schizophrenic, unmarried men are inadequate for the majority?

We have now introduced concepts: social isolation, support system, depression. We have also introduced evaluative judgments such as "adequacy." Any two social workers could argue vehemently on any of these questions; however, they could not settle the argument until the concepts were converted to a set of facts. If by depression we mean inability to sleep for three nights in a row, loss of appetite, or crying jags (or two out of three of those factors), we could then settle the question empirically. It is unimportant to agree about the set of facts that we name as depression (although that would be desirable), but it is crucial that each of us convert our concepts into empirical reference points. Otherwise we can communicate only tangentially with each other or with persons from other disciplines. I doubt that we can even talk to ourselves (known as thinking) unless we empirically define our abstract terms.

Converting our concepts into facts helps us strengthen our scientific base in several ways. Until we undertake the exercise, we are in danger of using fine-sounding terms such as "adequate social support system" without really coming to grips with what such a support system would be in concrete terms. We also will have trouble setting priorities for our services unless we can get some empirical idea of differential need. Finally, we need to be alert because other people are using our conceptual terminology and we cannot always assume that they mean the same set of facts that we mean.

All of this requires the social worker to take a hard look at the way concepts are defined. Numerous abstract concepts are used in our practice. Indeed it is often one of these abstractions that we strive for as a result of our practice. Examples come readily to mind—quality of life, decision-making ability, support systems, self-esteem, grief resolution, and many others. The scales used to measure such abstract qualities are nothing more than a series of questions, the answers to which were given a name. A horse named Speedster can still come in last! Not every self-esteem scale may really embody the facts we care about when we work to improve self-esteem (Kane and Kane, 1981).

Once dealing in defined concepts, social workers can do a number of important things to advance their science. First, they can study the psychosocial concomitants of common conditions. And—let me give a pitch for aging—these conditions might as well be at the upper end of the age continuum because the imperative is upon us. Especially in hospitals, we must be concerned with the upper end of the age distribution. We could take a look, for example, at the psychosocial conditions associated with failing hearing or urinary incontinence, to name common conditions. What is the onset of such problems? How do they affect the victim? Is social participation affected? Do the conditions create anxiety? We need to know about the natural history, if you will, of the psychosocial conditions that we care about. For this we need to define the concepts that we use.

Armed with measurable concepts, we can be on the lookout for relationships. If we notice that certain facts seem to occur frequently in the presence of another fact, we may have a hypothesis in the making. The hospital social worker is in a position to develop hunches about the conditions that are likely to be helpful in achieving the outcomes we consider as positive. Remember, however, the basic research precept that one cannot infer causation without testing hypotheses.

Testing hypotheses is definitely in order if we have an intervention that we think works. As Mr. Hoffman says (1981), the usual plea is that we have no time for such clinical research. I suggest we do not have time to neglect it. Social work should be perceived and perceive itself as a scarce resource in the hospital—it is our obligation to learn how to use it best. This may entail random trials of social work techniques with comparisons to control groups. The hospital social service department is the ideal location for such trials. The much-vaunted partnership between academe and practice should find its best expression in designing and implementing the studies that test hypotheses derived from practice itself.

Measures, Outcomes, and Values

At the outset I indicated that measures, outcomes, and values are an important trio that guide the development of our science. Each one merits brief attention here.

Measures

Clinicians will need to use measurements in a new and more precise way in their practice. Although social workers have the importance of assessment deeply ingrained within them, social work assessments often lack the precision of the observations we associate with measurement. Such precision serves clinical ends for a number of reasons:

1. It permits us to observe change, which, in turn, allows us to look at the natural course of the variables we are interested in and also permits us to monitor the effectiveness of interventions.
2. It permits us to determine service priorities, conduct screening, and assign cases on an equitable basis.

Measures used by hospital social workers must meet criteria of clinical relevance. First, they must measure the domains that are important to us (within the larger categories of physical, mental, and social functioning). Second, the intervals of the measure must fit the population we are working with and make it possible for us to show the effects we care about. Hair growth is not measured in miles, just as the distance between Los Angeles and New York is not measured in inches. However, in our field, we sometimes accept measures of functional status for chronically impaired populations that obscure the meaningful changes in quality of life.

As we refine our measurement capability, we must also develop thresholds for action. Rather than developing a perfect scale to measure increments of social support, for example, it is more practical to know how to determine when individuals have crossed a threshold that means their social support is inadequate or weak. Voluminous information about resources, social contacts, friends, confidants, and social activities is usually collected when we attempt to assess social support, but the challenge is now to identify those patterns that are problematic and suggest the need for social work intervention.

As social workers continue to develop their screening tools, they will need to be alert to questions of sensitivity and specificity of the measures they use. (This is related to the questions about access to our services and the cost of our services.) A sensitive screening tool minimizes false negatives at the cost of requiring follow-up of some who turn out not to have the condition. A specific measure minimizes false positives at the cost of missing some people with the condition. The kind of screening procedure needed depends on the frequency of the occurrence we are screening for, the seriousness of the occurrence, and the likelihood that our interventions can be helpful. In screening for elder abuse, a relatively rare but serious event, for instance, we would wish an instrument that picked up all cases, even if we have to reevaluate some false positives. But in screening to identify those recently bereaved who are depressed, our instrument would need to be specific enough that it did not pick up all mild depression. Otherwise we would spend so much time eliminating mild cases that the costs of the screening would detract from the actual service.

Furthermore, a clinically useful measure (especially when used in a study of social work effectiveness) should be one that gives a fair chance to demonstrate effects. Some traits are thought to be fairly stable and would not be likely to change as a result of social services. Other dimensions may be irrelevant to the program or technique being evaluated. For example, a well-known scale measures "morale" of the elderly by the answers to questions such as "I have as much pep as I ever had," or "As I look back on my life, I find I have accomplished most things I set out to accomplish" (Lawton, 1975). If such scales are used to measure the outcomes of a particular program—for example, a meal program for senior citizens—it is unlikely that the program will show much change. The scale is too weighted toward items unlikely to change as a result of the program implemented.

Finally, all measurement should be undertaken with the recognition that a change in status is more important than status at any given time.

This underscores the importance of baseline measurements in clinical work. The old story about the man recuperating from hand surgery is relevant here: he told his doctor that he was doing fine but could not play the piano. What he did not mention was that he could not play the piano prior to surgery, either. Social work must not get into the position of being responsible for achieving social outcomes that are at variance with life-long patterns of clients. In seeking to facilitate a positive adjustment to illness, the social worker should not be accountable for outcomes that surpass the preillness state.

Outcomes

When we have measurements in place, we can begin to determine if our interventions are associated with the outcomes we desire. As already indicated, clinical experiments may be necessary to examine these outcomes properly. Again, social workers need to take usual precautions (not to bias results) but to be sure that they have an even chance of showing an effect. To aid in this task, the following steps are important.

1. Carefully describe (in reproducible terms) the interventions being tested and monitor to insure they really do take place.
2. Do not claim too much for a social work intervention. A series of group meetings may do no more than make the participants more knowledgeable about their illness or more willing to raise questions with their doctor. Demonstrating the achievement of modest goals is worthwhile.
3. Be sure that the measures selected to document the outcomes are appropriate.
4. Describe the target population that received the intervention and do not generalize inappropriately beyond that target group.

Values

Even values—the hallmark of social work practice—can be examined scientifically. A useful economist's precept is that it is impossible to maximize more than one outcome at once. Therefore, it is impossible to strive simultaneously for optimum physical and social well-being, or for optimum quality of life at minimum cost. Our professional literature is replete with such contradictory statements of goals, a characteristic also found in the World Health Organization's definition of health as a state of optimum physical, mental, and social well-being.

What does this mean for soc⋮ l work? Simply stated, we or our clients may simultaneously be seeking contradictory outcomes. For example, we may want to maximize independence and minimize safety hazards, or maximize both physical comfort and activity levels, or maximize longevity and minimize functional disability. Hoffman (1981) has indicated that social workers can be considered the conscience of the hospital. In that exciting, at times unenviable, role, we can make more explicit the value dilemmas inherent in health care choices. We can systematically try to determine the value preferences of our clients. And we can participate in the difficult dialogue ahead as our society tries to determine whose value preferences—the taxpayer, the patient, the family, the caregiver—are most important and how much risk individuals shall be permitted to take with their own lives.

Conditions for Building Our Science

In closing, allow me to accentuate the positive. Hospital social workers were interested in the science of our art in Ida Cannon's day and still are today. This conference is a testimony to our commitment and our diligence in this area.

To continue expansion of the knowledge base for hospital social work, we need only combine skepticism about everything with inner security about ourselves. We need to be willing to ask questions about all our work and its utility, recognizing that it is useful just to ask a good question at times. But we also need the confidence to know that we can test our techniques and refine our interventions without testing the worth of social work as a discipline. We can appropriately ask, "Is this intervention useful with this target group to achieve this result?" but remain confident that, regardless of the answer to such questions, social work itself has an important role to play in the hospital.

References

Cabot, R. *Social service and the art of healing*. New York: Moffatt, Yard & Company, 1915. '

Cannon, I. *Social work in hospitals: A contribution to progressive medicine*. New York: Russell Sage Foundation, 1913.

Cannon, I. *On the social frontier of medicine: Pioneering in medical social service*. Cambridge: Harvard University Press, 1952.

Coulton, C. Don't just do something: Applying knowledge and research in hospital social work. In *Putting knowledge into practice*. Proceedings of the Sixteenth

Annual Meeting of the Society for Hospital Social Work Directors. American Hospital Association, Philadelphia, Pennsylvania. March 31-April 4, 1981, pp. 3-15.

Hoffmann, P. B. The social work director's responsibility for contributing to knowledge: A hospital administrator's perspective. In *Putting knowledge into practice*. Proceedings of the Sixteenth Annual Meeting of the Society for Hospital Social Work Directors of the American Hospital Association, Philadelphia, Pennsylvania. March 31-April 4, 1981, pp. 16-26.

Kane, R. A. Let's describe practice in reproducible units, *Health and Social Work*, Vol. 5, No. 2 (May, 1980), pp. 2-3.

Kane, R. A. Lessons for social work from the medical model: A viewpoint for practice. *Social Work*, Vol. 27, No. 4 (July, 1982), pp. 315-321.

Kane, R. A. and Kane, R. L. *Assessing the elderly: A practical guide to measurement*. Lexington: D. C. Health, 1981.

Lawton, M. P. The Philadelphia geriatric morale scale: A revision. *Journal of Gerontology*, Vol. 30 (1975), pp. 85-89.

Index